T0086704

Vittorio Emanuele Orlando

Vittorio Emanuele Orlando
Italy
Spencer M. Di Scala

HAUS HISTORIES

First published in Great Britain in 2010 by
Haus Publishing Ltd
70 Cadogan Place
London SW1X 9AH
www.hauspublishing.com

Copyright © Spencer M. Di Scala, 2010

The moral right of the author has been asserted

A CIP catalogue record for this book
is available from the British Library

ISBN 978-1-905791-79-8

Series design by Susan Buchanan
Typeset in Sabon by MacGuru Ltd
Printed in Dubai by Oriental Press

This book is dedicated to the memory of Vincenzo Di Costanzo, Southern Italian and my grandfather, who voluntarily returned from the United States to Italy, in his words, to help save the country from the Germans and Austrians in the First World War. He died in the fighting and left behind a widow and five children.

Contents

Acknowledgements

Authors incur many debts during the writing of a book, and I am no exception. I would like to thank publisher Barbara Schwepcke, whose vision has made this series possible and whose meetings with me I always found pleasant and informative. Jaqueline Mitchell's skill has served as a guide with regard to the technical aspects of this book and I thank her as well for her editing skills. I also thank Professor Alan Sharp, Series Editor, for his encouragement; Roberta Wollons, Chair of the History Department at the University of Massachusetts Boston for her continued support; Professor Nunzio Pernicone, Drexel University, for the stimulating discussions we have had on the First World War and on the Italian role in it; and Antonio Landolfi for helping me gain access to sources in Italy. I would like to thank my friend, former Prime Minister, and now President of the Treccani Institute, Giuliano Amato, for his constant support and thought-provoking exchanges. I enjoyed my many stimulating conversations on history and on this book with Ciro Morroni, former Deputy Consul General at the Consulate General of Italy in Boston.

I have had the help of many librarians in doing my research but would like particularly to thank Janet Stewart of the

Library of the University of Massachusetts Boston and Aldo Ricci, Director of the Archivio Centrale dello Stato in Rome, for their invaluable help.

In 2009 I had the honour of being chosen the Barbieri Fellow and recipient of the Barbieri Foundation Grant (Trinity College Research Grant in Modern Italian History). I thank the committee that selected me for the grant and particularly Professor Borden Painter, Honorary President, Cesare Barbieri Endowment for Italian Culture, and Professor John Alcorn, its Program Director.

My daughter, Ashley, kept life exciting outside of the academic realm. Finally, most of all, I thank my wife Laura, originally from Turin, who was forced to live with the Sicilian Vittorio Emanuele Orlando, in addition to the descendant of Neapolitans, for her constant support and for her creation of an ideal atmosphere in which to write.

Spencer M. Di Scala
Boston, Massachusetts
July 2009

Introduction

Italy has always been an anomalous country within the European community of nations. Its great history from Rome to the Renaissance has been acknowledged by Italians and non-Italians alike, but this history has also weighed down the modern nation in crucial ways. Foreign invasions destroyed the Italian Renaissance just when its culture began permeating Europe. From the 16th to the 18th centuries the country became a battleground between the Great Powers and after 1715 Austria dominated the peninsula. A movement for unification began in the late 18th century and finally united the country in the late 19th. Italy's historical tradition at once hampered and helped this movement. The memory of great achievements by Italians in the arts and the sciences encouraged many Italians to look backwards and bask in the glory of past accomplishments instead of focusing on the modern world and on the progress it made; but the same memories of greatness spurred patriots to fight for independence and unity as a means of modernizing the peninsula culturally and politically.

The Kingdom of Italy came into being on 17 March 1861, and in 1866 Venice and Venetia became Italian as a result of the Seven Weeks' War. The borders established as a result of that war, however, failed to bring all the Italian-inhabited areas into the new state, and, moreover, left the country vulnerable to attack. In the north, Trent and the Trentino remained in Austrian hands, putting the Austrian armies over the Alps in an arrow-shaped wedge of territory and making it easy for them to strike into the country's heartland. In the east, as well, the frontiers remained vulnerable because the Austrians retained Italian-speaking Trieste, Istria, and other areas from which they could launch offensives. Furthermore, the borders as drawn in 1866 put large, continually mistreated, Italian-speaking minorities into Austria. Unlike foreigners, Italians did not consider unity accomplished and chafed at the oppression under which the minorities lived, something the other European powers never understood or appreciated. The Italian situation with regard to these 'unredeemed territories' resembled the Alsace-Lorraine problem between France and Germany which, unlike the Italian case, stimulated great sympathy for France. Indeed, the Italian minority in Austria was treated worse than the inhabitants of Alsace-Lorraine and aroused greater passions among Italians than any other foreign policy issue.

On 20 September 1870, Italian forces entered Rome, which became the country's capital. Many Italians considered themselves the heirs to the ancient Romans, and with the conquest of the old capital believed that the 'Third Rome' would rapidly assume its 'natural' place among the Great Powers. However, the modern country was neither Ancient Rome nor Renaissance Italy. After centuries of disunity, conquest, and repressive rule, this should have been no surprise; but intellectuals, who as in other European countries had a disproportionate influence on policy, found that difficult to accept.

If Italy did not resume its 'natural' position among the Great Powers as a result of the heroic struggle for independence and unification, it was not due to centuries of backwardness but to the inadequacy of its leaders. The criticism of Italy's leaders and of the liberal democratic political system that put them into power poured out as writers, political scientists, and artists would not accept reality – Italy was neither a great nor a small power but somewhere in between.

This truth did not prevent intellectuals and some of the country's leaders acting as if Italy possessed more clout than it actually did, an attitude that encouraged them to have greater hopes for the country's aggrandizement than were possible. This brought criticism from the other powers. Nevertheless, in a situation of equilibrium Italy could make a difference depending upon which side of the scale it threw its weight, and its strategic position and growing industrialization meant that its authority within the European universe was increasing. In this situation, Italy's policies especially resembled those of Germany and Britain: Germany because it had a newcomer's brashness in trying to make its way, Britain because of its diplomatic policy shifts. However, while Germany's challenge aroused fear, Italy's stimulated scorn and resentment because of its inherent weakness. But unlike Germany, Italy followed the general assumptions and tactics of traditional European foreign policy. Italy's circumstances help explain why other countries courted it before and during the First World War.

Unless this context is understood, there can be little comprehension of Italy during and after the war. In fact, this lack of understanding even by diplomats caused resentment of its policies and the bias still pervades the historiography of Italy. The 'default' position with regard to Italy during the

First World War is that it put on a poor military performance; the 'default' interpretation after the war is that it nevertheless demanded vast and unjustified rewards at the Paris
Peace Conference. The method of this book is to put aside
'default' positions in order to seek interpretations of Italian
aims and actions in context and to consider them in a manner
that is similar to those by which the goals of other powers are
judged.

In order to reach this objective, I have examined the career
and role of Italy's wartime leader, Vittorio Emanuele Orlando,
who courageously took over leadership of the country during
the darkest period of Italy's and the Entente's struggle against
the Central Powers. Orlando did not come out of nowhere to
lead the country, as the scarce scholarship on him in English
makes it seem. He was born a week after Giuseppe Garibaldi
landed on Sicily to make that island part of a united Italy,
and died six years after Italy became a republic. The story of
Orlando's life and career is seamlessly integrated into Italy's
story and reflects it to a great degree. Orlando is the focus
of this story, and he stands tall in the panorama of modern
Italian history.

Vittorio Orlando

I

The Life and the Land

1

Less than Great

The homeland of the Roman Empire, Italy, remained a political unit after the 'fall' of Rome in the West in AD 476. It was not until the 6th century, with the Lombard invasion, that the peninsula came under control of the semi-independent Lombard chieftains, and that the ancestors of the independent Italian states appeared. The 8th-century Frankish invasions to aid the Popes against the Lombards, the divisions of the Middle Ages and the struggle between the Holy Roman Empire and the Papacy sealed the political division of the peninsula. With the decline of both the Empire and Papacy in the 14th century, five large states – Rome, Naples, Florence, Milan and Venice – and several minor ones consolidated themselves. In 1454, these states established the 'balance of power' both as a concept and as practice. None of the major states could dominate the peninsula because if one threatened to do so the others would ally against it. This recognition of Italy as a multistate system prevented the peninsula from being united while France, Spain and Britain created large, powerful and unified states.

In 1494, France invaded Italy and provoked the entrance

of its arch-rival Spain. For 65 years Renaissance Italy became a battleground between these two major powers and their Italian allies, now reduced to a minor role. This continual warfare impoverished the country, spelled the decline of Italian cultural influence and produced Spanish domination until 1715. The Spanish imposed their values on Italy and helped generate a decline of the cultural and economic enterprise associated with the Renaissance. Moreover, Italy entered the front lines in the wars conducted by the Spanish against the Turks, the French and the Protestants, debilitating the country even more. When Spanish domination ended, the Austrian branch of the Habsburgs took control. Through all of these wars, the states remained intact, even if dominated by foreigners, each continuing to evolve their own customs, laws, and practices. Their strong presence and their international connections made it more difficult to unify the peninsula during the Risorgimento, the term applied to this movement in the 19th century. In the 16th century, Niccolò Machiavelli exhorted the Italians to unite to expel the foreigner in the last chapter of *The Prince*, but in the following two centuries the idea of unifying all Italians fell into abeyance.[1]

Italian unification

During the 18th-century Enlightenment a number of positive developments led to a revival of the idea of unity. When the Austrians replaced the Spanish, they felt the need to establish themselves in the areas they ruled directly, especially since the Austrian Queen Maria Theresa (herself challenged during the War of Austrian Succession, 1740–8, because she was a woman on the Austrian throne) promised to collaborate with prominent subjects in the Habsburg possessions in order to introduce reforms.

In Italy, this policy produced its most important results in Lombardy. With the cooperation of the Lombard philosophes, the Austrians streamlined the region's financial and administrative structure, eliminated the residues of feudalism, took back the right to collect certain taxes and tolls that the Spanish had sold to landlords, conducted a land survey in order to impose fairer taxes, and in 1776, instituted freedom of internal trade in grain. These reforms presented the aristocracy with the dilemma of returning to business activities in which it had been engaged before the Spanish conquest or suffering a reduction in income. Part of the Lombard nobility resumed its tradition of engaging in business and founded efficient agricultural firms based on profit. The long peace between Austria and France that lasted from 1748 to 1792, when the former rivals for control of Italy became allied, combined with the reforms and fundamentally transformed the region's economy.

In other areas of endeavour the Austrians achieved mixed success, but their stimulation of the Lombard economy would powerfully influence the fight for unification, ironically against the Austrians themselves when they reversed their collaborative rule following Maria Theresa's death and after the French Revolution frightened them into abandoning their reform policies. The Austrians shut the Lombards out of government, exploited the region's growing economic development to pay for their Empire's deficit and instituted discriminatory regulations favoring Austrian enterprises.

In other areas of Italy, the rulers also attempted to institute Enlightenment reforms, but they failed because of the aristocracy's opposition and its successful defence of its privileges. However, Enlightenment culture penetrated all the Italian states, with the exception of the Kingdom of Sardinia (also called Piedmont). Nevertheless, this state remained the strongest native Italian power, and while conservative and pro-Austrian, would later develop into a liberal monarchy and lead the fight for unity. With the outbreak of the French Revolution, Italian rulers dropped their efforts favouring reform because, they concluded, Enlightenment reforms produced rebellion. This development resulted in a crisis in all the Italian states and left them susceptible to French Revolutionary influence because intellectuals – and in many cases the inhabitants – strongly supported the reforms that they felt certain the French Revolution would bring.

Although the Kingdom of Sardinia took its name from a large, lightly-populated island to the west of the Italian peninsula, the centre of the state was the northwestern region of Piedmont. Unlike the other Italian states, its ruling dynasty, the Savoys, did not expand from a large city to conquer the surrounding region but collected territories piecemeal over the centuries. Their capital, Turin, lacked the prestige and size of other Italian capitals and had to be built up during the 18th century.

Besides these political developments, cultural interactions between the Italians and the French during the Enlightenment were intense. The work of thinkers such as Giambattista Vico, Antonio Genovesi and Ludovico Antonio Muratori emphasized Italy's common language, cultural heritage, historical tradition and economic interests, making the period a 'preface' to the unification movement known as the Risorgimento or Resurgence.

The French Revolution gave enormous impetus to Italian unification. The French broke through into Italy under Napoleon in 1796. Despite setbacks they dominated the peninsula until the Emperor's first fall in 1814, and a Napoleonic general ruled in Naples as King until 1815. The French eliminated the vestiges of feudalism, reorganized the administration and ruled with the bourgeoisie. Over the long run, Napoleonic dominion disappointed the Italians and they eventually turned against the French, but two aspects of French control advanced the cause of Italian unification.

First, at the height of French dominance after 1804, only two kingdoms existed: the Kingdom of Italy in the North and the Kingdom of Naples in the South. Surrogates of Napoleon ran these states; but in both cases, Italians participated in the governments and the administrations, creating a native ruling class. In Naples, where Joachim Murat heeded his Italian advisors more than Napoleon, the Kingdom undertook the first war for Italian unity in 1815. These states gave the Italian bourgeoisie experience in governing and, by combining former inhabitants of separate states into larger units, demonstrated the economic advantages of unity. Second, intellectuals from different parts of the peninsula openly discussed the questions both of freeing Italy and unifying it, bringing together persons from diverse areas for the common purpose of uniting their country.

The French themselves destroyed this 'Jacobin-Patriotic' movement, but not before it had launched the idea of unifying Italy under a republican form of government. An important characteristic of this movement was that it identified a unified Italy with the left. This feature aroused opposition to Italian unity among Italian conservatives who feared for their economic and social superiority. The prophet of Italian unity, Giuseppe Mazzini, confirmed them in this opinion when he advocated formation of a unitary republic by means of insurrection and guerrilla tactics.

Mazzini had great popular appeal, but at the same time other models for Italian unification materialized. One of them, the brainchild of Vincenzo Gioberti, called for unification under the aegis of the Pope, something that seemed possible after the surprise election of Pius IX in 1846. A different model called for unification, or at least independence, under the leadership of the King of Sardinia. A lively debate ensued over which model should prevail, but the 1848 revolutions made the decision: they demonstrated the idealistic nature of Mazzini's solution and the reality that the rest of Europe would intervene to crush an Italian revolution. At the same time, Gioberti's solution collapsed under the ambiguous policy and then the reactionary shift of Pius IX.

This left the Piedmontese solution, but the kings of Piedmont had been reactionary, and its King during the 1848 revolutions, Charles Albert, had vacillated between supporting the Italian cause and defending the socially conservative *status quo*. After 1850, however, unification under Piedmont appeared as the only alternative. All the Italian states had been defeated, but Charles Albert had issued a constitution (the *Statuto*) that survived the 1848 upheavals thanks to his successor Victor Emanuel II. Surprisingly, this constitution quickly developed into a liberal instrument that protected Parliament and that, as a result of a political deal known as the *connubio* (marriage), brought the center-left to power under the most brilliant statesman of the age, Camillo Benso, Count of Cavour.

Cavour transformed Piedmont into a liberal state and the economic leader of the peninsula, wooing away Mazzini's supporters and securing their acceptance of a monarchy open to change. Following a bewildering series of diplomatic deals, reversals, wars and referenda, in 1859 and 1860, Piedmont annexed most of the peninsula and on 17 March 1861 proclaimed the Kingdom of Italy. Unfortunately, Cavour died three months later, depriving the new state of its most sophisticated leader.[2]

The 'Age of Prose'

King Victor Emanuel II labeled the Risorgimento as the 'Age of Poetry' and remarked that the 'Age of Prose' would follow it: state-formation and economic development. The peninsula lacked raw materials, particularly the coal and iron that fueled the first industrial revolution. Mountains and hilly areas represented 77 per cent of its territory and plains made up 23 per cent. The Alps with their high peaks crowned its northern frontier and the Apennines ran down its entire length and reached to the sea, limiting arable land and contributing to the high population density in the cities and towns and, later, to massive emigration. Abundant and unhealthful marshlands characterized the Veneto, Tuscany and Lazio, hotbeds of malaria and other diseases that hampered the country's economic development. Only the Po River Valley of the North and, in the South, small areas around some southern cities such as Naples and Catania included fertile areas.

In addition to these physical limitations, the costly wars of the Risorgimento and the assumption of the debts of the formerly independent states left the new state with enormous debts and necessitated imposition of new and sometimes unfair taxes that weighed most heavily on the poor. Despite these adverse conditions, the state did not renounce large expenditures on the armed forces. The warrior tradition of the Savoy dynasty made the kings loath to accept a modest diplomatic role for the new country. Moreover, Italian intellectuals had assumed that, once united, the country would take its rightful place as a great power as befitted the heir to the Roman Empire and the Renaissance.[3] These attitudes meant that, in addition to debt, military expenditures burdened the state; these would rapidly become the most onerous in Europe as a proportion of the country's wealth.

This handicap did not prevent Italy's rulers from wishing to play a major role in European politics. They entered the rush for colonies, challenging France in the competition for Tunisia, to which many Sicilians had emigrated. They lost the contest in 1881, setting off a quest to end their diplomatic isolation, a quest which would result in the formation in 1882 of the Triple Alliance (considered in detail in Chapter 2). In the long run, this constellation, a fixture of pre-war European diplomacy, did not work for the Italians: hostility towards France turned out to be temporary, Italian defeat at the battle of Adowa in 1896 after Italy attempted to take over Ethiopia (see Chapter 2, p 27) demonstrated that it did not support Italy's colonial ambitions, and the French, threatened by German power, worked hard to repair relations between the two Latin countries, and by 1902 had succeeded.

As the years went by, relations between Italy and Austria constantly worsened and only fear of an Austrian attack kept Italy uneasily in the alliance. Moreover, in the late 19th century Italy was in no shape to conduct a major war. It struggled to construct an efficient army from the military remnants of the old states,[4] although its navy became one of the world's largest. Industrial development did not take off until 1897 and then only in the northwestern 'industrial triangle' bounded by Milan, Turin and Genoa. The South's economy remained backward because it lacked raw materials, energy sources and roads. After unification, northerners dominated the new state and imposed the free-trade regime of Piedmont; this and a trade war with France resulted in the collapse of southern agriculture. High illiteracy and the Church's boycott of the new state prevented most of its men from voting (women could not vote), so only its large landowners had a say in national policy, and they followed their own interests.

In domestic politics, Italy confounded European predictions by not falling apart. After Cavour's death in June 1861, his political heirs (the Right) ruled and in 1876 the Left, which had advocated a republic during the Risorgimento, came to power peacefully. Despite disagreements, both agreed on the fundamentals of how to resolve Italy's problems. Cavour's heirs ruled until 1876, keeping the problems with the economy and the Catholic Church from getting out of hand (The Law of Guarantees). The Left – those who had advocated a republic during the Risorgimento but who accepted the monarchy – took over in 1876 and, when it became clear that the difference between them and their opponents was minimal, accepted exponents of the Right into their cabinets. This policy turned out to have negative connotations: instead of being saluted as a compromise, the opponents of both condemned the procedure as 'transformism', a selling-out of principles, touching off a fierce condemnation of the parliamentary system that later became enshrined in the political theories of Gaetano Mosca, Vilfredo Pareto and Roberto Michels (a German Socialist who taught in Italy). These thinkers argued that, no matter which party governed, and no matter what their ideology, an elite working for their own interests always ruled. This idea, which influenced sociologists all over Europe, became particularly prevalent during the 'Giolittian Era' (1901–15).

A son of Piedmont nurtured in the bureaucracy, the calm and deliberate Liberal statesman Giovanni Giolitti dominated Italian politics for 15 years,[5] coming to power briefly in 1893 as Prime Minister, in 1901 as Interior Minister in the cabinet of Giuseppe Zanardelli and as Prime Minister in 1903. Although he worked with the Socialists, Giolitti was equally ready to cooperate with Conservatives if political conditions made it impossible to collaborate with the Socialists. In fact, Socialist cooperation with Giolitti set off a fight followed by a series of splits between Socialist reformists advocating a gradual road to socialism and revolutionaries who advocated violence.[6]

Giolitti's tenure is fundamental to an understanding of Italy before the First World War. Fired by the idea that the country's foreign policy was too timid because it was ruled by timid leaders, a new culture of the Right emerged – one that demanded war to demonstrate the country's greatness. The most important intellectuals who propagated this view organized the Nationalist Association in 1910 under the leadership of Enrico Corradini. Corradini turned Marxism on its head, arguing that the revolution would be an international one in which Italy would lead the poor and exploited countries to victory against the rich nations of the world. These intellectuals hoped to unseat Giolitti but recognized their inability to do so through parliamentary means. They therefore condemned the parliamentary system that allowed him to govern. At the same time, members of the parliamentary Right who considered him too liberal also resented Giolitti because of their inability to gain control of Parliament.[7]

Even if Italy made important economic gains during Giolitti's tenure, the Liberal statesman's rule and that of Parliament came under intense attack not only from the extremes of the Right and Left, but also from politicians within Parliament who felt they were excluded from power. During the early 20th century, Italian thinkers subjected Parliament to withering criticism. This ironic and dangerous development would be played out fully following the First World War when perceived mistreatment of the country at the Paris Peace Conference of 1919 played a major role in mortally wounding the Liberal parliamentary regime.

Vittorio Emanuele Orlando

The man who would lead Italy to victory in the war and represent the country at the Peace Conference was a product of the Giolittian Era. Vittorio Emanuele Orlando, born in Palermo on 19 May 1860 to a family of lawyers, received a gold medal for his first-grade scholarly achievements, the beginning of a brilliant academic and political career. He followed his ancestors in the study of the law at the University of Palermo in 1877. The next year he produced his first literary work, a study of Prometheus and the transformation of myths, then studied anthropology and flirted with Herbert Spencer's positivistic philosophy, much in vogue at the time. In 1881, the University conferred its law degree on him along with its highest honors; in 1882 and 1883 he published two studies on parliamentary government and electoral reform that presaged his later Liberal political ideas. In 1882, Orlando became Professor of Constitutional Law at the University of Modena, the youngest in Italy. He returned to Sicily in 1885 to teach at the University of Messina and later at the University of Palermo. During the same period, he published important studies and textbooks on constitutional law and in 1890 founded the *Rivista di Diritto Pubblico*, a prestigious journal on public law.

Pictures of Orlando as a young man at this time show him sporting a full head of hair, but, strangely, less than he seems to have had later in life. His hair is greying, with lots of salt and little pepper, and evenly distributed; the shock of white hair that characterizes portraits of him during the Paris Peace Conference is missing, although there is a hint that it will soon make its appearance. He has piercing eyes, in contrast to the somewhat vacant, resigned look one notes in later pictures. His face is adorned with a full, turned-down handlebar mustache, giving him a vague resemblance to the young Georges Clemenceau, his French antagonist in 1919 Paris. Never really physically heavy until extreme old age, he maintained a slim appearance during his youth.

Following what seemed a natural development, in 1897 Orlando won election to the Chamber of Deputies representing Partinico, an agricultural district outside Palermo. At the time no one could be elected without Mafia consent, and Orlando was no exception. However, during this period the Mafia respected 'men of culture' more than it did later, and the Professor had made such a name for himself that his compromises with the organization are said to have been minimal. Nevertheless, he moved to Rome to distance himself from the 'ambiguous' world of his native island. He held the chair of Public Law at the University of Rome until 1931, when he refused to take the loyalty oath to Fascism and resigned. He resumed his position in 1947 and kept it until his death.

Orlando's juridical studies underpinned his Liberal political philosophy.[8] He rejected the theories of Mosca and Pareto, according to which minority elites always rule, and emphasized the importance of social legislation. In 1889, he published a well-regarded essay on electoral reform in which he favored universal manhood suffrage, legislation Giolitti passed in 1912. The Milanese riots of 1898 and subsequent arrests of opposition deputies found Orlando defending his colleagues; and in 1901 he supported the liberal turn of the Zanardelli-Giolitti cabinet by supporting the freedom to strike. Despite its dangers and inconveniences, he wrote, a modern state had to be neutral in the conflict between capital and labour. He condemned the Italian bourgeoisie's attitude of declaring socialism conspiratorial and terroristic in its refusal to enter into a discussion with its leaders.

Orlando's liberal attitude and reputation brought him to the notice of Prime Minister Giolitti, who appointed him Education Minister from 1903 to 1905, and chose him for his Justice Minister on 14 March 1907. He held the position until the cabinet's end on 10 December 1909. During this period Orlando sponsored legislation guaranteeing judicial independence[9], and solidified his reputation as a Liberal. He took over the ministry again on 5 November 1914. His efficiency and insistence that civil liberties be protected even during wartime convinced his colleagues to support him for Prime Minister in 1917, by which time the country had been at war for over two years, and it was going badly for Italy.

> Sometimes the very delicate function of peaceful reform is neglected and governments delude themselves into thinking that they can attain immutability through immobility.
> **VITTORIO ORLANDO,** *C.* 1941

2

European Alliances and the Path to War

Italian foreign policy before the First World War is frequently misrepresented in general texts, which see Italy as betraying its Triple Alliance partners because it did not join them when the First World War began. The Italian situation, however, must be considered in the context of a new and weak state seeking, at first, to avoid isolation, then to affirm itself in foreign affairs and, finally, as a sensitive barometer registering subtle shifts in the European diplomatic atmosphere.

Italian foreign policy and the Triple Alliance

Immediately following unification serious diplomatic problems challenged the cabinets of the Right. From 1861 until 1871, Cavour's heirs sought to complete unification. In 1866 Venetia became part of the new state when the Italians allied with the Prussians in the Seven Weeks' War against Austria; and in 1870, during the Franco-Prussian War, the Italians took Rome from the Pope and made it their capital when the French withdrew their garrison. These developments caused internal debate because of the military failures of 1866 and

'Irredenta' means 'unredeemed land'. It was originally used for the Italian-speaking areas that remained part of Austria after the Kingdom of Italy's establishment. Italians never gave up hope of 'reuniting' the lands to the Fatherland. The Italian passion to acquire Trent and Trieste can be compared to the burning French desire to retake Alsace and Lorraine. Popular opinion resented the continuous mistreatment of the Italian population in the Irredenta, while intellectuals charged that a 'barbarian' Austrian policy aimed at wiping out the last remnants of Roman civilization there. The Irredenta inflamed emotions between Austria and Italy to fever pitch and damaged relations between them. It was clear from its diplomatic protocol that Austria never accepted Italian unification. In 1915 the Italian government cited grievances over the Irredenta as the reason for Italy's declaration of war against Austria. The word has entered the English language and refers to unredeemed lands in general.

charges by the Left that Italy had entered Rome in a 'cowardly' manner.[1] More importantly, these annexations did not 'complete' unification because substantial Italian-speaking territories remained in Austrian hands – the 'Irredenta' of Trent, the surrounding Trentino and Trieste. Foolishly exacerbating the situation, the Austrians continually mistreated the Italian populations of these areas while control of the Trentino deprived Italy of a defensible frontier in case of war.

It was not only the problem of the Irredenta that confronted the new kingdom. Powerful enemies stood ready to undo the peninsula's newfound unity for a variety of reasons. Most serious was the strong influence the Catholic Church had in Austria and, for a period after 1870, France. Austria would have relished reclaiming its lost Italian territories; and in the new century persistent rumors circulated that the heir to the throne, Franz Ferdinand, would try to destroy Italian unity. The Right and its longtime Foreign Minister Emilio Visconti Venosta attempted to meet this threat on both domestic

and foreign planes. Parliament voted the 'Law of Papal Guarantees', which gave the Church special privileges in Italy and
a sum of money to replace the lost revenues from the former
Papal State.

Internationally, Visconti Venosta viewed diplomatic isolation as Italy's most urgent foreign policy challenge and particularly feared the antagonism of the Pope. He tried to end
Italy's isolation by gaining the support of Britain and France.[2]
However, Britain had not yet abandoned its 'splendid isolation' and the French connection posed special problems. Italians complained that Italy had practically become a French
satellite after Napoleon III had helped unify it, but relations
worsened between the two countries after Napoleon's overthrow and the annexation of Rome during the Franco-Prussian War. The French complained about Italy's failure to help
them against the Prussians and resented the seizure of Rome.
Furthermore, in the early years of the Third Republic, the
Catholic Church wielded great influence, and encouraged
French hostility against Italy. For example, the French stationed a warship in the port of Civitavecchia despite Italian
protestations, in case the Pope decided to flee Italy – a slap
in the face. These hostile attitudes produced several crises
between the two countries, especially after the Left came to
power in 1876 – most notably the loss of the race to acquire
Tunisia in 1881. This encouraged Italy to seek allies against
French unfriendliness.

Above all, Italy needed peace and tranquility to construct
a state; and given this aim, an alliance with the Central
Powers seemed more advantageous, especially to the Left
that came to power in 1876. Leftist leaders such as Francesco Crispi admired Otto von Bismarck, whose anti-Catholic
crusade, the *Kulturkampf*, they considered more suited to

their aims than the mild anti-clerical policies of the Right. At the same time, Bismarck, in the process of isolating France diplomatically, offered the Italians an alliance. The Italians initially hesitated but soon changed their minds. The ruling Savoy dynasty was linked to the Habsburgs through marriage and preferred the Central Powers to France because of their conservative policies, and in 1881 and 1882 domestic political developments reinforced this desire. A new electoral law enlarged the vote and benefitted the extreme Left, which was more strongly anticlerical at a time when the new pontiff Leo XIII reinforced Pius IX's hostility toward the Italian 'occupation' of Rome and reiterated the *non expedit* policy prohibiting Italian Catholics from participating in national elections. Italian diplomats feared that exacerbation of the Roman Question would lead to increasing international isolation, while the strengthening of the extreme Left and increased demands for establishment of a republic would weaken Italy's international position because of the conservative orientation of the European powers. These factors boosted the chances of an alliance with the Central Powers because that solution would allow the government both to avoid isolation and gain the support of the most conservative powers against the perilous demand for an Italian republic. Paradoxically, even the Irredenta problem increased chances for agreement. The question of the unredeemed lands troubled Austro-Italian relations, and increased the possibility that Austria would make a move against Italian territory. An agreement with Germany and Austria-Hungary would win de facto German and Austrian recognition for the Kingdom within its present borders, while strengthening the monarchy and inserting Italy into Europe's conservative international structure. Accordingly, King Umberto I visited Vienna, fulfilling Bismarck's requirement of making up with Austria if Italy wished a German alliance; and on 20 May 1882 Austria-Hungary, Germany and Italy signed the Triple Alliance.

The new alliance obliged the partners to aid each other if attacked by third parties. The Triple Alliance had major advantages at the time for Italy because it reduced the chances of a French attack while the probability of the country being obliged to fight alongside Austria was miniscule. It was difficult to conceive of any aggression against the alliance signatories: Italy obtained a joint declaration stating that the alliance was not directed at Britain, Russia was allied to Austria and Germany, and a weak France would not dare to attack Germany. The treaty simultaneously reduced Austrian support for Papal claims, ended Italy's diplomatic isolation and reinforced the monarchy.[3]

Despite the factors that help explain why Italy joined Germany and Austria in the Triple Alliance, the treaty had a slim chance of long-term success because public opinion strongly considered it 'unnatural'. The extreme Left saw the alliance as a cooperative society linking a conservative monarchy and conservative foreign powers to keep liberal domestic forces in check, and vigorously objected to the arrangement. Although the extreme Left lacked a majority in parliament, it had considerable strength in the 'real country', influence that increased with the passage of time. Moreover, Radicals and Republicans, Mazzini's heirs, patriots who had fought against Austria and the Church to liberate Italy, and rising extreme Left forces resented the renunciation of the revolutionary and Liberal Risorgimento traditions. They would never fight on Austria's side against a France that incarnated liberal values and had helped the peninsula liberate itself from Austrian domination. As Socialist influence among the masses grew exponentially during the early 20th century, all wings of the Partito Socialista Italiano founded in 1892 (Italian Socialist Party, PSI) missed no opportunity to denounce the alliance, fearing it might produce a conflict involving Italians in fighting on the Austrian side. Revolutionary Socialists saw a direct link between the Triple Alliance and domestic reactionary policies: Arturo Labriola charged King Umberto I with plotting with his allies to undermine parliamentary institutions during the reaction of 1898–1900.[4] Reformist Socialists believed that the Triple Alliance obliged Italy to spend money on arms rather than on needed reforms.[5] In short, Italian Liberals and Leftists abhorred the Triple Alliance: if they had to fight, they supported the Triple Entente against their country's undemocratic allies whose policies had repressed them in the past and would have done so even more in the case of a victory to which, ironically, Italians might be asked to contribute.

Socialist divisions and anti-militarism

Italian Socialists advocated neutrality in case of war, but the movement increasingly split in its attitude toward an eventual conflict. The moderate reformist wing argued that Italy spent more on arms than other countries as a percentage of its wealth; and it advocated proportioning expenditures to the country's means and investing the savings in necessary reforms. Italy's military obligations under the Triple Alliance, however, precluded this solution.[6] At any rate, Italian Socialists, like their European brethren, believed in the impossibility of a major war because the peasants and proletarians who made up modern mass armies would supposedly turn their weapons against their bourgeois officers.

The reformists kept up a united front on these principles

until May 1905 when the Party expert on foreign affairs, Leonida Bissolati, led an Italian Socialist delegation to a 'summit' with Austrian Socialists in Trieste to discuss coordinating their response in case war broke out between their countries. The Italians vowed to resist 'militaristic bourgeois irredentism' and, should a war begin, pledged to call an immediate general strike and sabotage mobilization. Their Austrian colleagues led by Viktor Adler, however, refused to undertake a similar commitment, and the Italians withdrew their promise.[7]

This meeting fractured the reformist wing, producing deep divisions between Bissolati and his old friend Filippo Turati, the father of reformism. Both leaders advocated leaving the Triple Alliance, but because they were unable to change Italian policy they took different roads. Turati advocated Italian neutrality, but Bissolati became convinced of an imminent war with Austria-Hungary.[8] In September 1908, Austria annexed Bosnia-Herzegovina *de jure*, leading to a war scare. In the wake of this affair, Austrian students at the University of Vienna attacked Italian-speaking students demonstrating in favor of an Italian university in Trieste, killing two of them. Bissolati denounced the Austrian Socialists and cited the incidents as proof that Italian Socialists put too much faith in internationalism while, conversely, Turati blamed the Italian government for exploiting the Bosnia affair to increase arms spending.[9] As time went on, Bissolati and his friends became more convinced that if the Central Powers won a European war, the victory would spell the end of democracy. This conviction spurred them to refuse opposing increased arms expenditures and other policies that they believed would strengthen the country.[10]

Bissolati, however, represented only a minority of the PSI,

and although his old companion Turati could not bear to have him expelled, his policies alienated the Party's revolutionary wing. In 1911, Italy went to war with the Ottoman Empire for control of Libya. Bissolati did not oppose the war because he believed it strengthened Italy internationally, and domestically Giolitti linked it with universal manhood suffrage and other reforms. The Socialist left wing, out of power for several years, had been organizing a comeback, and profited from traditional anti-war sentiment to regain control of the Party. It attacked the reformist leadership – especially Bissolati – as a major contributor to the Libyan War.[11] Indeed, the divided reformists had posed only an ineffective opposition to the conflict, and proved too dispirited to meet the revolutionary challenge.[12]

After 1911, when the Libyan War broke out, revolutionary Socialists led by Benito Mussolini demanded the government's overthrow; Mussolini condemned the parliamentary system and universal suffrage on the ground that these institutions maintained the capitalist system in power.[13] In June 1914, the eve of the First World War, revolutionaries gained control of the Romagna, one of Italy's most important regions, in an insurrection that Mussolini encouraged. The revolt failed, but it instilled in Mussolini a desire for revolution at any cost.[14]

At the Socialist Congress of Reggio Emilia, 7 July 1912, Mussolini denounced the policies of the Bissolati wing and proposed its expulsion; and the delegates accepted the motion overwhelmingly.[15] Bissolati established his own party (Partito Socialista Riformista), and when the First World War broke out, supported Italian intervention in the war in order to defend democracy. He joined the cabinet during the First World War and opposed Italian aims he considered expansionist after the conflict. His party, however, remained miniscule and had little influence on the Socialist movement.

Although Mussolini was not the major leader of the traditional PSI left wing that won the Reggio Emilia Congress – indeed, its leaders regarded him with suspicion – the future Duce skillfully exploited traditional Socialist anti-militarist sentiment to reinforce his influence. He utilized his position as editor of the Party daily newspaper, *Avanti!*, to advocate violence and to campaign against militarism. He increased PSI membership to 50,000 while membership in the Party's collateral organizations grew to a million, and he linked up with anti-militarist Republican and anarchist associations. On 7 June 1914 the government banned anti-militarist demonstrations in Ancona and set the stage for the most spectacular part of Mussolini's crusade: 'Red Week'. Protests against the government's action spread after the army killed three demonstrators. Egged on by Mussolini's *Avanti!* – WORKERS OF ITALY, STRIKE! – the demonstrations spread to the Romagna and revolutionaries seized control of the region.[16] The government trod softly to minimize casualties, but suppressed the revolutionaries. In response, Mussolini planned to strengthen the unity of groups dedicated to revolutionary action, but the First World War altered the situation.

When the war broke out, the Italian Socialist movement demanded that the country remain neutral. All Party factions opposed war on principle, 'Red Week' had just demonstrated the depth of anti-war feeling among the Italian masses and Mussolini's influence was at its height. However, Mussolini proved to be part of the left wing but not of it. In reality, Red Week disappointed him and revolution at any cost became his primary goal – not necessarily Marxist revolution.[17] The outcomes of the First World War and the Paris Peace Conference would provide him with the opportunity to put his ideas into practice.

Orlando and the Catholics

Unlike the Socialists, the Catholics formed a united front in adhering to the Pope's desire for peace almost at any price. Thus, Catholics as well as Socialists supported neutrality when the First World War began. Relations between the Vatican and the Italian state were bound to become problematical after the outbreak of war, given the government's possible intervention in the conflict; but luckily Orlando had established cordial relations with the Vatican, and as Justice and Interior Minister he directed relations with it during the conflict.

Orlando's governmental experience with the Church dated from his days as Education Minister in 1903–5 and, more importantly, as Minister of Justice between 1907 and 1909. Orlando's most significant impact on Italian Catholics as Education Minister was his staunch opposition to Leonida Bissolati's motion banning the teaching of religion in primary schools during the debate on Orlando's reform of elementary education, necessary to combat the high illiteracy rate. As Minister of Justice, he resolutely defended the autonomy of the universities and of the magistracy. With regard to the Catholic Church, he used his office to balance an officially non-confessional Italy under the Law of Guarantees, existing anti-clerical legislation, Catholicism as the traditional religion of Italians and Vatican interests – a very controversial task at the time. Orlando tried to blunt the extreme Left's strong anti-clericalism and his parliamentary duels with Republican deputy Eugenio Chiesa have remained legendary.

Orlando exhibited diplomatic finesse in continuing his

friendship with Romulo Murri, head of the Christian Democrats and later condemned by the Church for modernism,
with the theologically rigid but politically flexible Pius X and
with his more difficult successor Benedict XV, Pope during the
First World War. Despite their religious orthodoxy, however,
the popes recognized that the interests of the Vatican dictated
a resolution of the conflict with the Italian state. Orlando's
policies as Justice Minister, and later as Interior Minister and
Prime Minister, made him a leading practitioner of the 'tacit
reconciliation' between the Church and liberal democratic
Italy.[18] Under the difficult conditions of Italy's relationship
with the Church, Orlando opened an unofficial dialogue with
the Vatican during his tenure at Justice and set the stage for
later developments in Church-State relations.

A deep recession that began in 1907, and the disastrous
Messina earthquake in late 1908, made the period in which
Orlando held the Justice Ministry a particularly turbulent one
that highlights the success of his policy toward the Church.
Convinced that intermediaries aggravated the thorny relationship with the Vatican, Orlando and Pius X sidestepped
them and established direct communication with each other
through a young Sicilian priest with extraordinary access to
the Pope. Orlando wrote that from then on communications
between him and the Holy Father were *rapid, secure, and
direct, as if by means of an intelligent telephone*. This direct
dialogue with the Pope allowed Church and State to resolve
delicate problems peacefully, such as reducing the enormous
number of Italian dioceses and other potentially destructive
issues. How Orlando differed from his predecessors in the
office, he recalled, was his elaboration of a national ecclesiastical policy to replace the unofficial one that had been left to a
special class of lawyers favored by the Vatican.[19] In December

1909, as Orlando prepared to leave his post, the Holy Father bestowed an Apostolic Blessing on him.[20]

With regard to the First World War, the crucial difference between Catholics and Socialists was that while Catholics opposed Italy's intervention because of the Church's humanitarian tradition, once their country entered the conflict the Catholics supported the war effort, and Orlando's pre-war dialogue with the Church facilitated Italy-Vatican dealings during the conflict.

Dissolution of an alliance

In international affairs the Church had such good relations with Catholic Austria that they threatened Italy. While Italian membership in the Triple Alliance avoided diplomatic isolation, it did not defuse the difficult Church issue. For example, Emperor Franz Joseph promised the Pope that he would never visit Rome.[21] The Italian king had visited Vienna, but a return visit by the Emperor would have constituted formal Austrian recognition of the city as Italy's capital, and the Emperor's rejection of Italian invitations remained a sore point in the relationship. Nevertheless, until 1896 the treaty functioned reasonably well, despite the traditional antagonism between Austria and Italy. In the late 1890s, however, Italian colonial activities increased, reaching a high point when Italy tried to take over Ethiopia. After complicated diplomatic maneuverings a war

> Italy has been able to overcome the dangers of a situation of frightening difficulty, and it has prevailed over them so well that, if not chronicle, always partisan and passionate, then certainly history, that serene and impartial judge, will consider it the most glorious page [in the history] of the Italian state.
> VITTORIO ORLANDO, C. 1936

ITALIAN DIPLOMACY
The uncritical acceptance by historians and even the public of the alleged disloyalty and double-dealing by Italy has unfortunately marred the understanding of Italian pre-war diplomacy. Already during the Paris Peace Conference it had a strongly negative effect and afterwards it had serious implications because the statesmen in Paris frequently acted on their prejudices, and ironically those of the Austro-Germans, and wound up playing an important role in the rise of Fascism.

A counterbalance to this comes from diplomatic historian William C. Askew, who wrote in an essay on the Austro-Italian antagonism: '... Italian diplomacy was not the evil and dishonest thing which German and Austrian historians have pictured it as being. Italy, as the weakest of the great, could not afford diplomatic failure. Her diplomats, mostly aristocrats, were, with a few significant exceptions, among the finest in the world. The Foreign Office followed the practice of leaving its ambassadors and ministers in the capitals of Europe for a long time to learn the language and customs of a country, and to build up contacts and friendships. They were well informed. If Italy had any slogan which summarized her diplomacy it was that coined by Visconti Venosta: "Independent ever, isolated never".' [22]

broke out on 1 March 1896 and the Italians were defeated at the Battle of Adowa.

Several reasons account for the Italian failure, but Italian diplomats attributed part of it to the lack of German and Austrian support against France and Russia. Italy's partners made no attempt to halt smuggled French weapons from reaching the Ethiopians, and Austria's signing of a commercial treaty with France regarding Tunisia without informing Italy brought complaints from Italian diplomats. Bismarck's contemptuous reply, that the Triple Alliance was a conservative instrument and not a profit-making association, deeply offended his ally. This remark was one of a series of scornful statements and threats that German and Austrian leaders made when referring to Italy that alienated the country. In short, the fraying of the Triple Alliance began in the late 1890s.

In the aftermath of Adowa, the Italians expressed fear that Austria would expand its influence in the Balkans while Italy was tied down in East Africa and in Tripoli, in which it was also interested. Lack of support from its allies, they felt, also encouraged a hostile French policy toward them. Leftist deputies in Parliament continually denounced the Triple Alliance, inflaming Italian popular opinion. In 1901 when the Liberal government under Giuseppe Zanardelli and Giovanni Giolitti came to power, relations between the two allies worsened. Zanardelli, worried about commercial treaties, cited deteriorating relations with the allies and commented that Italy would think long and hard before renewing the Triple Alliance; in the same interview, he praised the visit of an Italian naval squadron to Toulon.[23] Relations with France warmed to the extent that in 1902 the Foreign Minister in the Zanardelli government, Giulio Prinetti, always cool to the Triple Alliance, reached an agreement with France in which the two countries promised not to attack each other. Sometimes cited as an example of Italian 'duplicity', Prinetti acted because his allies refused to discuss changes in the treaty and presented Italy with a 'take it or leave it' attitude.[24] This agreement did not violate the Triple Alliance, in which Italy was obligated to join its allies *only* in case of an attack on them; but it did demonstrate diffidence toward Austria-Hungary in the same way that Bismarck's Reinsurance Treaty with Russia (1887–90) had done, illustrated Italian sensitivity to changing power relationships and signaled that Germany no longer had overwhelming power on the continent. Italian Liberals, in the meantime, advocated that Italy drop out of the Triple Alliance and promoted an Anglo-French-Italian pact uniting the large democratic powers of the continent.[25]

Besides the special problems of the Austro-Italian relationship, Italy's position reflected the changing nature of the European balance of power. In the 1870s and 1880s Bismarck had successfully isolated France and the Central Powers seemed dominant. By century's end, Bismarck had been fired, German diplomacy had become arrogant and British decline and fears had induced it to abandon its 'splendid isolation' and seek allies. In the new century, France emerged from its isolation and led the way in forming the Triple Entente. The European balance of power slowly shifted in favor of Britain and France, and this change affected Italy, weakest of the Great Powers and therefore a sensitive barometer in measuring diplomatic change most of all.

Italy had always had cordial relations with the British, who controlled the Mediterranean; and its strong cultural relations with France and the increasing influence of the Left in domestic politics now coincided with Italian national interest and encouraged a rapprochement with the country's 'Latin sister'. The crisis over Bosnia-Herzegovina in 1908–9 in which Austria-Hungary refused Italy compensation led to an agreement between Russia and Italy in 1909 at Racconigi. Russia and Italy established friendly relations by declaring their interest in preserving the Balkan *status quo*; Italy voiced sympathy for Russian ambitions in the Straits while Russia did the same for Italian goals in Tripoli. In the wake of Italy's mistreatment after the Bosnian affair by its allies, the Racconigi meeting cast doubt on its continued commitment to the Triple Alliance.[26]

At the same time that Italy's relations with the Entente Powers warmed, its relationship with the Triple Alliance worsened. At the 1906 Algeciras Conference following German blundering during the First Moroccan Crisis (1905), a mal-adroit German challenge to France in colonial affairs, Italy did not lend support to Germany and stuck with previous agreements it had with France and Britain. This attitude so incensed the Kaiser that he told the Austrians he would 'seize with real enthusiasm' the opportunity to concentrate all his military might against Italy if that country should show hostility to Austria. By this point, both Germans and Austrians already considered the Triple Alliance a dead letter.[27] Given the changing European balance, however, Germany and Austria-Hungary could not afford to let Italy go; but succeeding years would only confirm the crisis of the Triple Alliance. In 1908 and 1909 Italian resentment reached a peak as the result of the crisis that broke out after Austria annexed Bosnia-Herzegovina; Italy felt entitled to compensation under Article 7 of the Triple Alliance, but received nothing. Popular hatred of Austria on this and other occasions regularly erupted into rioting, and the Austrians reciprocated. At the same time, the two countries engaged in fierce competition in Albania, which sought its independence from the Ottoman Empire and had become a battleground between the two allies. Both countries were involved in an intense commercial rivalry in the area. The Italians supported the nationality principle in the Balkans, opposed by the Austrians. Both dueled over the interpretation of Article 7 requiring compensation if either altered the Balkan *status quo*. This hostility was no secret. Europeans recognized that Austrians and Italians had become 'enemy allies', and diplomats reckoned that they would have gone to war if they were not in the same alliance – indeed, that they might do so anyway.

The Triple Alliance not only failed in the diplomatic arena but proved unsuccessful in resolving the old problems that existed between Austria and Italy, which in fact worsened. The Irredenta poisoned relations more than ever. The Austrians rejected the two major demands made by the Italians – autonomy for the Trentino and establishment of an Italian University at Trieste – which might have resolved the issue. Riots in which Austrians assaulted the Italian minority, promptly answered by anti-Austrian demonstrations in Italy, strained relations. In August 1913, decrees mandated dismissal of Italian citizens from public jobs in Trieste, which Italian diplomatic intervention just managed to stop. The 'allies' even failed to resolve the Roman Question and the continued refusal of the Austrian Emperor to make an official visit to Rome exacerbated the problem. In contrast, in 1904 French President Émile Loubet had visited Rome to a warm welcome despite the displeasure of French Catholics.

The Austrians cited their own grievances over the Irredenta. They charged that Italy promoted an influx of Italians into the area to strengthen its claims, while the Italians believed that the Austrian government encouraged Slavs to move into Italian areas to dilute the Italian population. Rumors circulated in Austria that the Irredenta would be ceded to Italy when the old Emperor Franz Joseph died, although no evidence for this existed. Moreover, the Austrians were convinced that an Italian attack to take over the region would come whenever the opportunity arose. These attitudes encouraged a faction of the Austrian military, headed by Chief of Staff Franz Conrad von Hotzendorff, to demand a pre-emptive attack on Italy. The army accused the Italians of spending enourmous sums to reinforce their border defenses against Austria, while the Italians claimed the Austrians had moved troops to their southern border to prepare an attack on their ally. Von Hotzendorff advocated a military invasion of Italy with such gusto when an earthquake destroyed the city of Messina and while the Italians were engaged in fighting the Ottoman Empire that he had to be removed as Chief of Staff on 30 November 1911; he was reinstated in December 1912 on condition that he not engage in politics.[28]

Italian public opinion, parliamentary debates and the press expressed so much anger against Austria, especially on the extreme Left, that it became abundantly clear the Italian people would never allow their government to drag them into an aggressive war on Austria's side. By 1914 the Triple Alliance was dead, and – apart from a crystal-clear unprovoked attack on the Central Powers that would fulfill the original defensive purpose of the Triple Alliance – the possibility of getting Italians to support Austria in a war did not exist.

3
Neutralists versus Interventionists

On 28 June 1914, Slav nationalists assassinated Archduke Franz Ferdinand. By early August, fighting had broken out and involved all the major powers except Italy, which declared its neutrality. The bad relationship between Italy and Austria-Hungary and the animosity of Italian public opinion and Liberals precluded the entrance of the country into the war on the Austro-German side, but as far as Italian officials were concerned, the violation by its allies of the Triple Alliance's terms justified a declaration of neutrality and compensation for any Austro-Hungarian gains in the Balkans under Article 7 of the Alliance. The Italians notified their allies that both polices were based on ironclad legal rights and that they retained their freedom of action depending on their country's national interest.

When the First World War broke out, the Italian government immediately stated that the *casus foederis* by which Italy would join its allies had not come into effect: the conflict did not break out as the result of a direct provocation by another power but rather because of an aggressive war initiated by Austria-Hungary against Serbia. This position did not come out of the blue. The Italians had clearly informed the Central Powers several times that the Triple Alliance did not contemplate their joining their allies in a war resulting from a provocation of another power. The Italians had done so most recently in August 1913, when Vienna requested Italian support in an eventual military action against the Serbians during the Second Balkan War. Foreign Minister Antonino di San Giuliano, backed by Prime Minister Giolitti, responded that the Triple Alliance did not come into play if one of the allies attacked another country.[1] In October 1913, the Austrians initiated a new and dangerous policy toward Italy that violated another of the Alliance's terms: they sent Serbia an ultimatum ordering them to withdraw from Albanian territory without informing or consulting with the Italians. Disputes continued between Austria and Italy in Albania with regard to new discriminatory measures and violence against the Italian minority in Austria, even if the two powers together guaranteed Albanian independence. Despite the worsening relations, neither side advocated leaving the Triple Alliance, due to good relations with Germany, a temporary deterioration of relations between Italy and France during the Libyan War, and widespread fears that a breakup of the Alliance might

> The fundamental article of the Triple Alliance controlling whether or not Italy would be obliged to join its allies in a war was Article 3. This article stated that the trigger for Italy's coming to the aid of its allies in case of a conflict (the *casus foederis*) or whether Italy could call on the aid of its allies, must be an unprovoked, direct attack by a third country or countries on one of the allies. Here is the full text of the article (emphasis added):
>
> ARTICLE 3. If one, or two, of the High Contracting Parties, <u>without direct provocation on their part</u>, should chance to be attacked and to be engaged in a war with two or more Great Powers non-signatory to the present Treaty, the *casus foederis* will arise simultaneously for all the High Contracting Parties.

precipitate a war between Austria-Hungary and Italy.

On 5 December 1912, the three allies renewed the Triple Alliance ahead of schedule.[2] Why did Italy consent to this renewal despite the tendency of the Triple Alliance to change from a defensive instrument to an offensive one? Asked that question in January 1916, Giolitti acknowledged that the observation was a fair one, but he cited the special circumstances under which the renewal had come about. The Italians had been fighting the Libyan War, which caused a crisis with France. German backing had been beneficial to the Italians in that situation and in return the Germans requested that the Alliance be renewed; Giolitti responded by asking for German recognition of Italy's annexation of Libya. The Germans could not oblige during the war but pledged to do so after it ended. They kept their word and the treaty was renewed. Giolitti then remarked to his interlocutor: 'Frankly, I'll confess to you that I never would have believed that there could have been two governments that were so far out of their minds so as to undertake this monstrous war so lightheartedly. I was aware of the intrigues and restlessness of the Austrian military faction; but I would never have expected it from Germany, having had repeated occasions to ascertain that it exercised a moderating influence on Vienna.'[3] So unpopular was the renewal among Italians, however, that Premier Giolitti publicly cautioned its allies that Italy's bond to the treaty could 'only be counted on in case her partners kept her fully informed of diplomatic negotiations which might make the terms of the alliance operable'.[4]

Italy's allies ignored this warning, and all of the problems that had dogged the Alliance erupted with a vengeance during the crisis preceding the First World War. The Austro-Germans consulted with each other – but not with Italy – after the

Article 7 of the Triple Alliance, not present in the original treaty but added later, required the country contemplating a change in the Balkans to consult with the others and to communicate its intentions, as well as those of any other power, to the others. The treaty stated the intent of both powers to favor the *status quo* in the Balkans (among other areas), but stated that if this maintenance became impossible, the country benefiting from any change should compensate the other. Thus the obligation of each ally to consult with the other <u>before</u> taking action was clearly spelled out, in addition to the requirement for compensation.

Here is the text of Article 7:

ARTICLE 7. Austria-Hungary and Italy, having in mind only the maintenance, so far as possible, of the territorial *status quo* in the Orient, engage to use their influence to forestall any territorial modification which might be injurious to one or the other of the Powers signatory to the present Treaty.

To this end, they shall communicate to one another all information of a nature to enlighten each other mutually concerning their own dispositions, as well as those of other Powers. However, if, in the course of events, the maintenance of the *status quo* in the regions of the Balkans or of the Ottoman coasts and islands in the Adriatic and in the Aegean Sea should become impossible, and if, whether in consequence of the action of a third Power or otherwise, Austria-Hungary or Italy should find themselves under the necessity of modifying it by a temporary or permanent occupation on their part, this occupation shall take place only after a previous agreement between the two Powers, based upon the principle of a reciprocal compensation for every advantage, territorial or other, which each of them might obtain beyond the present *status quo*, and giving satisfaction to the interests and well founded claims of the two Parties.

assassination of Franz Ferdinand, and the Germans agreed to Austria's ultimatum, which was framed in such a way that Serbia must either refuse – which meant war – or become an Austrian satellite. The Austro-German partners deliberately chose not to consult or inform their Italian ally of their planned action precisely because Italy had emphasized that the defensive pact uniting them in no case justified aggressive wars. The Central Powers reckoned (rightly enough) that the Italians would object to the ultimatum and sandbag their plans for a war against Serbia by citing the Alliance's terms and by claiming compensation for any change in the Balkan *status quo* as specified by Article 7. But, by intriguing and refusing to consult Italy, the Austro-Germans clearly violated the treaty.[5]

For two weeks following the assassination of the Archduke and his wife, the Germanic powers kept Foreign Minister San Giuliano uninformed regarding their intentions; but, being suspicious, the Italian Foreign Minister informed the German ambassador in Rome that no Italian support for Austria would be forthcoming if the Austrians presented Serbia with demands 'incompatible' with Italy's liberal traditions and motivated by 'tendencies, not yet dead either in Vienna or in Berlin, inspired by the Holy Alliance'. By 17 July, San Giuliano had got wind of Austro-German intentions to present Serbia with an ultimatum whose terms could not be fulfilled. He contacted the Russians and made proposals in a futile attempt to defuse the crisis and to avert the conflagration he expected. On the evening of 23 July 1914 Austria presented its ultimatum to Serbia without informing its Italian ally, letting it know only the next day along with the other European countries.[6]

When the Italian Prime Minister, Antonio Salandra, and San Giuliano, in the company of German Ambassador Hans von Flotow, heard the terms of the ultimatum (read to them over the telephone because they were in Fiuggi, where San Giuliano had gone because he was ill), all three blanched. In a heated exchange summarized by San Giuliano, the Italians made clear their opinion:

[Under the treaty] Austria did not have the right to take the step it had ... without previous agreement with its allies.

Austria, in fact, both because of the way in which the note is conceived and because of the demands it makes, which are ineffective against the pan-Serb danger and are profoundly offensive for Serbia and indirectly for Russia, has clearly demonstrated that it wishes to provoke a war. We therefore informed Flotow that, as a result of Austria's actions and because of the defensive and conservative character of the Triple Alliance treaty, Italy had no obligation whatsoever to aid Austria in the case that, as a result of its move, it finds itself in a war with Russia, because any European war, in this case, will be the consequence of a provocative and aggressive act on the part of Austria.

The Italians also informed von Flotow they would demand compensation under Article 7 should Austria change the *status quo* in the Balkans and that national interest would dictate their future actions.[7]

The Italians were firmly convinced that if a war broke out Britain would be involved, and considered German doubts on this point to be their greatest error. The British connection was fundamental in Italy's decision, given Italy's friendly relations with Britain, Italian assertions that the Triple Alliance could never be considered as directed against that country (to which Germany and Austria had agreed), the vulnerability of the long Italian coastline and its major cities to British bombardment, and Anglo-Italian agreements on the Mediterranean. It pointed to, and eventually determined, Italy's switch from the Triple Alliance to the Entente.[8]

The grievances the Italians had against their erstwhile allies pour out in the memoirs of Prime Minister Antonio Salandra. In addition to not having been informed about the plans of the Central Powers in the 1914 crisis and having been treated as inferiors for years, the Italians had endured insulting remarks from German leaders from Bismarck to Wilhelm II and threats of attack from the Austrians. A victory of these powers against Serbia would mean the triumph of German power and culture and the suffocation of Italian commerce and influence in the Adriatic, Salandra wrote. Even if Italy should join the Central Powers in a war and be on the victorious side with them, Italy would be 'at most, the first of the vassal States of the Empire'. Italian public opinion would never sanction the shedding of Italian blood for a war provoked by Austria exclusively in its own interest.[9]

As the terrible crisis played out, the Germans notified the Italians to do their duty under the Triple Alliance; San Giuliano responded that the agreement did not oblige Italy to take part in an aggressive war. On 2 August, Italy declared its neutrality and asked the Austrians to acknowledge their thesis that they should be compensated under Article 7 for any Austrian gains, and the Austrians eventually did so, though only under German pressure.

Neutralists

As might be expected in a country not directly attacked, a national debate quickly developed between proponents of continued Italian neutrality and advocates of interventionism. A large majority of the population favored neutrality, but parties and groups soon split on the question, with significant differences among both neutralists and interventionists and positions that varied with the shifting fortunes of war and increased reflections on how the conflict might affect the country.

The Liberal establishment, the most important political group, initially supported neutrality, but opinion soon diverged. Sidney Sonnino, longtime leader of the Liberals' conservative wing to which Premier Salandra belonged, passed from neutralism to interventionism because he felt that Italy's national interests dictated it. Following San Giuliano's death on 16 October 1914, Salandra urged Sonnino to replace him at the Foreign Ministry.[10] The Italian Liberals (both conservative and further to the left) were pro-British (Sonnino, of Jewish origin, had a Welsh mother and was an Anglican) and opposed the militarism and authoritarianism of the Germanic powers. They had thought it necessary for Italy to remain in the Triple Alliance for diplomatic reasons only. In fact, their first inclination was to remain loyal to their allies – the exact terms of the treaty were still secret – and they changed their minds only gradually. They came to believe that Italian interests would be damaged if the country remained neutral while the European order was shaken up, because Italy stood to lose influence in the Irredenta and the Adriatic where it confronted Austrians and Slavs. If Italy remained neutral and Austria won, the Austrians would gain control of the Balkans and shut Italy out; if Austria lost, a new South Slav state would emerge and perhaps even annex the Italian-populated Trieste. These considerations convinced many Liberals to switch from neutralism to interventionism. By the end of August, the mainstream Italian press controlled by the Liberals – particularly Luigi Albertini's *Corriere della Sera* – initiated a campaign favoring Italian intervention on the Entente side.

Despite this change in attitude, the Liberals led by former

longtime Prime Minister Giovanni Giolitti (further to the left), supported neutrality for pragmatic reasons. Giolitti and his friends argued that skillful diplomacy and threatened intervention could achieve the Irredenta's cession to Italy as compensation under Article 7 because the Italian minority represented such a small percentage of the Austro-Hungarian population and the Austrians would not risk Italian intervention for such a small number of people. Giolitti dismissed the argument of conservative Liberals who believed that the war would end in three or four months because Italian intervention on the side of the Entente would be decisive. The war would last more than three years before the Germanic empires, militarily the best organized in Europe, could be fatally weakened. Intervention would cost Italy enormous sums in lives and treasure, while the extremely difficult terrain of the Italian front and the complexity of securing raw materials would greatly hamper the war effort.[11] Giolitti, however, labored under serious handicaps. His supporters in Parliament could have voted Salandra out of office, but as a known neutralist Giolitti lacked the credibility to threaten war if Austria did not meet Italy's demands, so he would not personally take over the government and conduct negotiations to secure the Irredenta. Furthermore, he had dominated Italian politics for so long that conservative Liberals, Socialists, Nationalists, intellectuals and other resentful groups that had been unable to unseat him now aimed to eliminate him by defeating his neutralist policy. Thus, domestic and foreign considerations were inextricably intertwined, as his enemies calculated that defeat on this issue would destroy Giolitti's domestic influence.

Similar cracks appeared in the Catholic and Socialist movements that would become crucial in the post-war Italian milieu. The majority of Catholics followed the Vatican's lead. Newly-elected Pope Benedict XV condemned the war in his first encyclical as violating Christian and human principles, consistently professed his own neutrality and continually condemned the raging conflict. He hoped Italy would remain neutral, but he cautiously avoided taking sides in the debate, remained preoccupied about the effects Italian intervention could have on the Vatican and refrained from damaging the country's war effort when it did intervene. Italian bishops urged their flocks to follow the decisions of the government on the matter of intervention, which they did. Most Italian Catholics favored neutralism but distinguished between the absolute neutrality advocated by the Church for religious reasons, and the neutrality conditioned by the welfare of the nation that, at a certain point, may have to decide to enter the conflict for its own ethical reasons and national interest. Lacking a great organized political party (founded only in 1919), the Catholics followed the lead of the Liberal establishment and loyally supported the war effort once Italy joined the conflict, even sending representatives to participate in the war government.

The 'official' Socialists of the PSI presented a totally different picture. They quickly announced a policy of 'absolute neutrality' and declared they would not fight for their country if it should enter the conflict. The Socialists feared Italy would intervene on the side of the Austrians and Germans, but they did not modify their policy even after it became clear that the country's leaders had excluded that option. They hoped to collaborate with other Socialist parties of the Second International, impossible because the major parties – including the German and the French – supported their countries' war efforts. Many Socialists sympathized with the Entente, especially after the German invasion of Belgium, but they maintained a rigid attitude in opposing the war even after Italian intervention, adopting the slogan 'Neither a man nor a penny [for the war]'.[12]

The revolutionary Socialist leader Benito Mussolini, editor of the Party newspaper, initially agreed with his Party. He proclaimed his unalterable opposition to the war and conducted a survey that demonstrated the hostility of the majority of Party members toward joining the conflict. However, Mussolini had been drifting away from the Party hierarchy for some time. Most of the Party establishment objected to the violence of his language and his demand for immediate revolution; in addition, the failure of 'Red Week' in June 1914 demonstrating that the PSI was not ready for revolution alienated Mussolini.[13] Quite aware of the war's revolutionary potential, and insisting that the Party risked ruin by isolating itself from the greatest problem in the modern world by sticking to 'absolute neutrality', Mussolini wavered. He expressed his doubts to friends in the revolutionary syndicalist movement who urged him to come out into the open. On 18 October 1914, Mussolini published an article in the Party newspaper in which he argued that 'absolute neutrality' had become obsolete after developments disproved the Socialist fear that Italy would join its Triple Alliance partners. The Irredenta was a real national problem, Italian intervention could help end the war, and the Socialists could not remain inert while the world passed through a fundamental crisis, he wrote.[14] Although this article did not advocate Italian entrance into the war, it was a major step in this direction and in clear opposition to Party policy. On 20 October, Mussolini presented a motion to the Party Directorate to renounce 'absolute neutrality', but it received only his own vote. He

resigned as editor of *Avanti!* and accepted money from industrialists to found his own newspaper advocating intervention,
Il Popolo d'Italia. On 24 November, the Milanese Socialists
expelled him from the Party and on the 29th the Directorate
ratified the decision.[15] Destined to have major repercussions
after the war, the Mussolini defection turned out to be a
minor one at the time, and the Party remained as a powerful
bulwark opposing the war.

Interventionists

The interventionists represented a minority of the Italian
people; but, in contrast to the neutralists, their skill in propaganda and their effectiveness in maneuvering the country
into war immediately strikes observers. Like the neutralists,
the interventionists consisted of several groups to which must
be added those neutralists such as Mussolini who eventually joined them. Most of the country's major intellectuals
favored Italian entrance into the conflict, with the notable
exception of philosopher Benedetto Croce. Divided into Revolutionary and Nationalist groups, these latter served as the
shock troops of that part of the Liberal establishment that
eventually decided to intervene on the Entente side. Italy's
celebrated poet and novelist, Gabriele D'Annunzio, became
the most visible personage advocating war, but so also did the
leaders of the avant-garde Futurist art movement and editors
of the country's most influential journals. The Nationalist
movement founded by Enrico Corradini in 1910 supplied an
ideological framework for these factions. The Nationalists
transposed the Marxist revolution onto the international
plane and identified revolution with war, which they greeted
as necessary and salutary, the 'hygiene of nations'. Although
they were a small group, their propaganda had been essential

in pushing Italy into the Libyan War in 1911 and would be again in 1915. In love with war, they considered the Libyan conflict too small and demanded war on the side of the Triple Alliance led by warlike Germany; when they understood that Italy would never fight on Austria's side they switched with no regard for their ideology and demanded war on the side of the Entente. They insisted that Italy exploit the conflict not only to gain the Irredenta but to expand in the Adriatic and the Mediterranean, thus creating a strong link with conservative Liberals who disagreed with Giolitti's view that Italy should limit its aims to gaining the Irredenta. The Nationalists, Futurists and other groups that supported them used violence against anyone who opposed their ideas, and the Liberals had no objection to exploiting Nationalist-organized riots to bring the country into the conflict against Giolitti's wishes or to allying with them in the future in order to achieve other aims. After the war the Nationalists would lead the charge against the Versailles settlement, shouting down and beating up opponents, and pioneering the methods that the Fascists used to gain power. The Liberals who cooperated, hoping to exploit the chaotic post-war situation, instead ended up being defeated by them.

Paralleling Nationalists and Futurists, leftist revolutionaries such as revolutionary syndicalists, anarchists, and sundry dissident Socialists agreed with pro-war Liberals that reaction in the form of the Germanic powers required Italian intervention in the conflict. However, they believed that defeating the Austro-Germans would finally produce conditions favorable to a worldwide revolution and to the implementation of Socialism. June 1914's 'Red Week' served as their model for direct revolutionary action, and they shared with the Nationalists the desire to implement their aims through violence.

Representing a small minority, this faction was important because its most visible members had influenced Mussolini to abandon the absolute neutrality policy; its ideas attracted the future Duce. Many revolutionary syndicalists would join the Fascist movement and, along with the Nationalists, contribute to its style and its ideology.[16]

The most interesting faction advocating intervention consisted of the 'democratic interventionists'. This group is best characterized as being made up of pre-Wilson Wilsonians. A small minority like the other interventionist groups, they were sensible in their approach to the war and to managing its aftermath at the Paris Peace Conference, but they were cursed with Cassandra's gift. They were ignored even though (on the whole) they correctly interpreted events, and had the misfortune of quickly meeting defeat.

Made up of former Socialists such as Leonida Bissolati and Gaetano Salvemini, and with the support of the Freemasons, this faction advocated Italian intervention on the side of the Entente because Italy needed to contribute to the survival of democracy by helping defeat the authoritarian powers led by Germany and Austria-Hungary. They opposed the PSI's 'absolute neutrality' on the grounds that, in practice, it helped the Central Powers whose defeat would open the way to a more peaceful, democratic Europe sensitive to the just aspirations of oppressed ethnic nationalities such as the Slavs. Salvemini argued that only an Entente victory could resolve the problem of the Irredenta and work out a peaceful relationship with the Slav population that bordered Italy on the Adriatic. Given that war had broken out, Salvemini wrote, Europeans had to ensure that it would produce the best results possible by settling the major outstanding problems, creating a stable international order, and furthering the peaceful association of peoples. In short, Salvemini concluded: 'It is necessary that this war kill war.' [17]

Leonida Bissolati, head of the democratic interventionists, had been expelled from the PSI in 1912 because he objected to the Party's ingrained pacifism. Bissolati, who had denounced the Triple Alliance, distinguished between a pacifism that accepted the *status quo* and one that directly confronted foreign policy issues in the hope of creating a durable peace. He had already laid the groundwork for the position he took when the First World War exploded. In a series of articles in July and August 1914, Bissolati denounced the Austrian and German Socialists who, instead of acting to head off the war, had supported it. He reiterated the idea common to the Left that Italy could not make war on the side of the authoritarian powers. He warned that while neutrality was the proper course to take in the early stages of the conflict it could not remain a reference point. Addressing himself to his former Socialist comrades, neutralist champions, he wrote: 'Who can exclude that, in the course of this gigantic European crisis, there is about to be presented to the Italian Socialists, who today all insist on neutrality, the precise duty of demanding Italian intervention to steer the crisis toward a solution that is favorable to the interests of democracy and the proletariat?' Bissolati identified the moment as a decisive one in world history. It had been presented with a choice between the strengthening of authoritarianism and the intensification of military expenses on the one hand, and disarmament, peace and social justice on the other. Thus, while discussions revolved around the Irredenta and the technical issue of whether Italy was or was not bound by the Triple Alliance to support its partners, Bissolati focused on the wider question of the conflict as a struggle for democracy.[18]

The democratic interventionists had an important role when the war broke out, demonstrating against a possible intervention on the Triple Alliance side and then advocating joining the conflict on the side of the Entente to defend democracy from extinction. True to their principles and cognizant of Italy's isolation, they opposed Italian expansionism in the Adriatic and advocated negotiating with the Slavs, after the war ended, for reasonable borders. For this reason, after the conflict they became the prime targets of nationalists of all stripes, who – wilfully confusing them with their former Socialist comrades – accused them of wishing to 'renounce' Italian gains after having, supposedly, refused to fight in the war. To show his support for the war, Bissolati volunteered to fight at age 57 as a private and served in the war cabinets. That they were more in tune with Allied thinking and might have averted the disastrous consequences for Italy at the Paris Peace Conference was another calamity for the country.

Politics and war

The international crisis that led to war caught Italy in the midst of important internal changes. After rapid industrialization between 1896 and 1907 the country entered a recession followed by slow recovery, and it was also affected with greater severity than the more advanced industrial countries in the worldwide economic crisis of 1913. The recessions contributed to greater political extremism, resulting in the defeat of the reformist Socialists in the PSI by the revolutionaries and by the revival of revolutionary syndicalist fortunes in the labour movement. During the early years of the new century, an intense concentration of industry had taken place in Italy, and powerful industrialists turned against Giolitti's moderately leftist policies. Thus the reformist leaders and the unions that had been Giolitti's principal interlocutors had been weakened. Giolitti had dominated Italian politics since 1901, but in 1913 he confronted not only the problem of weakened allies but the prospect of an election under quasi-universal manhood suffrage that greatly strengthened the Catholics. Giolitti felt bound to ally with them in a secret agreement (the 'Gentiloni Pact') in order to win the elections, but the Pact became public soon after and provoked a strong political backlash that led him to resign.

Giolitti had been in similar situations before, when he had left power but soon returned because he retained a majority in Parliament on which his successor was dependent. No doubt Giolitti believed that it would be just a matter of time before the revolutionaries on the Socialist left would be defeated and his successor would prove ineffectual, allowing him to resume the Prime Minister's office. Giolitti suggested a rightist Liberal, Antonio Salandra, to the king as his successor after the leader of that faction, Sidney Sonnino, refused to accept the position. Giolitti judged that the right Liberal faction did not have much support and would be easy to unseat. Salandra, however, did not intend to play the role of seat-warmer for Giolitti and named a cabinet that excluded his followers, even though he remained dependent on the support of Giolittians for a majority in the Chamber of Deputies. This government, which took power on 21 March 1914, indicated Salandra's intention to reinforce the power of conservative Liberals and establish a non-Giolittian majority that would prevent the old Premier from returning to power in the future.[19] In the intervening months before the outbreak of the First World War, in fact, Salandra managed to strengthen the position of the conservative Liberals. Whether his strategy would ultimately have worked had war not broken out

San Giuliano's seven principles were: no separate peace to be concluded by any of the four powers (Britain, France, Russia, Italy); common action by the British, French, and Italian navies to seek out and destroy the Austro-Hungarian fleet; annexation by Italy of the Trentino and possibly of the other Austrian 'Italian provinces' to be determined by the war's outcome; no Italian opposition to participation in the division of Albania by Serbia and Greece, except for the neutralization of the Albanian coastline and an internationalized administration for Valona; Italian renunciation of the Aegean islands it conquered during the Libyan War in case Ottoman integrity were maintained, or compensation for Italy in the Ottoman Empire's Mediterranean provinces in case the integrity were not maintained, economic concessions in Adalia and maintenance of Italian inspectors in the Aegean islands in case these were returned to the Ottomans; an Italian share in any war indemnity; a pledge by the four powers to maintain the post-war territorial and political equilibrium.

is a moot point, but it established a link between Salandra's desire to oust Giolitti and the international crisis: if Giolitti's neutralism could be defeated, his domestic influence would crumble as well.

That crisis caused by the war was becoming acute for the Italians because, although they had promptly asked the Austrians for compensation under Article 7, the Austrians at first refused to negotiate, then stalled after the Germans urged them to open talks.[20] At the same time, the Russians and British made advances to Italy, and in a 9 August 1914 secret letter to Salandra, San Giuliano set out seven principles that must be satisfied if Italy were to consider joining the Entente, and these eventually formed the basis for Italy's intervention.

During the negotiations, San Giuliano's death, problems in the government relating to military affairs and the continuing struggle between neutralists and interventionists produced a cabinet reshuffle in which Salandra consulted closely with Sidney Sonnino, Giolitti's arch-enemy.[21] Sworn in on

When, at the beginning of November 1914 Salandra turned to me and offered the opportunity to enter the Cabinet as Justice Minister, I answered him playfully: 'During my entire scholastic career, I never repeated the same class; since I was Justice Minister for a very long time (more than three years), I don't relish the idea of resuming the same occupation'. All kidding aside, I added, it was not because of misplaced ambition that returning to an office that I had held for so long was repugnant to me; my mentality is such that it is the newness of a job that excites and elates me, while repetition depresses and bores me.

Salandra answered that in this case there certainly would not have been any repetition: given the grave historical moment, one of two things would happen: either Italy would receive territorial compensations, in which case I would be the Justice Minister who promulgated Italian legislation in new provinces; or the compensation [accrescimento] would be refused, in which case it would be war.

VITTORIO ORLANDO *C.* 1941–5

5 November 1914 the new cabinet included, among others less friendly to Giolitti, Sonnino as Foreign Minister and, as Justice Minister, Vittorio Emanuele Orlando, who had become less tied to Giolitti.

Sidney Sonnino had been the leader of the conservative Liberals and sworn enemy of the Left since 1897. He had presided over two cabinets in an anti-Giolittian vein, in 1906 and 1909, and both had collapsed after only three months. Inflexible, domineering, and undiplomatic, he unfortunately remained in office throughout the conflict and the Paris

Peace Conference, during which he would 'solidify his major claims to be Italy's worst-ever Foreign Minister'. His blunders exceeded those of Salandra who branded Italy by remarking that the country would be guided by its 'Sacred Egotism' (Sacro Egoismo) during the negotiations.[22] Although Sonnino came into office as a convinced supporter of the Triple Alliance, he changed his mind as the Austrians stubbornly refused compensation and as he took up negotiations with the Entente. These finally culminated on 26 April 1915 with the Treaty of London. This agreement committed Italy to enter the war in a month, ruled out a separate peace, and spelled out Italian gains in case of victory. Italy was to receive the Irredenta and a defensible frontier up to the Brenner Pass; initial Italian requests in Dalmatia were whittled down to about half, and Italy was to get equitable compensation if the Allies made gains in the colonies.

In light of the future dispute at the Paris Peace Conference, it should be noted that the Treaty gave the city of Fiume – Italian-speaking but surrounded by a Slav hinterland – to 'Croatia, Serbia, and Montenegro'. Guglielmo Imperiali, Italian Ambassador to London who conducted the actual negotiations regarding the Treaty under the direction of his superiors, foresaw that not claiming Fiume while requesting areas of Dalmatia not inhabited by Italians would cause grave problems. Examining a long memorandum sent to him by Sonnino, he wrote in his diary for 6 March 1915: 'There is perhaps too much Dalmatia [in the requests] while Fiume, incontestably Italian, is left out. This omission could cause us serious internal complications at the time of a victorious peace. I will recall for the record that in my talks in Rome with Salandra and Sonnino in November, I alluded to Fiume. The former rebuked me saying that you could not strangle a country depriving it of access to the sea. "Live and let live!" However, I stick to my opinion.'[23] At the Paris Peace Conference, the question of access to the sea for Yugoslavia was a powerful argument for assigning Fiume to that country despite the Italian majority in the city (if the population in the hinterland was counted, the Italian majority became slight or doubtful). However, the Italians considered the domination of the Adriatic as absolutely necessary to their security, explaining their demands in Dalmatia.[24]

The territorial gains that Italy would realize in case of victory have been considered excessive, but while the British and the French adopted this view when the war ended, they were willing enough to negotiate at the time. It was the Russians who objected to Italian demands most strenuously because of their support for the Slavs in the area;[25] in fact, Sonnino received criticism from some quarters for not gaining enough territory while sowing future problems by accepting territory inhabited by Austrians and Slavs.[26] However, by this time the Salandra government had come to the conclusion that Italy stood to lose if it remained neutral no matter who won the war because the major problems of the day would be settled without its participation; the Italians, to their detriment, always remained focused on the Adriatic, considering that if Austria won, it would dominate the area, and if it lost the Slavs would, but paying too little attention to the war's wider issues. Thus, the most important aspect of the Treaty of London was that it gave Italy the security it had sought in the Adriatic, if not control.[27] It is important to recall two crucial 'givens' at the time that history completely altered. There was no idea of Austria-Hungary's disappearance as a result of the conflict, nor did the Allies, including the Italians, desire it because of the problems that would ensue.[28] Moreover, the supposition that Russia would become a major Mediterranean power, and its close relationship with the Balkan Slavs, influenced Sonnino's obstinate demands for gains in the Adriatic in order to offset the supposed increase in Slavic authority and to protect Italy's post-war strategic position.[29]

There was a major obstacle to be overcome before Italy could enter the conflict. The Treaty had to be ratified by Parliament – no easy task given the anti-war majority (Giolittians, Socialists, and Catholics). Given their majority and the country's sentiment, Giolitti's supporters could have voted Salandra out of power, recalled Giolitti, and then voted against ratification. Since Parliament was closed, about 400 deputies (out of 508) left their calling cards at Giolitti's house as a sign of their support for his neutralism. Giolitti, however, who was quoted in the press as saying that Italy could get 'plenty' [*parecchio*] in return for its neutrality, quickly discovered that Salandra had outmaneuvered him. Salandra resigned on 13 May, but pro-war demonstrations led by a small number of nationalists broke out, and the police suppressed anti-war manifestations.[30] Informed about the London agreement, Giolitti judged that Italy's honour demanded that it be fulfilled and withdrew from the political scene,[31] even though the Austrians had finally decided to make concessions, Parliament had manifested its support for his position and the military situation of the Entente had drastically deteriorated. Salandra returned as Premier, and on 20 May the Chamber of Deputies convened to ratify war and voted the government full powers in view of intervention. Italy then declared war on Austria, citing the Irredenta as the cause. This dramatic switch to a declaration of war by representatives opposed to it only a few days earlier gravely damaged parliamentary institutions, creating a precedent and leaving them subject to overthrow during the post-war period.[32]

Writing about these events many years later, Justice Minister Vittorio Emanuele Orlando fully approved Salandra's actions and criticized Giolitti. Orlando vigorously disputed the argument that the government had resigned on 13 May 1915 as part of a plan to set off the demonstrations that led to war. However, he admitted that the episode had weakened the authority of parliamentary institutions, leaving open the question of whether it eventually contributed to the rise of Fascism.[33]

Orlando's agreement to join Salandra in November 1914, despite the Salandra cabinet's anti-Giolitti orientation, illustrates his drift away from Giolitti and the at least temporary change in his political orientation toward the conservative Liberals who had undone his former mentor. In preparation for Italy's entrance into the conflict, it fell to him to prepare the concrete restrictive legislation that would rule the country during wartime. In March 1915 Orlando presented his bill for the 'economic and military defence of the state'. The bill gave the government wide powers in military matters and greatly increased penalties for the unauthorized exportation of goods, spying ('direct or indirect'), the publication ('in whatever form') of military information and other matters having to do with war. Orlando eloquently defended this bill, which took three days of heated debate to pass and which witnessed charges from the opposition that Orlando lied in his defense of the provisions. The Socialists

> If for a moment I would be forced to choose between liberty and the security of my country, then on that day, with anguish but without hesitation, I would sacrifice liberty.
>
> VITTORIO ORLANDO, 1915

accused the government and Orlando of murdering Italian liberty, and were the only ones to vote against the law.[34] The government quickly followed up this legislation with exceptional provisions adopted under the full powers granted to it by Parliament on 22 May. The grave charges against Orlando have little foundation. He did his duty and had little choice but to establish the legal framework for a country about to enter a major conflict. Despite the criticism launched against him, his later actions demonstrated that his core belief in Liberal values and freedom remained strong.

4
Fighting the War

All of the states fighting the First World War found it necessary to increase the power of the central government and
to restrict the freedoms that citizens enjoyed during peacetime. Given the circumstances under which Italy had developed, and especially those in which it entered the war, this
question took on particularly grave importance. The fra-
gility of Italian democracy and the strong conflict between
interventionists and neutralists that continued during the
war quickly brought the issue of balancing civil rights and
military efficiency to the fore. Vittorio Emanuele Orlando's
successive posts as Justice Minister, Interior Minister and
finally Prime Minister made him a major figure in this delicate balancing act.

Justice Minister
Orlando served as Antonio Salandra's Justice Minister from
5 November 1914 to 18 June 1916. During his first term in
that office, in 1907–9, Orlando had concentrated on important reforms such as guaranteeing an independent magistracy. In contrast, his second tenure focused on altering the

legal system in preparation for war and then guiding it during the fighting. Orlando followed up proposed legislation to the Chamber of Deputies on 'the economic and military defense of the State' with laws addressing the 'exceptional' needs required by the war. Afterwards, the Chamber granted full powers to the government. Orlando promised to use the extraordinary powers 'parsimoniously', but they very quickly affected all five of the country's law codes.[1] Aimed at the Socialists and other anti-war activists, these groups protested vigorously, but the majority of the population seems to have accepted the measures.

Orlando had begun his political career as a follower of Giolitti, who had expanded civil rights. He had broken with the longtime Prime Minister on the question of Italy's entrance into the war, but he remained a Giolittian when it came to civil rights. He tried to defend them from erosion during the conflict, but he had to be mindful of protecting the country from domestic opponents of the war and commercial interests that tried to profit inordinately from the conflict, while combating pacifism and defeatism. On the whole, Orlando succeeded well, probably better than the other Allies did given his more difficult circumstances and criticism of his policies by rightists and leftists.

Domestic divisions

Italian divisions stemmed from splits between the interventionists and neutralists which continued after war broke out, and, indeed, after it ended. The minority nature of the Salandra government and the refusal of its leader to open up his cabinet to different currents until it was too late exacerbated the internal situation.

The 'official' Socialists, i.e. those that had remained in the

PSI, were steadfast in their opposition to the war. They adopted the slogan 'Neither adhesion nor sabotage' to summarize their views. The Italian Socialist Party was instrumental in organizing two international congresses, Zimmerwald and Kienthal, held in neutral Switzerland, in an attempt to implement the Socialist injunction against support for 'capitalist' wars that had been a major policy of the Second International but which the major parties had violated. These congresses advocated an immediate peace without annexation, which the Italian party accepted, but important differences split the 'official' Socialists as well. The reformists moderated their demands and, while they criticized the war, gave unofficial support to the government in order to prepare the terrain for the post-war era. The 'revolutionary' Socialists hoped to transform the conflict into an upheaval, and continually attacked the government, refused all cooperation, and hoped to convince the masses to abandon support for the war. Despite legislation hindering anti-war propaganda, the Socialists conducted a campaign against the conflict, sometimes underground but more or less openly. Dissatisfaction spread among the masses, occasionally leading to riots, and worsened as the fighting dragged on. In August 1917 in Turin the discontent reached its high point in a series of riots that caused sixty deaths and 200 wounded. However, economic hardships were primarily responsible for the riots, not Socialist propaganda.[2]

The freedom allowed to war opponents infuriated the Nationalists and other rightists who accused the Socialists of treason. They attacked all neutralists including Giolitti's supporters, who, they contended, exploited parliamentary maneuvers to hamper the war effort because they had been defeated in their effort to keep Italy neutral. The 'interventionists of the right' advocated shutting down organizations and newspapers that criticized the war, and curtailing the civil rights of critics.

In the meantime, Salandra's refusal to make his cabinet more representative by adding spokespersons of different viewpoints only brought increased political opposition. In May 1916, a serious Austrian offensive brought together diehard interventionists and a Giolittian group in order to vote him out. Salandra consulted with Bissolati, the 'democratic interventionist' leader, to widen the cabinet's basis, but the attempt failed. On 10 June the cabinet lost a vote in the Chamber of Deputies, and Salandra resigned.

Salandra explained his version of events in notes he sent to the King dated 15 July 1916. As well as disparaging his enemies, Salandra objected to the workings of parliamentary government during wartime and to 'the penetration of the government itself by parliamentary democracy'. Incredibly, he praised the authoritarian framework of the Central Powers as being better suited to war than the parliamentarian democracy of Italy and its allies. Salandra's notes also focus on another problem that he let slide, and that Orlando had to confront when he took over the Ministry of the Interior in the national unity cabinet that came to power after Salandra's resignation: civilian control of the military. In May 1916 the Austrians made advances and the Italian military commander Luigi Cadorna requested more troops. The cabinet agreed but proposed a kind of war council, to meet in Padua, consisting of several ministers and army commanders so the government could become better informed about the situation on the front. Cadorna categorically refused the request, although he did consent to a visit of some ministers provided they came to him. Eventually, the war minister met with Cadorna and reported back to the cabinet.

This incident pointed to a general problem described by Salandra as an important factor in his resignation, namely the lack of trust that existed between Cadorna and the government. He wrote 'it is indispensable that this trust between the head of the government and the head of the army remain intact. It is necessary that General Cadorna coexist with a head of government who is more submissive than the Hon. Salandra.' [3] In fact, Cadorna had strict links to the interventionists of the Right and supported their demands for greater civil rights restrictions in the country. He would soon lock horns with the new Interior Minister, Vittorio Emanuele Orlando.

Minister of the Interior

A national unity cabinet under rightist Liberal Paolo Boselli succeeded Salandra on 18 June 1916. Boselli opened up his cabinet to different factions in the country, including the democratic interventionists represented by Bissolati, and an 'unofficial' Catholic representative. The Foreign Minister, Sonnino, remained in the cabinet as leader of the right Liberals, while Orlando represented the left Liberals. His takeover of the most important post in the government, the Interior Ministry with responsibility for internal affairs, illustrates the growing importance of this group. At age 78, Boselli lacked the energy to handle this post and ran the government as a kind of mediator. Since Italian Prime Ministers were normally named Interior Ministers, the failure of Boselli to secure that office indicated his weakness. Orlando's assumption of the post pointed to his future designation as Prime Minister in the normal course of events. [4]

Unlike Salandra, Orlando did not despise parliament, nor did he admire the style or supposed military efficiency of the

It is somewhat of a mystery as to why Paolo Boselli was named Prime Minister in 1916. It probably indicates that Salandra's political influence was not completely spent at the time of his resignation, and certainly not with the King, because it was Salandra's choice that Boselli replace him. Boselli, a Turinese born in 1838, had been the first Professor of Business at the University of Rome, was elected for the first time to the Chamber of Deputies in 1870 as a member of the old Right party, and had served in various capacities in the cabinets of Francesco Crispi and Luigi Pelloux in the 1880s and 1890s. He supported Italian intervention in the war, and at the time of his appointment as Prime Minister was the Dean of the Chamber. It was clear from the beginning that he could not handle the demands the war would place on him. Ironically, the new national unity government took on the aura of a caretaker during a crucial period because Boselli, while he presided over a more representative cabinet than had Salandra, gave it little direction. The ministers ran their departments themselves and he allowed Cadorna to retain sole control of the military effort.

Boselli resigned on 30 October 1917 following the Caporetto defeat. He sympathized with the rise of Fascism after 1922 and in 1924 received honorary membership in the Fascist Party. In 1929, he reported favorably on the Lateran Accords, the agreements negotiated between Mussolini and the Catholic Church that ended the dispute between Church and State. Boselli died on 10 March 1932, beating Vittorio Emanuele Orlando for the title of longest-lived Italian Prime Minister by a little more than three months.

Central Powers, later emphasizing that democracy accounted for the victory of the Allies in the struggle. Italy found in Orlando a leader who understood how the First World War had transformed war into a modern conflict of peoples – a total war. Although he most clearly demonstrated that capacity on a worldwide stage after he became Prime Minister following the military disaster at Caporetto, his thinking was already clear as Interior Minister.

The beginning point: war among peoples; therefore 'unity among the people'...Union achieved by force: final failure. Interior unity: spiritual.[5] With these words, Orlando

During the debate as to whether or not Italy should have intervened in the war, a famous letter written by Giolitti appeared in the newspaper *Tribuna*. This letter stated that Italy could gain *parecchio* ('plenty') in return for staying neutral. The furious interventionists interpreted the letter as an attack on the Salandra government and as an unpatriotic attempt to weaken Salandra's negotiating position while he was in the midst of delicate talks with Austria-Hungary in order to gain as much as possible in return for Italian neutrality. Orlando, however, revealed that Giolitti did not intend to publish the letter and only agreed to do so, with modifications, with the intention of helping the government. The thinking was that publication would blunt the strategy of the Central Powers in standing firm against Salandra in order to split the country and negotiate with an eventual Giolitti government that would settle for less. Orlando also states that in the original letter the famous term *parecchio* did not appear but the stronger *molto* ('a lot'). Giolitti agreed to the change with the idea of softening the letter and avoiding damage to the negotiations.

demonstrated his conviction that the war was one of peoples and not solely of armies, necessitating unity of purpose among the people, government, and armed forces. This need, he maintained, required walking a fine line between military efficiency and democracy.

In contrast to Salandra, Orlando defended Giolitti from the charge that he had opposed Italy's entrance into the war because of pro-German feelings. Orlando emphasized their profound differences on Italian intervention but strongly defended Giolitti's patriotism, releasing important details showing that Giolitti had recommended what was best for his country and that, far from attacking Salandra – as the former Prime Minister believed – he had gone out of his way to help him during the period of neutrality. This point was important because of the demands by extremists who wished to implement laws restricting civil rights so that Giolitti and his supporters could be tried, wishing the same treatment for them, or worse, as had been meted out to Louis Malvy and Joseph Calliaux in France. Orlando, unlike Clemenceau in France, refused to endorse such policies.[6]

With regard to civil rights, Orlando began from the principle that the state must fight the war and combat tendencies that threatened to weaken it and the war effort, but that repression must not go beyond what was needed to assure both freedom and military efficiency. According to Orlando, the normal coercive force of a state was not enough to keep it together when a conflict involved the entire population of a country; therefore, a delicate equilibrium must be established between measures necessary to keep the state safe under pressure and the liberty that is desirable in a free country. An important aspect of this balance was the absolute requirement that concrete evidence be produced when treason was alleged, because charges became inflated and distorted during wartime. The apparatus of the Italian state was up to the task, Orlando wrote, and so were the Italian people whose actions, he argued, compared favorably to those of the other belligerent states. This certainly is true despite the application of the 'Sacchi decrees' after the panic following the military disaster at Caporetto during the last year of the war.[7] Italian legislation, for example, can be favorably compared to the infamous Espionage Act of 15 June 1917 and its amendment of 16 May 1918 in the United States prescribing long jail terms for anti-war proponents.

How did Orlando judge his own actions and himself? In the historical literature wartime Italy is famously portrayed as divided. Orlando viewed the extremists on both sides as a minority in the country, but a majority of those who were politically active. Therefore, since he had been a supporter of intervention, the neutralists opposed him; but the

> A psychological study of statesmen and ... why they are considered either "strong" or "weak" would be most interesting ... . A politician who speaks with a surly frown, who accompanies his words by banging his fists on the table or emphasizes them with violent and rude expressions is defined as "strong", even if behind this curtain is frequently hidden a surrender to another's will. The person who, however, even when saying "no" does not depart from a friendly smile, is gentle, even deferential, softens his refusal with courteous manners ... is a "weakling" even if he is firm – very firm – in sticking to his ideas ... . I belong to this second category. ...
>
> VITTORIO ORLANDO, *C.* 1941–5

interventionists did as well; that is – in a statement that summarizes his thinking as Interior and Prime Minister – those who wished to use the war as a reason to repress with violence *all freedom of thought, of speech, of the press, of association ... According to this faction, I should have refused political existence to all parties that had opposed or still opposed the war, dissolved the official Socialist Party, suppressed its newspapers, imprisoned its leaders, declared striking a crime, and so on, with all the therapies of despotic dictatorships.* Thus Orlando viewed himself as having the support of the majority of the Italian people and being opposed by the vocal political elite: *But I didn't care about them, and I still don't care about them.*

This attitude is Orlando's answer to being attacked during his tenure as Interior Minister for being too liberal. The violent diatribes against him no doubt explain why in his memoirs he discusses at length why politicians are seen by observers and historians as either 'strong' or 'weak', and why there seemed to be a nostalgic feeling in his country for a 'strong' personality such as the French leader Georges Clemenceau.[8]

Even though he might have seemed 'weak', or perhaps because of it, Orlando achieved the delicate balance that he recognized as essential during wartime between military efficiency and the preservation of democracy. He put down anti-war demonstrations, but at the same time resisted the attempts of extreme rightists who 'tried in every way to install a new *Holy Office* [Inquisition] against their adversaries'.[9] Certainly, his confrontation with General Cadorna – hanging fire from the Salandra administration – did not give the impression of a weak leader.

Facing down the military

The disorders that hit Italy during the First World War, even if fewer than in some belligerent states, brought about a dangerous conjunction between groups who wished to suppress civil rights because they believed that domestic traitors impeded the war effort and Supreme Military Commander General Luigi Cadorna, who had already been interfering in internal affairs during the Salandra administration. Cadorna argued that Socialist propaganda was weakening the army's resolve to fight. In what could have developed into a very dangerous situation and possibly led to a coup d'etat, he challenged Orlando's liberal policies and demanded that the Interior Minister crack down on the opposition which included not only Socialists but Liberal elements tied to Giolitti. Had this challenge succeeded, it would have spelled disaster for the country, but Cadorna ran up against Orlando's determined resistance.

In his memoirs, Orlando expresses no doubt that the newly

> This so-called weakling has ... always confronted the powerful and the bullies: from Giolitti (when he exercised a parliamentary dictatorship) to Cadorna (when he sent to Rome a Minister for War who was absolutely loyal to him to say that, if necessary, he would have commanded an armed detachment of troops to occupy Palazzo Braschi [the Interior Minister's offices]); from Clemenceau to Wilson. And that's not even talking about twenty years of totalitarian government!
> **VITTORIO ORLANDO** *C.* 1941–5

formed Boselli national unity government revived the old tensions between neutralists and interventionists, with the army openly encouraging and supporting the latter and re-energizing the dispute over civilian control of the military. This fight emerged as one between General Cadorna and Interior Minister Orlando, exacerbated by the hands-off attitude of the Prime Minister and his surrender to Cadorna's strong will and intransigent temperament which Orlando described as *sincere to the point of fanaticism, [convinced as he was] that any attempt at interference on the part of the civilian government in his sphere of competence was to be considered an intolerable usurpation.*[10]

On 6 June 1917, Cadorna wrote to Boselli informing him that the Austrians had made gains in a counteroffensive against the Italians on the Carso battlefield, taking 6,500 prisoners. Most of the captured soldiers belonged to three infantry regiments made up primarily of Sicilians, Cadorna specified, and they had defected to the enemy. If his information turned out to be accurate, Cadorna continued, it

'It would be useless, because the thing is so evident, if I undertook to demonstrate – in difficult moments – the necessity of concentrating political action in only one person, just as it is essential to concentrate military action in only one hand. When time is of the essence and very rapid, frequently bold, decisions are required, these cannot be taken except by one person who, having a wide vision of events, courageously takes responsibility. In [obtaining a] consensus, instead, responsibility is diluted among many people; they are by nature slow, do not agree, and are oriented toward the most prudent party, and there are cases in which the most prudent party appears to be the boldest. This inconvenience is attenuated (only attenuated) when these parties are led by a man with superior intelligence and character who, having achieved a great ascendance, becomes a true dictator not by right but in practice.'

SUPREME MILITARY COMMANDER GENERAL LUIGI CADORNA, 1921

was the result of anti-war propaganda in Sicily that 'has reduced the island to a dangerous den of draft-dodgers and deserters that, according to the War Ministry, number over 20,000 [*sic*]'. Not only Sicily was subject to such propaganda, according to Cadorna, but all Italy, and therefore the civilian population was infecting the army and threatened Italy's security. More alarming, the incidents of indiscipline, desertion and mutiny were increasing, and had led to trials, death sentences and summary executions. If the incidents continued or worsened, Cadorna asserted that he would reinstate 'decimation' of the contaminated units. In a 'decimation', the soldiers of a unit were lined up counted and every tenth man was taken out of the ranks and shot; Cadorna did indeed institute this technique, making the Italian army the only one subject to this punishment.[11] Cadorna considered 'decimation' as 'a supreme act of repression that had been irresponsibly removed from the military penal code' but a necessary weapon given the poison with which the troops were infected whenever they came into contact with civilians.

Cadorna then blamed Orlando's liberal policies for the current state of affairs, informing the government, with 'rude frankness', of the effects the 'weak management of [our] domestic policy will inevitably have on the fortunes of our war'. On 13 June, Cadorna followed this letter up with another informing the government of the number of executions the army had carried out and insisting that the government take immediate action against subversives in the country, and attached a detailed report on the action of military and special tribunals describing an alarming increase in cases of desertion, mutiny, disobedience and other behaviour that threatened the country's safety.[12]

Particular importance may be attributed to Cadorna's focus on the supposed disloyalty of Sicilian soldiers, because Orlando himself was Sicilian. On 4 May 1917, the army's Deputy Chief of Staff sent out a circular to all units suspending leave for Sicilian soldiers. According to this document, once on leave Sicilian soldiers were convinced by subversive elements on their home island to desert their units.[13] The army followed up this provision with others denigrating the patriotism of Sicilian troops and threatening retaliatory measures against their families.[14] Only on 25 May 1917 was the ban on leave for Sicilian soldiers partially lifted.[15]

On 17 June, Prime Minister Boselli wrote to Orlando informing him of Cadorna's letters.[16] Orlando flatly refuted Cadorna's thesis that subversive propaganda in the country was affecting the army in any substantial way. The general contradicted himself with his own evidence. The military tribunals' report on the problem of indiscipline stated that the causes were many and that war weariness caused much of the problem. Orlando observed that first, the increases during May in the crimes reported occurred in categories typical in large, wartime armies and could not be explained by political factors; second, with regard to the Sicilians, the disloyalty occurred only in some units that included them, as the military command itself recognized, and it was probable that the army's suspension of leave contributed to the discontent. Finally, Orlando pointed to a critical error in the evidence relied on by Cadorna: the report stated that the War Ministry counted 20,000 deserters and men who did not report for the draft, while the real number did not exceed 2,400. This figure did not include Sicilian emigrants abroad, which would influence the number for Sicily and for all Italy.[17]

Orlando noted that the problem raised by Cadorna was much greater than one that involved the Interior Ministry, and called for a cabinet discussion on the issue. He did not deny his concern, but insisted that after three years of hard battle the matter implied economic, morale and military issues and not just one area of activity.[18]

Orlando's reasoned response did not end the matter. On 18 July Orlando received a note from War Minister General Gaetano Giardino reiterating the lack of discipline in the army. Giardino was presumably the same War Minster who had conveyed Cadorna's threat to lead 'an armed detachment of troops to occupy Palazzo Braschi [Orlando's Interior Ministry offices]'.[19] In a harsh communication to Giardino on 25 July, Orlando repeated his contention that the issue implied a general revision of governmental policy, and he challenged

the War Minister to cite specific cases where offices dependent on his ministry did not do their duty with regard to maintaining the morale of the troops. Orlando could make the
same charges made against him by the War Minister, *with
an exhortation that the complex military policy over which
Your Excellency presides succeed in better guaranteeing
against the bad feeling and discontent that has effects on the
civilian situation.* Giardino not only had failed to prove that
discontent in the country had a serious effect on the army's
morale, but excluded it by concluding that intensified military campaigns and the army's enlargement accounted for
the increased incidence of criminal behaviour. In an attachment to his letter, Orlando called attention to the case of
the other belligerents, where war weariness of the kind seen
in Italy caused problems similar to those in the Italian army
but on a proportionately much greater scale.[20] A few hundred
troublemakers printing up a few thousand manifestos and
holding a few disorderly meetings could never explain the
myriad and complex reasons for what was happening at the
front and in the country.[21]

The dispute between Orlando and Cadorna came to a
head at a meeting of the Council of Ministers held on 28
September 1917. In addition to restating his reasoning as to
why subversive anti-war propaganda had little effect in the
country, Orlando turned the tables on Cadorna by claiming
that bad conditions at the front affected the entire country.
It was not the civilians who subverted the soldiers, but the
soldiers who infected the civilians. Orlando showed that demonstrations by women against the war always coincided with
the return of soldiers on leave from the front. Letters from
soldiers asking civilians to try to end the fighting had important effects. If strict wartime censorship under strict military

control could not control the spread of dissatisfaction with the war, how could the Interior Ministry control an entire civilian population? Orlando complained about the vagueness of charges against the civilian authorities that supposedly had not been doing their duty, and he insisted on hard, concrete evidence – which was not forthcoming – to back up any charges. The army's problems, he concluded, were purely military and pointed to the danger to the army itself if Cadorna kept thinking that the problem of army morale could be attributed to the action of subversives in the country.

After Orlando had finished what amounted to a condemnation of Cadorna's military administration, he asked the General to correct him if he was wrong; Boselli also asked him to respond, but Cadorna remained silent and the session ended without his having said a word. Walking out of the session, Cadorna turned to Orlando and said: 'All right. You secure my rear lines and I'll take care of the soldiers.'[22] The clash with Cadorna and his army supporters demonstrates Orlando's commitment to civil rights and to civilian control of the military, and his skill in defending these principles. If it can be argued that the young Italian democracy remained fragile, especially because of its exposure to great tensions caused by the conflict, it had worthy advocates in leaders such as Orlando. It is impossible to know if Cadorna was planning a serious coup d'etat, of which Orlando gave a strong hint. In a conversation with journalist Olindo Malagodi on 17 September 1917, Orlando stated that the agitation against him was *fictitious* and aimed at taking over the Interior Ministry in order *to govern Italy with partisan criteria and goals, organizing demonstrations with the [help of] the police in order to instill terror in their opponents [anti-war groups].*[23] Cadorna's authoritarian character and his actions toward the government make him suspect, although he never tried to overturn the government, and his behaviour can be interpreted as that of a soldier worried that the interference of civilians would weaken the war effort.[24] On the other hand, his harsh disciplinary style and obtuseness hindered the military effort, failed to appreciate the link between popular support and war, and would soon produce the disaster at Caporetto.

Besides the military, civil rights and civilian control issues brought to the fore in the struggle between Orlando and Cadorna, the clash revealed another weakness of the Italian war effort. Boselli had in effect kept out of the fight, if he was not sympathetic to Cadorna's arguments. There is no evidence that the cabinet meeting of 28 September, which was supposed to discuss general problems related to the war, made any changes in the government's policies. Boselli was incapable of altering the way in which the war was being fought, of resolving the continuing dissension between neutralists and interventionists, or of augmenting popular support for the war effort. Orlando's experience as Interior Minister confirmed his thinking that popular backing would increase support for the war, and this would be his main accomplishment as Prime Minister.

Orlando and the Catholics

Besides the Socialists, the Catholic Church presented a subtle problem for the Italian state. Italian Catholics had favored neutrality even though they supported their country during the conflict. The Vatican, however, opposed the war and made constant efforts to end it, especially in 1917 when war weariness affected all warring parties. Another problem, especially for Italy, was the widespread feeling that Pope Benedict XV favored the Central Powers, and especially Italy's main enemy Austria, which had been the Papacy's major ally. Italy's circumstances were particularly delicate because, as a Catholic country, if the war worsened relations between Church and State and caused them to relapse to the antagonistic state of affairs in which they languished in the late 19th century, they could have adversely affected the war effort.

As a known quantity who had dealt successfully with the Vatican in the past, Orlando's presence in the government was essential in managing the extremely delicate situation. The immediate and most important issue was the legal status of the Church in Italy, given that the Law of Guarantees regulating relations between the two was silent on what would happen in wartime, with the country in mortal danger and government powers greatly increasing. Orlando, who in his capacity of Minister of Justice oversaw Church affairs, quickly announced that the Law of Guarantees would continue to guide Church-State policies in wartime. In fact, he stressed, the privileges given to the Church needed to be enhanced precisely because of the crisis situation. This policy meant, first and foremost, that the Vatican would retain its diplomatic prerogatives to receive ambassadors and other representatives, including those of the enemy powers at war with Italy. Orlando also allowed high ecclesiastical officials and other persons having business with the Vatican – citizens of enemy states – to travel freely to Rome to conduct their affairs with the Church. In addition, Italy refrained from applying wartime regulations to citizens of enemy states working for the Holy See and living in Italy. Finally, the rules regarding military exemptions for persons rendering valuable service to their country were also applied to persons, religious or lay, who worked for the Pope. Orlando notes that he did not interfere with the Vatican's business even when certain persons violated the good faith extended by ecclesiastical and Italian officials.

Clearly there was a mutual understanding expressed by Papal Secretary of State Cardinal Pietro Gasparri, who said that the Vatican would not cause Italy any embarrassment. In fact, during the conflict, Catholics served loyally in the armed forces, Catholic chaplains were attached to fighting units, and priests prayed for an Italian victory in the churches.[25]

Domestic problems between Church and State thus remained minor, depriving the Central Powers of a lever they could have used to split the Italians, and of a propaganda issue that might have badly embarrassed Italy. Probably the most serious problem that arose during the war was the Italian expropriation, in August 1916, of Palazzo Venezia, site of the Austrian Embassy to the Vatican, and the anticlerical backlash the Papacy provoked when it protested.[26] Cardinal Gasparri wrote to Orlando objecting to the cabinet's supposed manipulation of events, but the situation soon blew over. When Orlando left the Justice Ministry to take over as Interior Minister, the Vatican asked if he could remain its interlocutor, and the government agreed.[27]

Orlando went out of his way to defuse another potentially explosive issue when he defended Pope Benedict XV from charges of pro-Germanism.[28] When the Pope called for international peace on 1 August 1917, his appeal had an effect on war-weary Europeans who agreed with his definition of the war as a 'useless massacre'. The peace that Benedict called for mirrored President Woodrow Wilson's Fourteen Points and served the propaganda aims of the Central Powers, which accepted the Pope's suggestions (with conditions). The Entente powers did not answer, except for Italy in the form of a speech to the Chamber of Deputies by Foreign Minister

Sonnino on 25 October. The gruff Sonnino pronounced the message a reflection of Austro-German propaganda and useless as a basis for discussion. This attitude angered Italian Catholics and embarrassed Filippo Meda, their unofficial representative in the cabinet.[29] By this time, however, the Boselli government was at the end of its rope, and the Caporetto defeat would be the last blow, bringing in Orlando as Prime Minister.

5
Military Affairs

The military history of the First World War is hardly brilliant. All belligerent armies made errors, suffered defeats and endured hundreds of thousands of casualties for trivial gains; disaffection, desertions and mutinies afflicted all armies. Italy's military underwent the same kind of trials, exacerbated by the country's industrial and economic weaknesses. However, given the context in which it fought the war, Italy's military effort hardly deserves the dismissals it received from its allies after the conflict (and still receives in the English-language literature) and which coloured the disputes at the Paris Peace Conference.[1]

The person who would represent Italy at the Conference, Vittorio Emanuele Orlando, was the major political figure in the government. He was the only person who served in important posts in all the war cabinets, from the Salandra administration that took the country into the conflict before Sonnino succeeded San Giuliano as Foreign Minister, to the Boselli cabinet. Both Salandra and Sonnino were strongly disliked, and Boselli stood out for his weakness. Orlando had support in all the Liberal camps, left and right, and maintained his friendly relations with Giolitti, still one of the country's most important politicians. What seemed to puzzle him most was the opposition of the groups that had pressed for Italy's intervention in the war, which he had supported. He understood the opposition of those who had advocated neutrality, but constantly tried to understand why the interventionists disliked him and his policies. He finally came to the conclusion that they expected him to repress all dissidence harshly and to set up a dictatorship, something he consistently refused to do both before and after he became Prime Minister, because he was convinced it would damage the country's war effort instead of enhance it. Indeed, Orlando personified this principle.

At the outbreak of the First World War the Italian armed forces suffered from several serious handicaps. The country was poor and primarily agricultural, with heavy industry mostly confined to the triangle formed by Milan, Turin and Genoa. Italian industry could not produce weapons in the unprecedented quantities required during the First World War, developing that capacity only later in the conflict. In addition, while the country spent proportionately more of its budget on the armed forces than the other large European powers, its poverty meant it could not hope to keep up with them. They had a much larger industrial base and could easily outspend the Italians while devoting a smaller percentage of their budget to armaments. This problem created enormous political tensions in Italy, because the monarchs pressed for a big army and the Socialists demanded that less be spent on the army and more on reforms. Yet, while even the Liberals of the Right understood the need to restrict military expenses which by 1912 had risen to 29.4 per cent of the budget, the secret commitment that Italy had undertaken under the Triple Alliance to send half its army to fight with the Germans in case of a war with France made it impossible to initiate a new policy according to which the army would become smaller but more efficient.[2] The result was that the Italian army seemed large on paper, but only a few divisions were at full strength even when Italy entered the war.

Well aware of the country's military inferiority in an increasingly turbulent Europe, Italian army Chief of Staff Alberto Pollio and Minister for War Paolo Spingardi proposed a program to reinforce the army, but the Libyan War and the subsequent guerrilla fighting threw their plans awry. Eventually, in late August and September 1914, with Europe at war and Italian military recovery urgent, the cabinet appropriated 120 million for the armed forces, less than a quarter of the original sum they had sought.[3]

During the neutrality period, the Italians did their utmost to make up their deficiencies by using the increased funds to intensify officer training, to make up for the serious scarcities in equipment and to transfer troops from Libya and Albania to Italy. Given the lack of time, this effort could hardly succeed; and although better prepared, the Italian army entered the war at a significant disadvantage when compared with its enemies. The most serious lack was heavy artillery (which numbered only 132 pieces) and machine guns (of which the army possessed only 618). The rifle situation was better, although the army did not possess enough modern rifles to arm all its projected one million men with them. Ammunition presented an even greater problem, its scarcity imposing a quota on artillery shells that could be fired, while bullets were in short supply. One army corps was allotted only four rounds per mortar.[4] It would not be until 1917–18 that Italian industry had expanded to a great enough degree to make good these shortages; and even then, given the lack of raw materials, it needed considerable help from its allies. In addition, the lack of winter clothing meant the army could not undertake an autumn campaign. Consequently, the army's Chief of Staff informed the government that the army could not commence a military campaign in 1914, and this consideration contributed to the political and diplomatic factors postponing Italian intervention until spring 1915. This delay had a crucial military consequence because the Italians had lost the element of surprise when they did intervene.

Political factors also had an important impact on military strategy, especially at the beginning of the war when Italian intervention would have been most effective. There was an amazing lack of coordination between armed forces and government. Luigi Cadorna succeeded Pollio as Chief of Staff on 27 July 1914 after his sudden death on 1 July, leaving the country without a military commander for three weeks in the midst of the grave European crisis. When Cadorna took over Italy was still in the Triple Alliance, and he worked out plans to concentrate Italian forces against France and to send part of the army to fight on the German side on the Western Front. Just as the cabinet prepared to declare Italy's neutrality, the King approved Cadorna's plan in principle. Only afterwards, convinced that Italy would be fighting against Austria instead of on its side, did Cadorna turn his attention to prepare a war plan against that country. The best military scenario would have been to mobilize quickly and attack the Austrians while their army was on its way to the Russian front, but this turned out to be impossible for other reasons in addition to the critical shortages plaguing the Italian army.

Several important factors slowed down Italian mobilization, including the length of the Italian peninsula, the scarcity

of railroads due to the mountainous terrain and the station-
ing of soldiers on a regional rather than on a national basis.
Political reasons determined this setup. After unification, the
army was an important instrument for melding the populations of the different Italian regions. Post-unification governments required that regiments be composed of soldiers
coming from at least two different regions speaking different
dialects and be stationed in a third, with its location changed
every four years.[5] When intervention finally came, mobilization and concentration of troops in the war zone, estimated
to take twenty-five days, took more than forty.

Military myths

More than the history of any of the Big Four Allied powers,
Italian history immediately before and during the war, and
especially its military performance, is replete with myths. It
is necessary to consider some of these legends because Vittorio Emanuele Orlando, Italian representative to the Paris
Peace Conference, found them already well entrenched when
he arrived at the meeting. The myths and misunderstandings
of the Italian context – particularly the privileged defensive
position of the enemy, the mountainous character of the front,
and the treacherous nature of the terrain that made that front
the most difficult on which to conduct military operations
– not only affected the French, British, and United States
officials. They and their representatives actively exploited
them in order to combat Italian claims that threatened either
their colonial or ideological interests, so that they have come
down to our own times, if anything, augmented. Orlando
and especially Sonnino seemed unaware of the worst effects
of these misinterpretations – or they were powerless to dispel
them – and they certainly failed to win the propaganda and

the public relations battles that took place in Paris. These myths then spread to their own country, spurring resentment, helping set the stage for extremism and, eventually, favoring the rise of Fascism.

In the attempt to undermine Italian claims, the Allies began by denigrating Italian motives for entering the war, an attitude which has persisted. The primary purpose attributed to the Italians for their intervention was territorial gain – as if the other combatants did not have similar motives. Yet in comparison to Britain, France,[6] Russia,[7] Germany[8] and Austria-Hungary,[9] Italian aims were petty (except in colonial areas, where they received only vague assurances of compensation in case their allies made gains, and which they did not gain). Moreover, little or no heed was paid to the Irredenta and the mistreatment of the Italian minority there, or of the security issues regarding Northern Italy, which was subject to invasion, issues always mentioned in regard to France. Certainly the Italians overreached in terms of their power, as the Allies and Germans never tired of noting, but so did they; it was common in the diplomatic world of the day and perhaps even now.

The United States did not fight for territorial gains, but to 'make the world safe for democracy', suspiciously only beginning to do so in 1917. At that point the nature of the war changed, but the Italians were slow in getting on the bandwagon, and perhaps were not quick enough to switch gears as the British and French did. And they suffered for it, because their allies viewed them as cynically declaring their neutrality although they were part of the Triple Alliance, bargaining for the best deal and then betraying their allies. However, the United States stayed neutral for most of the conflict's duration, and when it entered the war it did so primarily on the basis of safeguarding neutral rights. In his speech declaring war on Germany, Wilson condemned unrestricted submarine warfare, reiterated neutral rights, objected to German interference in US affairs and said little about democracy. Yet the three-year neutrality of the United States goes unmentioned while the Italian period of neutrality is consistently condemned.

The so-called 'betrayal' by Italy of its Triple Alliance partners has already been discussed; this legend was an important undercurrent at the Paris Peace Conference, and is still commonly referred to.[10] Yet this is to misconstrue the nature of the Alliance. When the war began, Germany demanded to know how Italy would stand, and San Giuliano answered that Italy was not committed to join its allies because Austria had begun an aggressive war. Here is the relevant article from the Triple Alliance with regard to Germany (emphasis added):

ARTICLE 2. In case Italy, <u>without direct provocation on her part</u>, should be attacked by France for any reason whatsoever, the two other Contracting Parties shall be bound to lend help and assistance with all their forces to the Party attacked.

This same obligation shall devolve upon Italy in case <u>of any aggression without direct provocation by France against Germany</u>.

So, Italy was not in fact bound to help its partners if they provoked an aggressive war, and neither the Germans nor the Austrians were bound to aid the Italians if they undertook an aggressive war.

Another episode commonly held against Italy during the war, at Paris and down to the present, was the failure of that

'Germany could be induced to fall upon us before it otherwise would do [if Italy declared war immediately]. As far as the Allies are concerned, frankly I do not see what right they have to complain about us, who are the only ones who have loyally adhered to the April agreement [Treaty of London], while they, both with regard to the financial and military conventions, have given us as little as possible, one could say nothing.

'While all should have now been on the offensive, we are the only ones on the offensive. The others blandly talk about August or September [1915]. What right do they have to demand that we, and only we alone, commit ourselves everywhere, immediately and to the hilt?'

PRIME MINISTER ANTONIO SALANDRA, 27 JUNE 1915

country to declare war on Germany until 1916. Here is the way one historian puts it: 'Surfeited with riches still to be earned, Italy declared war against Austria on 23 May 1915, but didn't pronounce against Germany until 27 August 1916.' [11] The dates are correct, but the implications are not. The Treaty of London obliged Italy to declare war on Germany (and Turkey, which it did on 21 August 1915). The treaty did not specify the date by which Italy was bound to declare war on Germany, and countries normally look to their interests in cases of this kind. Sonnino proposed that a declaration of war be sent to Germany and Turkey soon after Italy intervened, but Salandra opposed him not because he planned to evade the obligation (German forces were already fighting the Italians on their front and German submarines had sunk Italian ships), but because, once he realized the gravity of the military circumstances, he believed a declaration of war might cause the Germans to send more troops to the Italian front while the country was relatively weak. He was awaiting the right moment and was upset because he believed the Allies had not fulfilled their own commitments toward Italy; he certainly did not realize the hostility his reticence aroused in the Allies.

Choosing the date on which to enter a conflict according to a country's national interest is normal; and an interesting, though hardly mentioned, comparison may be made with the United States. The Americans declared war on Germany on 6 April 1917, but not on Austria-Hungary until 7 December 1917; furthermore, they refused to declare war on Turkey or Bulgaria despite the wishes of a Senate Committee to do so.[12] A reason for this lack of action may have been the indications that the US was interested in Near East trade after the conflict, and the American belief that Turkey would still be a major player. As late as June 1918, a Turkish attack on an American Consulate and hospital provoked demands in Congress for a declaration of war, but Wilson objected saying that there had been 'no actual collision' with Turkish or Bulgarian troops. Indeed, it was the Turks who suspended relations with the US in April 1917.[13] Given these facts, it is curious to see the persistent accusation against the Italians because they did not declare war on Germany when they did so against Austria-Hungary. This propaganda perpetrated by the Allies in the days of the Paris Peace Conference remains a black mark against Italy in the historical literature on the First World War.

The capstone of the case against Italy is its allegedly poor military performance, but all the Allies demonstrated less than brilliant generalship, if not downright incompetence, as well. The French, British, Germans, and Russians, in addition to the Italians, all sacrificed the lives of hundreds of thousands of soldiers for insignificant gains, employed mistaken tactics and privileged the offensive, while failing to understand that new weapons gave the overwhelming advantage to the defense over the offense. French and British generals were despised by their own soldiers, dismissed and, after the war, shunned by their own people because of the carnage their tactics wrought on their armies. The Italians shared in these errors, both qualitatively and quantitatively, but whether on average they were so much worse than their colleagues – given their more limited resources and their less industrially-advanced society – remains to be established.

Criticism of the performance of Italian soldiers in the First World War has its origins with the Italian commander, Luigi Cadorna, who consistently excused his own incompetence by blaming his soldiers for their supposed failure to fight adequately because of subversive propaganda. Modern historical research has consistently disproved his thesis.[14] The incident in 1917 in which Cadorna attempted to convince his government of the pernicious influence of anti-war propaganda has been discussed in Chapter 4, but, as the person responsible for the defeat at Caporetto, Cadorna redoubled his efforts to blame others. Cadorna's political astuteness and ability to manipulate the press exceeded those of his British and French counterparts, and his arguments unduly influenced foreign observers, probably because they knew so little about the Italian front. The Caporetto defeat is a major reason for the decline of Italy's military reputation, although the Allies suffered similar defeats. Caporetto ruined the country's military reputation and, as John Keegan states, 'Gibes at the military qualities of the Italians have been commonly and cheaply made ever since. Unfairly …'[15]

Stories abound of Italian soldiers surrendering while hailing the Austrians, the Germans or the Pope; but, besides the normal human wish to survive (and examples can be cited for other nationalities), the stories should be treated cautiously and not all uncritically accepted as fact. For example, the soldiers of the Reggio Brigade, cited as surrendering without fighting and while shouting 'We want peace' were not even stationed on the Isonzo.[16] Moreover, since it is incomprehensible that an army that refused to fight and whose soldiers ran away like cowards successfully resisted the triumphant Austro-Germans only a few days later at the Battle of the Piave, another myth developed: that the Allies saved them. Reality, however, is quite different.[17]

Another reason for the prevalence of these military myths is ignorance of the nature of the Italian front, so that even the heavy casualties suffered by the Italians are held against them. However, the front was the most difficult of all the fronts in the First World War. The mountainous terrain stretching to stony plateaus, were full of natural defenses which the enemy reinforced, and the ground itself accounted for many casualties: '… Shellfire in the rocky terrain caused 70 percent more casualties per rounds expended than on the soft grounds in France and Belgium.'[18] Yet, Italian casualties, it was implied, resulted from a significantly greater incompetence than that demonstrated by their allies.

In the highly charged atmosphere of Paris in 1919, during which Orlando's dispute with an anti-Italian Wilson – furtively supported by French and British leaders who aimed to sabotage a new competitor in the Mediterranean and in Africa – provoked the most serious split, the myths regarding Italy carried enormous weight and caused massive resentment in the country afterward, partially accounting for the idea of the 'mutilated victory' and helping fuel the rise of Fascism.[19] Unfortunately, the legends have also persisted; only recently has a book appeared that discusses the 'forgotten sacrifice' on both sides of the Italian front in an objective manner that should be proper to all historians;[20] but, sadly, it is unlikely that this reappraisal will find its way into the popular consciousness any time soon.

The fighting

When the Italians entered the war on 23 May 1915, they faced an unexpectedly serious military situation that had reversed the one existing at the time of the negotiations that resulted in the Treaty of London a month earlier. Italian intervention was supposed to have been coordinated with Russian and Serbian offensives and Romanian intervention. However, just before the Italians entered the fighting, the Central Powers had overturned the previous military balance favourable to the Entente. They routed the Russians in the East while the Turks defeated the British at Gallipoli. The Russians thus could not coordinate the planned offensive with Italian intervention, while the Serbians preferred to move into Albania, not against the Austrians, and the expected Romanian intervention did not materialize.[21] These developments allowed the Austrians to transfer troops from the Russian front to the Italian frontiers. Had this situation existed before the signing of the Treaty of London, it is possible Salandra would not have intervened, as his letter to Sonnino of 27 June 1915 suggests.[22]

Cadorna had drawn up a war plan that called for a breakthrough on the Isonzo River, his right wing, which would have allowed him to threaten Vienna, Trieste and the Adriatic littoral. Even though he was supremely convinced he would succeed, several factors held back Cadorna's army. These included the lack of arms and munitions, especially artillery, which, when the offensive began on that section of the front, consisted of 52 medium and ten heavy guns hampered by the lack of air reconnaissance.[23] The Austro-Hungarian army, in the war for a year, was much better equipped, better experienced and had the advantage of superb defensive positions. The Italians also lost the element of surprise because when hostilities began on 24 May, only two of 17 army corps were at full strength and could not undertake a planned offensive. Moreover, Cadorna's war plan was flawed because he did not concentrate his offensive on a limited front on the Isonzo while staying on the defensive along the rest of the line; instead, he also went on the offensive at different points further west at varying times. This technique divided his forces and split up the few heavy guns he had at his disposal, making him too weak to break through at any one point.

In addition to these factors, the practically impregnable Austrian defenses stopped the Italian offensives and caused extremely high casualties. The terrain on the left bank of the Isonzo, occupied by the Austrians, was higher than the right bank, where the attacking Italians were located. In addition, the Italian front included some of the highest mountains in Europe and some of its most rugged terrain, making fighting very difficult and favoring the defense. Cadorna, at age 65, had been trained in the same tactics as the other First World War generals, that is, to favor a war of movement and the quick offensive – with élan counting the most. The war on the Western Front, however, had demonstrated that the machine gun made mobile warfare impossible because it favored the defense, and that a war of attrition and fighting from trenches was the only kind of combat possible. Cadorna

Count Luigi Cadorna (1850–1928) came from an illustrious Piedmontese family. His father, Raffaele Cadorna, born in Milan, immigrated to Turin and became a hero of the Risorgimento. He led the attack on Rome that resulted in the annexation of the capital to Italy on 20 September 1870. Before then, he distinguished himself in the armed forces during the Italian wars of independence in 1849 and 1859, in the Crimean War in 1855–6, and in the fight against brigandage in southern Italy in the 1860s.

Luigi Cadorna attended military school as a boy, then Turin's military academy and took part in his father's siege of Rome in 1870. Originally attracted to the artillery, he transferred to the infantry, made exhaustive military studies of Italy's rugged frontier conditions, writing monographs that became standard texts, and participating in peacetime maneuvers with the *Bersaglieri* (crack infantry). These endeavours established Cadorna's reputation and brought him steady promotions in the army. In July 1914, he succeeded General Alberto Pollio as Army Chief of Staff after his sudden death. Cadorna was a skilled politician, and maneuvered very well not only in his native country but also abroad. An example of this talent is how favourably he impressed Lord Kitchener, who, after an inspection of the Italian front in November 1915 wrote a laudatory report on Cadorna's handling of the war. In the same year, Great Britain named him an honorary Knight Grand Cross of the Order of the Bath. During the First World War, Cadorna became famous for using harsh discipline to keep his troops in line, orders for the summary execution of his own soldiers, his penchant for the offensive, his dismissal of more than 200 officers and his haughty attitude toward politicians. His reputation suffered after Caporetto, but the Fascists rehabilitated him in 1924 by conferring on him the rank of Marshal of Italy. He died on 21 December 1928.

did not incorporate these lessons despite reports from Italian observers describing the drastic change in warfare,[24] despite the inadaptability of the terrain to the older ideas of how to conduct military campaigns and even though he understood that the war had changed character.

Playing into this situation was the fact that Cadorna was obliged to take the offensive for political reasons: to retake the Irredenta, the stated basis for Italian intervention; to establish

Italian security on the eastern littoral of the Adriatic Sea; to achieve a breakthrough that would knock Austria out of the war and end it by opening up the German citadel to an attack from the south-east; and, at various junctures, Allied pressure.[25] Cadorna proved unequal to the task, and proved himself as incompetent as the typical First World War commander;[26] though taking into consideration the more limited time the Italians were in the conflict, Italian casualties were proportionate to those of the other Allies.

The battles on the Italian front seesawed between May 1915 and September 1917, with both sides winning small areas of territory, losing them and then winning them back again, as was the case on the Western Front. Cadorna kept trying to break through on the Isonzo, unleashing eleven offensives without achieving his objectives, but halting a determined Austrian attack known as the *Strafexpediton* (punitive expedition) designed to drive Italy out of the war.[27] The temporary military success of this campaign was a factor in Salandra's resignation, and his replacement by Boselli with Orlando as Interior Minister. There was talk about replacing Cadorna, but it went nowhere because of uncertainty about who would succeed him, and the wily general survived.

Given their mutual antagonism, it is interesting to note Orlando's interpretation of military events. Cadorna has consistently been criticized for the number of his offensives. Orlando points out that the action of all the Allied armies were predicated on the success of the offensive, thus wasting an enormous number of lives and resources. As far as the Italian defeat at Caporetto is concerned, Orlando points to numerous 'Caporettos' suffered by all armies: Charleroi, the Aisne (Nivelle offensive), Chemin des Dames for the French; Passchendaele and Saint-Quentin for the British; and the disastrous Franco-British offensive of the Somme. The losses had repercussions on the Italian front. According to Orlando, these defeats had their origins in the Allied failure to fight the war in a unified manner, which stemmed from the military commanders' downgrading of the proper role of civilian authorities and the consequent lack of military coordination on the different fronts. Thus the Caporetto defeat in Italy stemmed from the inability of the Allied commanders to see the war as a joint effort, which produced the Allied defeats on the Western Front in 1917. Here Orlando cites his British colleague David Lloyd George who argued that 'The Flanders campaign was directly responsible for the Italian disaster' and who put the blame for Caporetto (and Passchendaele) squarely on British commander Douglas Haig.[28] The war was won, Orlando wrote, only after the great military defeats of 1917 spurred the Allies to remedy their organizational defects and to restore the authority of civilian leaders.[29]

As in the other military defeats that marked 1917, Caporetto also had its origins in the hubris of the Italian military commander, and his well-known disdain for, and independence from, civilian authority. Although Cadorna's military responses had stopped the Austrian *Strafexpedition* in 1916, the fighting revealed fatal flaws in his generalship that he never remedied: a consistent underestimation of the enemy and a lack of imagination. The Italian offensives had gained territory in 1915 and 1916. The war of attrition that prevailed on that front exhausted the Austrian army by the fall of 1917, and a fresh Italian offensive was in the offing for the spring.[30] The Austrians feared their enemies might finally break through, and in order to prevent the new offensive, they proposed to their German allies a joint offensive strong enough to knock Italy out of the war. Their reconnaissance showed that a weak ɔoint existed in the Italian lines at the upper Isonzo River, and they asked for German help to unleash an overwhelming attack there that would allow the armies of the Central Powers to overrun the plains of north-east Italy, to capture Venice, and end the war in Italy. The Germans, fearing the defeat of their allies and that the Austrians would renew a previous bid for a separate peace, overcame their initial hesitation and agreed.

In the meantime, Cadorna had concluded that it was too late in the year for the enemy to consider an offensive, despite ample information from his own intelligence services that the enemy was preparing a major push; the more intelligence that came in signalling an attack, the more he ignored the threat, and he especially did not believe it possible that any attack would come through the mountainous region of the upper Isonzo. On 18 September Cadorna issued generic orders for his army to assume the defensive and to prepare for winter quarters. These orders did not change the distribution of the troops holding the front, which left the upper Isonzo lightly guarded. Cadorna then left for two weeks' rest behind the lines, and returned to his post five days before the enemy attack. The Austro-Germans exploited the element of surprise, and the poor deployment of the Italian forces allowed them to gain an enormous local superiority at crucial points when they began their attack on 24 October 1917. For example, in one sector, four defending Italian divisions were attacked by ten German divisions, and one division that cracked found itself overwhelmed by three German divisions.

The battle began at 2:30 a.m. with an intense artillery bombardment, hardly answered by the Italians who had been ordered by their commander Pietro Badoglio not to fire except on his orders, and by a poison gas attack. Badoglio hoped to draw the attackers into a trap, but fog hid the true nature of what was happening from the Italian command. Surprise contributed to a series of confused orders and the isolation and envelopment of crucial units. Cadorna remained optimistic and failed to realize until evening that the enemy had broken through and was cutting off, surrounding and annihilating isolated Italian units. As a result, he did not send reinforcements quickly enough. The speed of the enemy advance also surprised him. The lines collapsed and panic spread through the ranks, and a disorderly retreat began as discipline broke down and hundreds of thousands of troops dispirited by years of intense warfare threw away their arms and headed for the Venetian plain. The first line of planned resistance at the Tagliamento River broke down. However, the Italian line held at the Piave River, stopping the offensive. French and British troops were rushed to the scene but remained in reserve.[31]

The human and material cost of the Battle of Caporetto was terrible for the Italians: 11,000 dead, 275,000 prisoners, 350,000 disbanded soldiers and 400,000 evacuated civilians. The Italians lost about 3,150 cannons and 3,000 machine guns, in addition to other losses. But, by holding at the Piave, the Italians denied their enemies the capture of any major city, especially Venice, which would have added to the psychological blow they had already received. Despite the severe defeat, the objective of knocking Italy out of the war failed, and the country demonstrated that it could hold the enemy off even if the Italian front became the major focus of their war effort after the Central Powers had defeated the Russians, Serbians, and Romanians. The Italians were not the only ones to lose a major battle in the First World War,[32] and their dogged resistance and recovery prevented the Central Powers from shifting millions of Austro-Hungarian soldiers to the Western Front. Moreover, a new unity government headed by Vittorio Emanuele Orlando was determined to lead an Italian military recovery and to fight until victory.

Worse than the Caporetto losses, however, was the damage done to Italy's reputation, which would have pernicious repercussions at the Paris Peace Conference and beyond. Although there is no doubt that military reasons accounted for the defeat, as has been abundantly proven since the battle, Cadorna defended himself by immediately blaming the troops and subversive propaganda. In his official communiqué of 28 October, spread far and wide abroad by his telegraph service, he wrote, 'The failure of units of the II Army to resist and their cowardly withdrawal without fighting, or their ignominious surrender to the enemy, has permitted the Austro-German forces to break our left wing on the Julian front.' Orlando removed the most offensive statement from Cadorna's report, but it still created indignation in Italian public opinion, and he regretted that he had never thought of reviewing such communiqués before they became public.[33]

In England, the Italian Ambassador, Guglielmo Imperiali, noted the pernicious effects of Cadorna's communiqué in his diary: 'Had a hellish time last night. Cadorna issued a bulletin in which he talked about the *cowardice* [in English and in italics in the original] of some units that surrendered without fighting (Fourth Army Corps). God only knows what a terrible blow this rash and disgraceful telegram caused me.' The government sent Imperiali a more moderate version of the story and he succeeded in getting this account published by the British newspapers. But, 'unfortunately, it [Cadorna's telegram] has already circulated. Cadorna has made an enormous error and must assume the grave responsibility of inflicting a terrible stigma on the soldiers and on the nation.' At a meeting with the British King, George V attributed the defeat to a 'preordained defection' and demonstrated how Italian myths circulated in Britain at the highest levels: 'When His Majesty alluded to Southern troops I respectfully protested, saying that they had always behaved valorously.' [34] Cadorna's telegram and similar attempts by other Italian commanders to dodge their culpability by erroneously blaming the Caporetto defeat on a supposedly inherent lack of military proficiency, as noted, seriously damaged the Italian reputation.

Despite his attempt to blame the troops, this time Cadorna did not survive. On 9 November he was 'kicked upstairs' and sent to be part of the Supreme War Council at Versailles. Armando Diaz replaced him; the new army chief had commanded a corps and had headed the operations office of the Supreme Command. Diaz, from Naples, treated the troops with greater respect as human beings, and instilled an efficient military style into the army. The armed forces would go on the defensive, repair their wounds and, this time, would not take the offensive again until they were more than ready.

6
Prime Minister

On 28 October 1917, when news of the Italian catastrophe at Caporetto began circulating, King Vittorio Emanuele III summoned Interior Minister Vittorio Emanuele Orlando to his Rome residence and asked him to form a government. Orlando notes wryly in his memoirs that he had no competitors for the job.

The reason was clear: with the enemy speedily penetrating into the country and the army supposedly crumbling, the new Prime Minister would hold the most unenviable post in Italy. Indeed, herculean tasks faced Orlando. Besides organizing the military resistance and, eventually, victory, Orlando had to unite the country – but only unity could bring victory. The country's profound political divisions had contributed to the weakness of popular support for the war, and it was up to him to try to heal the wounds that the enemy hoped to exploit and debilitate the country. Moreover, the differences between him and Cadorna raised serious questions of civilian control of the military[1] and the maintenance of civil rights during a total war – a problem with which all the Allies struggled. Finally, the 'breaking of armies'[2] in 1917, the Allied crisis of that year, the American entrance into the conflict and the Bolshevik Revolution would profoundly change the war's nature. These issues and, in late 1918, the impending breakup of the Austro-Hungarian Empire, made an alteration of Italian foreign policy necessary. Orlando confronted these issues with success, with the exception of foreign policy, which was steadfastly guided by Sonnino who successfully resisted efforts at change.

Caporetto's political effects

There has been discussion among historians as to who wanted Cadorna fired, Orlando or the Allies. Orlando states in his memoirs that he posed it to the King as a condition of taking office. Consistent with the historiographical pattern downplaying the Italian role in the First World War, English-speaking historians tend to affirm that Allied pressure at the Rapallo Conference, called after Caporetto to discuss Allied aid, forced Cadorna's dismissal. Sonnino reports in his diary that the Allies were not disposed to entrust their troops to the existing military leaders, and this statement is frequently cited to affirm the Allied role in firing Cadorna. However, Sonnino goes on to quote Orlando as saying at the same meeting that the government had already decided to reorganize the General Staff, and had full powers to do so.[3]

This account is consistent with Orlando's claim to have made Cadorna's dismissal a prerequisite for his accepting the Prime Minister's post. There were three reasons why he could not allow Cadorna to continue as head of the army, he told the King: first, commanders have to take responsibility for defeats; second, the public and violent manner in which Cadorna had placed the blame for Caporetto on his soldiers; third, he believed in the intimate collaboration between the armed forces and the government that Cadorna denied.[4] Earlier in his memoirs, Orlando stated that under no circumstances could he rule without affirmation of the principle of civilian control of the military, which made Cadorna uncomfortable, and stopped just short of accusing the general of cooperating with the Nationalists to prepare a coup d'etat.[5] Be that is it may, Cadorna resisted leaving his post despite Orlando's attempt to soften the blow by sending the soon-to-be former commander gentle telegrams and naming him to the Supreme War Council in Versailles.[6] The King had to pressure Cadorna.[7]

> Between that party [the Nationalists] and General Cadorna there had been established a relationship of political solidarity that could be labeled an alliance. I do not know, and it would be difficult to say, to what point those relations could have led. Certainly, they were very intimate when one thinks only of his special military police, set up by the Supreme Command and extended from the front to the rest of the country.
>
> VITTORIO ORLANDO, C. 1941–5

Orlando moved quickly to set up a cabinet, promising the King he would complete the process within 24 hours. In this achievement after the Caporetto disaster, Orlando 'demonstrated great political skill, putting together a cabinet that was a miracle of parliamentary equilibrium; had he not succeeded we would certainly have witnessed very grave and dangerous excesses that would have threatened the internal stability of the Nation'.[8] His government received a vote of confidence on 22 December and represented the victory of the left Liberal Giolittians even though it retained Sonnino as Foreign Minister. Most importantly, it obtained the unqualified support of the Catholics and the most influential Socialist leaders.[9] Orlando sent

Diaz, the new Italian commander, a telegram announcing his intention to tour the front immediately and to confer personally with him.[10] The Prime Minister quickly concluded that the causes of the Caporetto defeat had been purely military, that the army was not about to collapse and initiated several strategies to restore the country's military fortunes. First, he asked for immediate Allied reinforcements for the defensive battle to stop the invaders on the Piave River, *it seeming to me that the effect of the troops on morale could be incalculable*.[11]

Eleven British and French divisions arrived in November, but were held in reserve. Ward Price, British press representative at Italian headquarters, described for *The New York Times* readers the crucial battle taking place to stop the Austro-Germans, noting the gratitude of Italians but also their wonderment that British and French forces were not participating in the hard fighting: 'Some people are asking in Italy, and perhaps in England too, "Why don't we hear of English and French troops taking part in this important fighting? Where are the Allies' reinforcements?"' Price believed this lack of participation was due to the time it took the troops to arrive, to their need to settle in and to their getting to know 'the lie of the country'. He reported that the reserves were important because 'it would not be too encouraging a position for an enemy General who had at length succeeded in opening a gap in the stubborn front of our Italian allies to find his exhausted troops faced by a mass of French and English divisions of the first quality, seasoned to war, yet refreshed by months of rest and change of scene.'[12]

The fact that the Allies held back these soldiers 'refreshed by months of rest and change of scene' caused Orlando and Italian officials to seethe with anger. Orlando's papers include an angry telegram addressed to the King's aide-de-camp

General Cittadini for transmittal to Bissolati: *Enemy pressure north of the Piave line has initiated. This determines the evident and immediate danger of a repetition of encirclement [aggiramento]. The policy of the allies in keeping troops inactive that could save the situation is absolutely incomprehensible. I am making the same point in more detail to His Excellency Diaz, with whom His Excellency Bissolati can confer. As a politician, he can more easily convey [to the Allies] the pitiful impression that [the Allies] are already making because of the inexplicable fact that [their] forces are not being utilized while there hangs over [us] the most grave danger from which their intervention could effectively provide a defense.* The telegram gave a secure route by which troops could be ferried from France to Italy on *from four to six large transatlantic liners that would be enough to transport about a division in a single voyage*, and requested that the information be passed on to the French General Ferdinand Foch. Orlando must have thought better of the criticisms he made because he suspended the telegram [the original is marked 'sospeso' with his initials].[13] The Prime Minister instead sent a more moderately framed communication to Cittadini, again meant for Bissolati, and again calling for Allied troops to be put into the front line; it glumly states: *You know that [Lloyd] George is of the same opinion, but experience has demonstrated that he will not overrule the technicians [military commanders].* Orlando's telegram gives Bissolati suggestions on how to convince the Allies to move their troops to the front line.[14] The British and French rebuffed all Italian efforts to commit their troops to battle, and they had only a marginal role in stopping the enemy offensive.[15] This was, indeed, the feeling of the British Prime Minister, who frequently could not control the military policy of his generals. Lloyd George told the Italian

King: 'If our forces were not at your side during this test, the fault, you know, is not mine.'[16] The Italian army had to do the fighting itself and be content with the morale boost the presence of Allied soldiers provided, while Orlando enjoined its commander to hold on to the Piave line *at all cost*.[17] The fierce fighting proved Orlando right because it demonstrated that the army was not near collapse following Caporetto; had it been so, it could not have successfully resisted the Austro-Germans at the Piave two weeks later. More than soldiers, Italy required economic, financial and food aid to make good the material losses suffered at Caporetto and to prepare the ground for a future victory.

Reorganization of the Supreme Command to make it less dictatorial, more inclusive of different viewpoints and more responsive to the civilian government was also part of Orlando's plan for eventual victory. First he transferred Cadorna's functions to another general and then named Armando Diaz to replace him as Supreme Commander. Diaz, who had the King's confidence, carefully coordinated military policy with the government and constantly communicated with Italy's allies, reversing his predecessor's policies. Two generals [*sottocapi*] flanked Diaz; Pietro Badoglio focused on army reorganization while Gaetano Giardino directed operations at the crucial Battle of the Piave that stopped the emboldened Austro-Germans, who at this point outnumbered the embattled Italians.[18] Under Orlando's political leadership, Italian battle-ready divisions, which fell from 65 before Caporetto to 38 after the battle, rose to 52 by June 1918, just in time to confront and defeat the Austro-Hungarians, who, thanks to the collapse of the Allies in the East, concentrated all their efforts on a last, great offensive against the Italian enemy in a second battle on the Piave. The government, moreover, efficiently organized Italian resources and it only took a few months for the factories to replace the equipment lost at Caporetto.[19]

Orlando's second task was to calm the panic that had seized Italian officials, alarmed by a report of the Minister for Military Assistance and War Pensions, Leonida Bissolati. Orlando describes the cabinet's consternation when it read what Bissolati wrote while on a tour of the front: the line at the Tagliamento River would not hold and probably resistance at the Piave would also fail; this would require a further retreat to the Mincio River, meaning the loss of northeast Italy. Confusion and disorder reigned among the military commanders, who had lost contact with the fighting units. Orlando believed, accurately, that Bissolati reflected Cadorna's views that the soldiers had not fought[20] and worked hard to calm his cabinet colleagues, some of whom wanted to take extraordinary measures to restore authority. First the military situation had to be addressed, Orlando said; and he was prepared to retreat even to *my Sicily* if necessary and resist the invaders from there. In his memoirs written long after the fact, Orlando acknowledged that confusion was a key problem, but considered it a normal effect of a major defeat, not a breakdown.[21] He judged it especially urgent to ease the fears of Bissolati, one of the most energetic ministers in the cabinet. He communicated with Bissolati through Cittadini in the previously-cited telegrams, urging him to employ a special cipher to avoid their being seen by the prefects, who might then alarm the country. He enjoined Bissolati to *keep your calm at all costs* and urged him to refrain from portraying the military situation in dark terms without citing concrete events. He had had long talks with Allied commander Ferdinand Foch, Orlando wrote, and was convinced that the Allies recognized Italy's predicament unconditionally *and with great energy* and understood the need to send reinforcements. The only doubt Foch expressed was whether the country was politically prepared to resist, a point that directly addressed the call for greater 'authority' on the part of some politicians. But the country was tranquil, Orlando assured Bissolati, even if officials must prepare for an emotional reaction when news of further losses as a result of Caporetto became known. *I think that it would be a good policy to prepare public opinion for the coming territorial sacrifices in a manner that is not brusque but gradual*, wrote an unruffled Orlando, suggesting the Italians follow the French example of explaining the war through communiqués, and concluding that he himself had a duty to remain more serene as the situation worsened.[22]

A high-level meeting scheduled with the British and French Prime Ministers and other high officials at Rapallo on 5–7 November encouraged Orlando's confident tone, but this feeling gave way when he learned at that meeting exactly how little direct military aid would be forthcoming from the Allies; few Allied soldiers would be sent to Italy and they would not be stationed on the front line because the Allies feared that their soldiers would be overwhelmed if the Italians failed to stop the Austro-Germans. As Caporetto was shaping up to be a disaster for the Italians, the Italian Ambassador in London, Guglielmo Imperiali, sent a long memorandum to Orlando. This note began by explaining the debate between the Imperial War Cabinet and the British General Staff – the 'Westerners' who believed the war could only be won on the Western Front. Lloyd George himself was sympathetic to the Italian appeal for 300 heavy artillery pieces requested in a London visit by Bissolati, but the 'Westerners' won out. Furthermore, in a moment of pique, the British army withdrew the heavy pieces they had previously lent the Italians because Cadorna had not agreed to an offensive they wanted. However, Imperiali explained that the British had not understood the Italian predicament because, unfortunately, a communication Cadorna had sent to the British (consigned to an English general) took eight days to reach the British General Staff. In it, Cadorna explained he could not undertake an offensive because German and Austrian soldiers released from the East had been transferred to the Italian front. The Caporetto events, Imperiali optimistically judged, had weakened the 'Westerners' and he speculated that the tragedy might have the beneficial effect of establishing a united command of all the fronts in the West and that the Italian would be the most important of these fronts.[23]

Imperiali's optimism proved misplaced. The delegates at Rapallo did agree to coordinate military action and, in the general context of reviewing military policy in all theaters, ordered an advisory council to investigate the Italian situation and 'advise as to the amount and nature of assistance to be given by the British and French Governments, and as to the manner in which it should be applied'. Despite these encouraging words, however, the British and French military commanders had already decided by 31 October not to send a significant number of forces to fight on the Italian front because 'Allied forces in Italy could constitute only a support in favour of the Italian army, which is responsible for the defense of Italy, whose fate will later depend on the conduct and the holding power of the Italian army itself'. Cadorna informed Orlando that he told the Allies that their decision was 'petty-minded [*meschino*]' and that they did not understand how much an Italian collapse would damage the Entente.[24] Orlando could not produce any significant change of Allied hearts at the Rapallo meeting, in which the Italians

complained of being treated badly because of the deterioration of their military reputation, while their poor presentation
of their own case conveyed the impression to the British and
French that they were consciously exaggerating the amount
of help they would need to stop the Austro-Germans.[25] The
Allies finally relented and agreed to send troops, Sonnino
said, 'but they wanted first to make certain that their troops
would be safe, waiting to see what ours did; they subjected
us, in short, to a sort of make-up examination'. The Italians apparently passed the exam,
because the Allies promised to
deploy their troops to defend two
sectors of the Piave line beginning 25 November,[26] quite late
in the battle. The Italian image
problem worsened quickly, as
Italian ambassadors reported,
not only because of the Caporetto loss but also because of the
publication of the secret Treaty
of London by the Soviets.[27]

Orlando's third task was to
increase popular support for the
war. He took as his model the
ancient Romans, who in 216 BC
suffered a disastrous defeat at the
Battle of Cannae, the worst in their history, which threatened
the state's survival. Orlando determined to follow the example
of the Romans, who had not gone on a partisan witch-hunt
after the loss. The Nationalists and Cadorna blamed anti-
war opponents and the troops for the Caporetto disaster and
demanded laws repressing free speech and civil liberties in

The motives for establishment of
the Supreme War Council at
Rapallo seem to have been as
much political as military. British
Prime Minister David Lloyd
George, who had been feuding
with the British military
commanders and their domestic
supporters, wished to dilute the
influence of William Robertson
and Douglas Haig; the French
exploited the Council to
strengthen the command of
Ferdinand Foch; and, as Orlando
wrote in his memoirs, the Council
came at a convenient time to help
him ease Cadorna out of his post
as Supreme Military Commander
by naming him the Italian
representative to the Council.

order to suffocate their enemies; anti-war proponents in turn condemned Cadorna for eleven supposedly useless offensives and for his overly harsh discipline. Orlando avoided excesses, and flatly rejected demands from different sides of the aisle during closed sessions of the Chamber of Deputies calling for the general, war ministers, and other members of the war cabinets to be tried: *Our sons are fighting like lions to defend our country. May they never learn what has been said in this hall!*[28] But he dismissed Cadorna, traveled to the front and determined for himself that the reasons for the Caporetto defeat had been military and not due to subversive propaganda. On his tour of inspection Orlando found that even the troops that were no longer organized in units (*sbandati*) were tranquil and greeted him and the King with respect, not signs of seditious infections; they treated Cadorna the same way during an incident when he was lost and found himself among several thousand defeated troops who could have killed him with impunity and without fear of being caught. On 12 January 1918, Orlando ordered an investigation into the Caporetto defeat in a report that would emerge when passions had cooled. The report cited military reasons for the loss, but did not emphasize Badoglio's role in the defeat, because in the meantime he had become a military hero.[29] In the King's proclamation addressing the country, written by Orlando, there was a strong appeal for the nation to put aside political differences and unite:

All the energy of our spirits and all the energy of our work must be aimed at fulfilling, until the end, all our duties, even the most bitter, and in the meantime, disputes and internal divisions must be fraternally settled in a profound and loyal truce. All cowardice is betrayal, and all discord is betrayal.[30]

In short, Orlando aimed to pacify the various factions and concluded that, while he did not completely succeed, he came as close as possible.[31]

The Caporetto disaster, like the Cannae defeat, had the merit of uniting popular sentiment. After three hard years of sacrifice, the Irredenta perhaps was no longer worth fighting for – but saving the homeland was. The statement of Socialist leader Filippo Turati – 'Our homeland is also on the Piave' – encapsulated this sentiment. Orlando's proclamation for the King in his address to the country emphasized, in addition to unity, the people's support to save the homeland from the invaders and to save Italy's honour:

> Citizens and soldiers of Italy, become one army only, with one heart, with one will, with one faith: faith in our victory! For us, for our children, for the fate of Humanity, it is necessary to win.
>
> But above victory itself something burns that is dearer to us and more desirable than existence [itself]: national honour. May no stain contaminate the pure name of Italy! The Heroes … who have offered in a sacred holocaust their generous, vermillion blood have entrusted this legacy to us, have imposed this commandment. Think about the sacrifice of these our brothers: let it not have been in vain for us![32]

Caporetto also galvanized Italy, and it resurrected its army to an extent that surprised all observers; thus the success of the Central Powers in northeast Italy was short-lived and has been described as a 'Pyrrhic victory'.[33] The results of the battle also brought a new realization to Italy's allies, particularly the United States and Britain, that Italy needed economic and financial aid above all. The loss of important supplies and Italy's lack of raw materials could be made good by its richer allies. Food, iron, coal and other raw materials poured into Italy, along with the loans to pay for them, and were essential for the country's survival and the recovery of its war effort. Southern peasants had been unhappy with exemptions given to industrial workers while the peasants marched off to war leaving their wives to take care of the farms. More exemptions for peasants decreased the dissatisfaction, even as women continued to substitute for male labor both on the land and in the factories. New organizations supporting the troops sprang up in the country. Orlando's government also addressed land hunger, promising land reform after the conflict ended. The National Veterans' Organization established a fund to buy up land to allocate to returning war veterans.

The new government paid more attention to the well-being of its soldiers and their families than had been the case in the past. In the aftermath of Caporetto, on 1 November 1917, it established the Ministry for Military Assistance and War Pensions, put under the capable democratic interventionist leader Leonida Bissolati. Free life insurance policies were given to the soldiers to help their families. However, there was no increase in draftee pay, or in the subsidies their families received. The government addressed the morale issue among the soldiers as well, publishing numerous periodicals dedicated to them, establishing previously lacking propaganda services directed at the enemy, explaining why they were fighting and adding ten extra days' leave to the existing fifteen. In addition, Diaz softened the harsh discipline practiced by Cadorna and increased rations. These measures lifted the army's morale considerably. 'After three years of war, the Italian soldier at last had the material comforts that had been provided to the soldiers of other belligerent armies long before.'[34]

These changes greatly improved the will of the Italians to resist their hereditary enemy and save their country, although they could not completely eliminate the problem of desertions and dissatisfaction. Even though many people continued to fight the war more with resignation than fervour, Orlando succeeded in raising the country's morale and reorganizing the armed forces to the point of sending Italian soldiers to fight on the Western Front.[35] On 18 April 1918, Orlando announced in Parliament: *Italy, which follows with admiration the heroic efforts of the Anglo-French troops on the Western Front, could not remain absent from the battlefields of France.* Journalist (and former pacifist) Gustav Hervé commented: 'The Italian soldiers are to give us on our front the aid which the British and French soldiers gave after the retreat on the Isonzo.' The aid came at a crucial point, when the Germans reinforced their armies with troops from the East after the Russians had been defeated and launched a spectacular spring offensive designed to win the war before American soldiers could arrive in force. The Italians would send 500,000 troops to the Western Front, the *New York Times* reported, as part of a combined Allied army: 'This joint use of British, French, American, and Italian forces ... is expected from now on to have a most important bearing on plans now being shaped for taking the offensive away from the Germans at the proper moment.'[36] In France, the newspaper reported, Italian soldiers 'recently have taken over from the French and British contingents an important sector of the western front, lying midway between the Marne and Rheims,' where they repulsed the Germans in a critical area; they suffered 4,375 deaths in the fighting.[37] The Italian contribution to victory on the Western Front was forgotten at the Paris Peace Conference and thereafter by historians.

Missed opportunities and changing priorities

Had the Italians been able to capitalize on the goodwill created by their gesture and expand it, events at the future Peace Conference in Paris might have gone differently. Unfortunately, foreign policy was still run by an inflexible Sonnino preoccupied with Italy's security and, worse, fixated on the Treaty of London as the only means to protect that security. Orlando understood, at least at certain points, that the war had changed in nature, that Wilson strongly favored Yugoslav claims and that Sonnino's rigidity was causing problems with the Allies; but he was either unwilling or unable to overrule him, and this represents the major failure of his administration.

In 1917, the nature of the First World War changed because of the intervention of the United States and because of the success of the Bolshevik Revolution in Russia. Both of these events, despite their different ideologies, focused on supposed moral aspects according to which the war was to serve the greater good of humanity, not the territorial gain that hitherto had been the main preoccupation of the belligerents. For Italy, this change had major implications. The Allies now had a reason to consider that the gains Italy had hoped to achieve through the Treaty of London were out of tune with the times and, furthermore, that the decline in Italy's military reputation because of the Caporetto defeat made it appear as if it demanded more than its military effort was worth. The Italians, however, suspected Allied motives and believed that because of the Russian collapse in 1917, their armed forces made a major contribution to the war effort by tying down

Sidney Sonnino (1847–1922) illustrated the racial, religious and political tolerance of Liberal Italy. His father was of Jewish descent and was rumored to have made his fortune in Egypt as the head of a firm that collected garbage; his mother was Welsh. Sonnino was an Anglican in a Catholic country, which, however, did not prevent him from becoming Prime Minister in 1906 and 1909. Sonnino was noted for his stubbornness well before his long term as Foreign Minister and Italian representative at the Paris Peace Conference – and his ability to speak English probably made things worse there, even though he was an Anglophile. His activities as a politician suggest he considered himself dedicated to principle rather than being inflexible. In 1897, he published a famous article, 'Torniamo allo Statuto', denouncing the corruption he felt democracy inevitably produced. In a constitutional crisis lasting from 1898 to 1901, he guided the conservative forces that wanted to amend the Italian Constitution; Sonnino argued that his reforms would have made the Italian constitutional system more similar to the British. Neither of his terms as Prime Minister lasted more than three months, because of his inability to make or keep political allies. It is difficult to understand why he had so much influence, but he must have exuded a certain political charisma. Probably his standing on principle helps explain his influence in Italian politics. Even the Socialists voted for him as Prime Minister in 1906 because they believed his personal rectitude would translate into a campaign against corruption and make the Italian state more efficient. The reverence demonstrated by Salandra toward him and his insistence that Sonnino take the Foreign Minister's job following San Giuliano's sudden death – even though he had neither substantial diplomatic experience nor the character for the post – is explained only by the respect he enjoyed as the intellectual leader of the Liberal right wing. The manner in which he negotiated the Treaty of London, keeping it a secret from the cabinet except for Salandra, reinforces the feeling that the scarce respect for parliamentary government he betrayed in the 1898–1901 crisis remained a constant feature of his political outlook. The strong and consistent support of the other Liberals of the Right, a minority, allowed him to preserve his job after Salandra's fall and into Boselli's administration, and during Orlando's, even though these governments represented the increasing influence of Giolitti, his main political opponent. His prime argument during the Paris Peace Conference was his conviction that the terms of the Treaty of London must not be modified in the slightest way, not even if the change benefited Italy, because doing so would give the Allies an excuse to evade their commitments under that document. Sonnino died on 24 November 1922.

millions of enemy troops. The Italians suffered further blows when the Soviet government published the secret treaties in its archives, embarrassing the Allies, and the United States said it would not recognize these.

The new situation coincided with another development damaging to Italy: the opening of talks with Austria-Hungary for a separate peace. Although this attempt fell apart, a separate peace implied that the Italians had to renounce some of the concessions they had obtained in the Treaty of London. In a speech on 5 January 1918, British Prime Minister Lloyd George proposed the cession of Alsace-Lorraine to France but said that only 'legitimate' Italian aims for the unification of the Italian minority in Austria with Italy would be considered; what that meant exactly was unclear. On 8 January, American President Woodrow Wilson enunciated his Fourteen Points, which included the statement that the Italian frontier be established according to clearly recognized national lines; those lines were unclear and would set off a battle between 'experts' at the Paris Peace Conference. Both Anglo-Saxon leaders thus enunciated principles that contrasted with the Treaty of London, which put non-Italians into Italy on the grounds of military security. Indeed, Foreign Minister Sonnino's primary concerns were not only for the absorption of Italians into the homeland but for the country's security, and he considered strict fulfillment of the Treaty of London's terms as essential for Italy's safety. Less rigid than Sonnino, Orlando hinted that he was ready to give up some demands, and even to reach a compromise peace with Austria. Orlando even made contact with Austria through the Church, but the effort collapsed under the weight of the great German offensive on the Western Front that began in March 1918.

At the same time, the idea of the Habsburg Empire

remaining intact in some form faded and the Allies – especially the Americans – began focusing on the minority populations in the area. This change had major consequences for
Italy because of the sympathy that President Wilson had for
the Slavic cause, because of Sonnino's determination to keep
to the letter of the Treaty of London not recognized by the
US and because of Orlando's ambivalent attitude toward
Sonnino and his inability or unwillingness to drop his Foreign
Minister. The Allies began following a policy designed to
gain the support of the 'oppressed' nationalities of Austria-
Hungary, and these nationalities began organizing themselves
for a post-war world in which the Dual Monarchy no longer
existed. But Italy did not elaborate a foreign policy to deal
with the new conditions, and particularly the emergence
of a new state formed by a union of the Serbs, Croats and
Slovenes, under the leadership of the Serb dynasty, as decided
on by the different Slav factions at a meeting on Corfu on 20
July 1917. It became clear at this and subsequent meetings
that these factions coveted lands claimed by the Italians and
promised to them in the Treaty of London. This attitude provoked Sonnino's ire, and relations between the South Slavs
and Italians started off on the wrong foot.

Even though some Slav leaders showed themselves willing
to compromise, Sonnino refused any concessions. The Serbians approached the Italian Ambassador in London in an
effort to resolve the differences between the two countries,
and Imperiali was sympathetic. He wrote to Orlando: 'I don't
have to point out to Your Excellency how appreciated this
would be here and how beneficial [an agreement] would be in
increasing our influence on the disposition of the President
[Wilson] and of American public opinion … and how much
it would benefit our vital national interests following a variety

of circumstances that derive from the unhappy present situation.' Imperiali added that he had it from a good source that Wilson 'is completely favourable' to the aspirations of the Yugoslavs.[38] Orlando's Ambassador in Washington gave him the same message, but the Prime Minister either would not or could not change Sonnino's mind.[39]

The Foreign Minister, preoccupied by American opposition to the concessions won in the London treaty, considered it bad tactics to negotiate away some of the gains made in that agreement, thus weakening Italy's position after the war ended. Sonnino also did not believe that a large south Slav state would actually appear, and did not favor the breakup of Austria-Hungary which, he and other Italian politicians believed, would end up by bringing an enlarged Germany to the Italian border. Instead, Sonnino sabotaged all attempts at cooperation with the Slavs, even when encouraged by the Allied governments and influential foreign individuals who tried to act as negotiators between the two sides.

In January and February 1918 preparation took place for a congress of oppressed peoples to be held in Rome, but Sonnino made it clear that the Treaty of London was not to be touched and that he was prepared, at most, to make very minor concessions. He argued that the country had been through three hard years of fighting, and that popular support for the war would wane if the prospect of important gains vanished. The congress bringing together Italian, Yugoslav, and Allied representatives took place from 8–10 April and produced the so-called 'Pact of Rome'. This document substantially reproduced an agreement reached by the Italian Ambassador to London and the Yugoslavs on 7 March condemning Austria as the major obstacle to the freedom of peoples, and committing the Italians and Yugoslavs to resolve their territorial differences peacefully and to fight together for the independence of their peoples based on the principles of nationality and mutual respect for each other's culture and material interests.[40] Sonnino could not block the conference, but his refusal to participate deprived it of all official character. Sonnino also sabotaged efforts to create fighting units consisting of Austro-Hungarian prisoners of war who were from areas that might become part of a united Slavic state in the Balkans and which would fight on the Italian side. Although Sonnino endorsed a free and united Poland, he refused to sanction either a south Slav state or a Czech one, thus pitting Italy against its Allies in a propaganda battle it was bound to lose.

The prospect of Austria-Hungary's disappearance, the appearance of new states based on nationalities, and Sonnino's intransigence ignited a debate in Italy between nationalists of different political persuasions and democratic interventionists. Nationalists of all stripes agreed with Sonnino and advocated large gains for Italy. They saw no reason to give up the prospect of rewards they believed the country had earned. Their position hardened as time went on, as the prospect of an Allied victory loomed and as anti-Italian demonstrations broke out in Slovenia. Opposing them, the democratic interventionists believed that Italy stood to gain more from the goodwill of the emerging nationalities and that it did not need as much territory to ensure its security as the Treaty of London had demanded. Their leaders hailed from the left and were former Socialists such as Bissolati and Gaetano Salvemini. Salvemini, a historian of that prophet of nationalities Giuseppe Mazzini, distinguished himself by trying to convince the Slavs to drop their most extreme demands in an attempt to bring about an agreement. These differences between the two groups characterized the national debate in Italy during the Paris Peace Conference and afterwards during the rise of the Fascists to power. For example, the attempts of the democratic interventionists to secure the renunciation of some tenets of the Treaty of London earned them the epithet of 'the renouncers' from nationalists who used the term with great effectiveness after the war.

Sonnino's rigidity spurred an attempt by the democratic interventionists and their allies to remove him as Foreign Minister. According to Salvemini, it would only take six or seven articles in the *Corriere della Sera*, run by the Liberal Luigi Albertini, to 'get rid of the Jew [Sonnino] who is bringing us to perdition'.[41] The press campaign indeed occurred, and was coordinated with pressure on Orlando to fire Sonnino. However, Sonnino's newspaper *Il Giornale d'Italia* and Nationalist periodicals responded so successfully that the effort backfired. Besides the press battle, it was unrealistic to hope that public opinion so severely tried by the fighting would support an attempt to dump a Foreign Minister who was trying to get the most for the country after so many sacrifices.

Salvemini and Bissolati knew that they needed Orlando's help to get rid of Sonnino. Salvemini wrote that Sonnino believed that if he left his post, Italy would be ruined and that

> Orlando will not decide by himself: he sees things clearly but is weak [*la volontà è fiacca*]. In addition, we cannot exclude that he is playing a double game. Sonnino – he probably thinks – always winds up letting me do what I want; I am the one who is generous, and he is the usurer; if things go well, it is my merit; if not, there is always Sonnino to resolve the situation, and its my merit for keeping him as a parachute.

Salvemini considered this attitude a disaster, however, because Orlando did not realize the repercussions of his behaviour on the country's image: 'he does not see that in this way he discredits his own politics, putting Italy in the dock again under the accusation of Machiavellianism. He does not understand that we lose the moral merit of whatever politics we follow, even if, as the result of assurances and reassurances we delude ourselves by thinking that we always survive [*di cadere sempre in piedi*] ... . And on his own he will never understand major world currents, outside of which there are no grand politics.'[42]

Salvemini has the reputation of being a harsh and sometimes unfair critic, but his criticism of Orlando here has some merit. Orlando had indicated several times by his actions and words that he did not agree with his Foreign Minister and that he was receptive to a new foreign policy for Italy that would bring it in line with the one that Italy's allies at least professed. For example, he had opposed Sonnino and authorized the formation of Czech units to fight on the Italian front, although he never succeeded in doing the same for the Yugoslavs. In the end, however, he did not replace Sonnino because such a major change would have meant the government's resignation and a full-blown parliamentary crisis that could not be managed, he felt, with a parliamentary debate. Furthermore, in addition to creating a terrible impression abroad, Orlando asked, how could a debate take place in full wartime that would consider renouncing the country's claims in case of victory? In the end, no matter what differences may have existed between Orlando and Sonnino, Orlando kept his Foreign Minister.[43] In addition to Orlando's inaction, Bissolati could not find the strength to resign, ending all chance of provoking the crisis Salvemini hoped for.[44]

So 'Orlando continues the game,' Salvemini wrote. But the question of just how much Orlando disagreed with Sonnino remains open. In his memoirs, Orlando acknowledges their personal differences and their disputes, but mounts a full-blown defense of Sonnino's policies, especially at the Paris Peace Conference, stating that he was no imperialist but was concerned only with Italian security, and calling him a representative symbol of the war. Given that Orlando wrote his memoirs after the Second World War and had witnessed the events of the intervening 25 years, this defense of Sonnino is very significant.[45] Orlando did not take the opportunity in 1918 and before the Paris Peace Conference to alter Italy's foreign policy in order to bring it more in line with that of the Allies, overestimating the capacity of Italy to take them on and putting the country onto the road to 'losing the peace'.

Winning the war

When Orlando took over as Prime Minister after Caporetto, Cadorna sent him a glum report on the military situation. Again blaming the soldiers for the defeat because they lacked the will to fight and had capitulated to subversive propaganda, Cadorna called what had happened a 'military work stoppage [*sciopero*]' and a 'pacific rebellion' and did not believe the reports of his commanders who held out hope for an effective resistance. Should another enemy attack follow, he wrote, the army might be completely annihilated and would have to renounce any attempt at saving its honour.[46]

This report illustrated the enormity of the military problem facing Orlando, but the new administration responded to the crisis so well that it transformed the Italian army into a new force by 1918. As already described, Orlando responded to the emergency by firing Cadorna, reorganizing the General

Staff, and improving the morale and material conditions of the troops. After the Piave line held, the new administration set out to rebuild the army while keeping on the defensive. General Alfredo Dalloglio, Minister for Armaments and Munitions, increased the number of factories devoted to war production from 998 to 1,708 and efficiently resupplied the army by December 1917. Italy had no raw materials, but with these coming from abroad at enormous expense, Italian industry and its 800,000 workers put on an amazing perform- ance, making good in a brief period the artillery and other losses the army had suffered. The army had lost half of its artillery as a result of Caporetto, 3,500 guns for example; by April 1918 it possessed 5,900 and by the beginning of summer, 6,300. In 1918, 1,200 machine guns reached the army monthly, compared to 25 in 1915. From January 1918 to the end of the war in November the Italians fired more artillery shells than they had from 1915 to 1918.

Greatly increased armaments production was not the only change. The army renewed its doctrine and tactics, relying no longer on lines of defensive trenches but concentrating on defense in depth, combining its defense of strongholds with swift counter-attacks by small units, and the strategic placement of machine gun nests. It abandoned its previous technique of defending every inch of territory. The army significantly strengthened its intelligence services (in whose importance Cadorna did not believe), adopting modern tech- niques such as parachuting operatives behind enemy lines. It greatly expanded its air arm by replacing its 22 lost airfields with 26 new ones and improving its aeroplane models. It called up the 1899 class of soldiers early – the 'ragazzi del '99' – who acquitted themselves very well. It greatly increased the numbers of the distinctive volunteer assault units, known as

'Arditi'. These units worshipped violence and were notable for their boldness, daring and love of fighting.[47] They had the strong support of the interventionists and later many of the soldiers participated in the squads that helped Mussolini to power.

In the spring of 1918 the German spring offensive on the Western Front seemed headed for a stunning success, and Allied commander Ferdinand Foch asked the Italians to undertake an offensive to help take some of the pressure off the West. Because that offensive had important implications and much has been made of the Italian reluctance to begin, it is useful to look at the reasoning of Armando Diaz.

In responding to Foch on 14 May, Diaz stated that he agreed with the Supreme Commander that the Allies should coordinate their offensives at the proper moment (at the time the German offensive was still taking place). He then went on to describe the Italian situation. Austrian forces were equal to or even superior to the Italians, with 56 divisions and four more on the way so far, plus the arrival of new artillery. Foch had noted the internal difficulties being faced by Austria, but while Diaz agreed, he interpreted Austrian inaction as more probably, or at least partly due to the continued need for Austrian troops in Russia, and partly to the poor climatic conditions and to the difficult terrain of the Italian front. Because of Italian artillery and supply needs, an offensive could not begin for 20 days. Diaz then detailed the forces at his disposal and concluded that the operation would be very risky because he would not have adequate reserves available, thus leaving his forces open to a devastating Austrian counterattack because the enemy could concentrate its forces wherever it pleased. Therefore, Diaz concluded, the Italian attack should coincide as far as possible with an Anglo-French counter-attack on the

Western Front. In order to plan the offensive, he added, he would need to know how many Allied troops would arrive to help, and when.[48]

Diaz's reluctance to go on the offensive seems not unreasonable, because it soon became clear that the buildup he reported to Foch presaged a massive Austrian offensive. With the East subdued, the Austrians could concentrate all their elite forces against the Italians, and disturbing domestic events had not yet affected Austria-Hungary's still-formidable army. Aware of the rearmament progress of their adversaries, the Austrian commanders decided to unleash a great offensive designed to break through the front before the Italians could recover fully from the Caporetto defeat.[49] On 15 June, on a section of the front where they enjoyed numerical superiority, the Austrians hurled 48 divisions against 45 Italian. They made headway, but an unexpectedly hard Italian resistance stopped them. By 23 June, their offensive had clearly failed and they retreated to their positions. This Second Battle of the Piave[50] represented Austria's last offensive, 'the first victory of the anti-German entente after a long drawn-out succession of disasters', and, for the Italians, a triumph for their resurrected armed forces.[51] It had the 'same strategical and historical importance during the last year of the war,' according to historian Gaetano Salvemini, 'as the Battle of the Marne had during the first year.'[52]

More than recognizing this battle as an important accomplishment of Italian arms, the victory reinforced Foch's view that Austria-Hungary was crumbling and that the Italians should immediately unleash a knockout blow against the Austrian army. Responding to a congratulatory message from Foch on the performance of Italian troops in Italy and in France, however, Diaz informed the Allied commander that

Italy had severe manpower problems. Men born in 1899 were in the front line; those born in 1900 had been called to the colors but had not yet been adequately trained and needed to be held back in anticipation of the hard battles to come in 1919 (no one expected the conflict to end in 1918). Thus the shortage of troops could not easily be made good, and Italy was scrambling to increase its manpower in other ways. Diaz noted Foch's good news that the Americans would soon reach the Western Front in large numbers, and asked that a small proportion be sent to fight in Italy. In addition to the need for more troops, the Italians urgently requested 20 tons of mustard gas and at least 25 Renault tanks.[53] In short, Diaz was waiting for the proper moment to unleash a final offensive and would not be moved by pressure from Foch.[54] In his memoirs, Orlando lauds Italian resistance to French demands that Diaz launch an offensive in the spring of 1918, claiming that the refusal made possible the victory on the Piave in June of that year and saved the military situation for the Allies on the Western Front.[55]

On 15 July, the Allies elaborated a war plan for the autumn and winter of 1918 and the summer of 1919. On the Western Front, the major worry was how fast American troops could arrive in France and be readied for action. After consideration of various elements, the plan stated: 'For these reasons, it would appear that Allied offensive operation on the Western Front during 1918 should be confined to counter-attacks against enemy operations; and to local operations with limited objectives.' On the Italian front the plan agreed with Diaz. It noted the military parity there, the bad climatic conditions that hampered fighting after October and the risks that a failed or only partially successful offensive might release Austrian troops for action on the Western Front. 'If the above considerations be correct,' it stated, 'it would appear that Allied offensive operations in Italy during 1918 should be confined to the maintenance of such pressure against the enemy as would preclude the transfer of any of his forces to the Western Front, and to the improving of the line of resistance, or, if necessary, for the maintenance of Allied morale.'[56] Events on the battlefield, however, soon made this plan unexpectedly obsolete. An Allied counter-offensive against the Germans that began on 18 July had an unanticipated success and changed the military equation on both fronts.

In this context, Foch continued to believe that the Italians were too passive, and pressed them to take at least limited action. Orlando considered the dispute serious enough to warrant a trip to Paris. In a long dispatch to Diaz, he explained his dilemma: continued refusal to go on the offensive *constitutes a political fact that is very damaging to our interests.* In talks with Sonnino, two important points emerged. First was the contention that Allied troops would participate in an Italian offensive. Instead, Orlando emphasized, nine English battalions had been withdrawn from the Italian front and this action represented for the Italians an important loss that would not compensate for Italian troop deficits that might result from the action.[57] Second, given Foch's insistence on an offensive, any eventual lack of success would put the responsibility squarely on the shoulders of the Supreme Allied Commander, making him more susceptible to requests for aid in case of need. However, if the Italians continued to refuse to go on the offensive, they would, in effect, affirm their independence toward the general charged with the fate of the unified front, which meant that if the Italians ran into difficulty he would be less disposed to send aid, and could argue that the Italian setbacks were due to their desire for autonomy on their front. Orlando considered this last point particularly important because it *aggravated and worsened the current state of military isolation in which we currently find ourselves*. Orlando also stated that the Allies had not supplied the Italians with all the material they had requested. He asked Diaz to keep him informed on the military situation so he could decide whether to adopt an intransigent line on principle or reach some sort of compromise.[58]

Foch, however, kept pressing for Italian action, an insistence that prompted the protest of the Treasury Minister, in the form of an interview with the Associated Press, that Foch, focused on the French front, did not understand Italian necessities; the French blocked its transmission to the United States.[59] In an extraordinary letter that could be considered insulting, Foch lectured Orlando that he had been pressing Diaz for an offensive since May, that it was urgent that it be undertaken immediately given the approaching winter season, that he had considered all the difficulties of a limited offensive and that he had sent all the supplies requested by the Italians. He indicated that the Conference of Abbeville (held on 1 and 2 May 1918, which gave him the power to coordinate the action of the Allied armies) gave him the power to order one. He had neither the time nor the means, he wrote, to plan an operation 'that involves only a small part of the Italian army under the direct command of its Chief'. Foch went on to say that the divisions that the Italians requested to help in the offensive were all employed on the Western Front, and even if they were not, the time required to transport them meant that they would not arrive in time for an offensive. Then he wrote: 'I really don't know what to add because, if the question is to obtain from me advice that, according to what you have declared, would leave me "the entire responsibility for development of the operations on the Italian front", this is a hypothesis that no reasonable person could conceive.' Foch ended his note by writing that there is no war without risk and that the question was whether the Italian command was willing to run this risk given 'the current moral traumatization and disorganization of the Austrian army'.[60]

An irritated Orlando responded that he had no desire to fight over interpretation of the Abbeville accords, but that he agreed completely on the necessity for action. He informed Foch that he had immediately visited the front (from where he was writing), found that Diaz had already been making preparations and that the commander fully agreed that an Italian offensive should take place in the shortest time possible.[61]

The general consensus had been that the war would last at least until the spring of 1919, but in October the Germans and Austrians began sounding out the Allies for an armistice and on 17 October Austrian Emperor Karl declared the transformation of Austria into a 'federal' state. This fact altered the situation. After more than three years of hard fighting Orlando now feared *the liberation of our territory only through a diplomatic act* rather than military victory. Orlando worried, however, that although legally Italy had complete freedom of action to begin an offensive, politically the country could be put in a bad light if it suffered many casualties to obtain lands it would shortly gain anyway if it waited.[62] Diaz, who had informed the French of the advanced preparations for an offensive in early October, responded: 'In my opinion, new developments cannot and must not influence noted decisions, neither legally nor militarily. Allies continue [to fight] and I would not see any reason to behave differently where other exigencies do not impose it.' He added significantly: 'Our success would crown in a worthy manner our military and political action affirming once again the enormous value of the effort given by Italy in the common struggle and truncating malevolent judgments or discussions on the matter.'[63]

The Italian offensive began on 23 October; it was not the small one Foch demanded, but in full style. After a slow start, the offensive was completely successful. Although revolutions broke out and the subject populations began declaring their independence from the old Empire, the Austro-Hungarian army fought well till the last; the final battle took place at Vittorio Veneto and it broke the Austro-Hungarian army. The Empire shortly followed its dissolution by itself dissolving. On 4 November 1918, at 3.00 p.m. the armistice took effect.[64]

Diaz soon discovered that the Italian victory did not dispel 'malevolent' judgments on the Italian role in the war. Unlike the Battle of the Piave in 1917, foreign troops did participate in the final battle, which gave observers an excuse to credit their Allies for the victory. Inexplicably and more seriously, the Italians were criticized for undertaking the offensive when the war was 'over' because the Austro-Hungarian Empire was on the road to dissolution, even though the same was true for conduct of the Allies against the German Empire which was itself collapsing: the Kiel Mutiny began on 29 October, the Kaiser abdicated on 9 November and the German Republic was declared on 10 November. On 30 October, Diaz sent an angry telegram to Orlando objecting to a French communiqué stating that the Italian offensive coincided with Austrian war-weariness and with a request for an armistice and a separate peace and emphasizing the role of 'Anglo-French troops' (Anglo-French troops and one regiment of Americans represented a small proportion of the attacking force, but the British distinguished themselves). This view was indeed strange since

Foch himself had pressed the Italians to go on the offensive on 28 September precisely because he believed that the Austrian army was in a state of dissolution, and the request of the Germans for an armistice on 5 October did not induce the Allies to stop their offensive on the Western Front. In fact, the French had fired the opening salvo of a campaign that would contribute heavily to the poisoned atmosphere of the Paris Peace Conference. Diaz keenly felt 'the pain that this unjust and poisonous communiqué causes me and all Italians'.[65] The same day Diaz followed this communication up with another telegram to the Prime Minister listing seven points that provided a timeline of the Italian offensive demonstrating that it had been planned, prepared and begun prior to the important events culminating in the Austro-Hungarian Empire's dissolution.[66] Judging from two telegrams from Orlando to Diaz on 28 and 29 October, Orlando was keenly aware of and preoccupied by the criticism of Italy taking place in France. Orlando asked Diaz to emphasize the date the Italian offensive began and to cite the strategic reasons that had prevented an earlier campaign. Orlando wanted the reasons explained to the press, especially to foreign correspondents, and asked him to be generous by citing the action of 'some French units' in the Vittorio Veneto fighting, a request directed at mollifying the main critics of the offensive. The Italians then began a press campaign in Italy and abroad to defend their actions.[67]

Italy's war effort thus concluded on the discordant note that had marked its relationship with its allies from the time it intervened in the conflict. The dispute over Foch's insistence on an Italian offensive between May and September 1918 took on an ominous aspect much beyond its military significance, one that would have important implications after the war ended. It appeared to the Allied commander that the Italians were too timid in their approach and to the Italians that Foch made unreasonable demands. The idea stuck that the Italians had been reluctant to commit to the final battle on the Italian front and this conditioned the view of the Allies toward Italy at the Paris Peace Conference. French Premier Georges Clemenceau, 'The Tiger', 'fumed' at Italian 'delays' in launching the 1918 offensive to relieve pressure on the French and expressed great hostility toward Italy as France's representative to the Conference.[68] The British Ambassador at the Conference reported that, 'The attitude to Italy in Paris ... has been one of supreme contempt up to now and now it is one of extreme annoyance. They all say that signal for an armistice was the signal for Italy to begin to fight.'[69]

Because of diverse national interests, it is normal for allies to have disputes, but the Italian situation was different and ultimately boomeranged against the Allies. A superficial mocking of Italy's war effort in an attempt to blunt its demands for territorial gain fed neatly into the well-established myth that the country had 'betrayed' its Triple Alliance allies when the conflict began. This attitude prevented the Allies from foreseeing the results their short-sighted policy might have in the country, even though the signs were clear. The Allies ignored them because, after the victory, they no longer had much use for Italy the spoiler. The idea of the 'mutilated victory' thus had its origins in the outlook of the Allies, who indirectly contributed to the fall of the Liberal State, the rise of Fascism and the resentful Italian attitude that led the country to follow a revisionist diplomatic policy during the inter-war years with such dire consequences. The rise of Fascism and Mussolini's foreign policy, therefore, did not stem solely from the weakness of Italian liberalism, ideology or the Duce's irrationality but from the ill-feelings that arose at the Peace Conference.

On 4 November 1918 the armistice on the Italian front went into effect a week before the one on the Western Front, leaving the Italians as the only Allied army on enemy soil. The Prime Minister who had reorganized the armed forces for victory, calmed Italian political differences during the conflict's crucial phase and rallied his people to support an unpopular war, Vittorio Emanuele Orlando, could claim a significant measure of success.

The 'Big Four' caught in conversation, Lloyd George, Orlando, Clemenceau and Wilson at Versailles, June 1919

II

The Paris Peace Conference

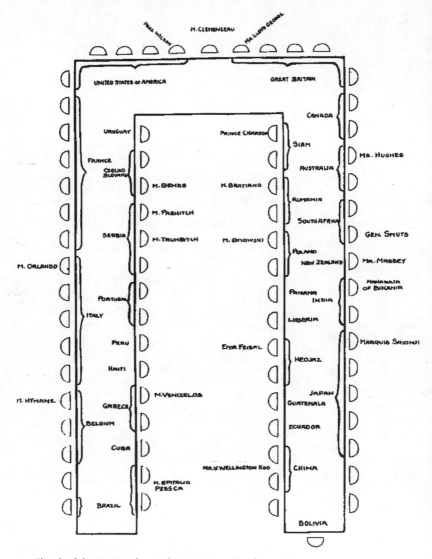

Sketch of the seating plan at the Paris Peace Conference.

7

Italy at the Paris Peace Conference

As Prime Minister Orlando headed to the Paris Peace Conference, he received a communication informing him that Italy's dead and disabled as a result of the First World War numbered 1,900,000 (modern assessments are in the same range).[1] The estimate on casualties was essential because of Allied contentions the Italians had not made a fair contribution to the war. From the viewpoint of population and considering that Italy had been in the war for ten fewer months, however, this figure demonstrated that the Italians had suffered losses proportionate to those sustained by the other major belligerents, and more than Britain. Orlando and Sonnino believed that the country should receive gains proportional to its war effort, but Italy failed to receive territorial or security benefits that counterbalanced and were in measure with its human and economic losses. This situation set off the greatest conflict among the Allies at the Peace Conference.

Italy proved unable to secure what it felt was essential for a number of reasons. Much of the blame is generally put on Sonnino's personality: the Baron managed to alienate the other Allies at every turn. Giolitti, who knew him well, said: 'He is only able to see in one direction and he digs in his heels like a mule; once he is fixated on an idea all the wise men of the earth would not be able to get him to change.'[2] All the major participants at the Conference noted this incredible obstinacy. In contrast to Sonnino, the representatives considered Orlando urbane, a gentleman; flexible, but weak. G A Borgese, literary critic and exiled professor at the University of Chicago during the Fascist era, pronounced judgments on both that are still accepted. Sonnino proved 'what little use there is in a resolute will if mind and heart do not inspire it'. As for Orlando, 'history most seldom had offered an equally striking example of how little avail brightness of mind and kindness of heart [are] if a resolute will does not choose the way'.[3] The Italian delegation was also considered to be divided, a flaw that favoured the Allies in discussing peace terms.

Poetry aside, it is hardly surprising that these two men did not achieve their aims against the stubborn opposition of the President of the United States, the most powerful man on earth, who could have at any moment cut off aid that Italy desperately needed. Italy went into the Paris Peace Conference as the weakest of the Big Four and woefully misinterpreted, with its military and diplomatic reputation in shreds and with strong enemies among the Allies. British Prime Minister David Lloyd George was perhaps the most sympathetic, but Georges Clemenceau was a noted Italophobe. After having wooed Italy into the conflict, both resented what they considered the hard bargain Italy had driven for its participation, despite the fact that it had been Russia that had objected the most to Italian requests during the negotiations on the Treaty of London, and despite their own overblown imperialistic aims. The attitude that Italian requests were excessive quickly rubbed off on the Americans: 'Italy came into the World War as the direct result of a bargain as to what she was to get,' wrote Wilson's confidant and biographer. 'She held aloof for eight months and dickered with both sides.'[4] Moreover, both Britain and France were long-standing colonial powers, fierce competitors for the former colonial holdings of Turkey and Germany, with economic interests to defend and resenting Italy as an interloper. They stated they would honour their obligations assumed under the Treaty of London, but provided ammunition to and let American President Woodrow Wilson resist fulfillment of that treaty's terms, even though he had not been a party to it, and were on the alert to seize opportunities to wiggle out of the agreement. Both had problems with those of Wilson's Fourteen Points that clashed with their interests (for example, for Britain, freedom of the seas) and Wilson generally gave in to them; ashamed, he determined to stand firm against the weaker Italians.

In his dealings with Italy, the self-righteous Wilson demonstrated some of the unattractive characteristics of his own personality and the bullying attitude that foreigners have frequently charged came to mark US foreign policy. The temperament of both men can be seen in the nature of their domestic policies. If a defense of civil rights marked Orlando, civil rights violations characterized Wilson's administration during and after the First World War. The American justice system imprisoned Socialists, comprising a negligible movement compared to Italy, because they opposed the war, and in 1918 jailed and prosecuted their ailing leader Eugene V Debs for making a speech that hardly mentioned the conflict.[5] The Wilson administration put 'aside the Constitution, jailing thousands of dissidents and suppressing the antiwar Socialists and Wobblies' and set the scene for the post-war 'Red Scare' driven by Attorney General A Mitchell Palmer.[6] In a period when racism characterized American leaders, Wilson provided a scholarly imprimatur to the bigotry in his bestselling textbook by denigrating African and Asian Americans and southern European immigrants, particularly southern Italians.[7] He was unlikely to form a good opinion of the Sicilian Orlando at Paris, and thought that Sonnino was 'as slippery as an eel or as an Italian'. He inclined toward opposing the Italians from the beginning because of the feeling that had by now become well established, that they had entered the war 'in a spirit of "cold-blooded calculation"'. Under these circumstances, things went wrong with the Italians from the first meeting, despite Orlando's good-natured optimism. 'He is very anti-Italian,' the British Ambassador noted. 'He was sick to death of Orlando and Sonnino and of all their ways and he did not want to have any conversation with them.' Wilson is supposed to have remarked that if territory should be given to the Italians just because they lived there, the US would have to cede Manhattan. The prejudices of the American delegation particularly emerged with regard to Sonnino. According to Wilson confidant Ray Stannard Baker, Sonnino 'was not really an Italian at all. His father was an Italian Jew, his mother a Scotchwoman [*sic*].'[8] In this case the astute Sonnino, who was suspicious of the President, was a better judge of character

'But now there came multitudes of men of the lowest class from the south of Italy ... men out of the ranks where there was neither skill nor energy nor any initiative of quick intelligence; and they came in numbers which increased from year to year, as if the countries of the South of Europe were disburdening themselves of the more sordid and hapless elements of their population ...'

WOODROW WILSON, 1902

than the good-natured Orlando, who also had the misfortune of being unable to speak English.[9]

Wilson remarked to Baker, Italian diplomats reported, that 'Italy is ruled by poets and orators that don't understand businessmen'.[10] During the Conference Italian informants continually reported that the Americans supported the Yugoslavs against the Italians over the port of Fiume and other disputed areas, indicating that they saw the Slavs as being helpful in favoring American exports to Eastern Europe and threatening that the US would use its economic clout to force Italy to agree to Wilson's terms.

It is interesting to note how quickly Italian leaders – distrustful of the US's supposedly altruistic motives – interpreted American intervention in the war not to 'make the world safe for democracy' but as an attempt to dominate it. On 13 November 1917, in a conversation with the well-connected journalist Olindo Malagodi, Giovanni Giolitti said, 'America will give us money and food; great quantities of munitions; but not its blood. ... It has entered the war for its own interests, especially to build an army to confront Japan in case of need. ...' Giolitti got some details wrong, but he saw the US as dominating the entire North American continent and, with its manpower, 'the entire world economically', a task rendered easier by the ruin of Europe, including Britain.[11]

The Italian political situation

In the three months between war's end and the formal opening of the Paris Peace Conference, the Italian political situation changed. The victory at Vittorio Veneto and the occupation of the territories pledged to Italy in the Treaty of London convinced the population that the country's war aims had been achieved. Unfortunately, this notion did not correspond to diplomatic reality. President Wilson did not consider himself bound by that treaty because the US had not been a party to it, even though it had hardly fought against Austria-Hungary, which had cost the Italians 689,000 dead. Wilson was determined to settle Italian borders on the basis of nationality as he and his experts saw it, and was unimpressed by Italian insistence on secure borders at the head of the Adriatic Sea.[12] On 11 January 1919, as the delegates to the Conference gathered, *The New York Times* was already reporting that the President 'favors only partial indorsement [*sic*] of Italy's ambitions'.[13] Two days later, Wilson informed Orlando that he did not deem the Treaty of London valid.[14] The British and French remained bound by their signatures but thought that at least some of the Treaty of London's provisions had been altered by events. They pledged loyalty to the treaty, Orlando saw immediately, because they knew that Wilson would oppose the Italians on it and because they would not press for its fulfillment.[15]

The looming struggle in Paris prompted Leonida Bissolati and his supporters to advocate a different approach when the Peace Conference met. Ambassador to London Guglielmo Imperiali had predicted in 1915 when Sonnino had left the city of Fiume out of the Treaty of London that it would cause major internal problems after the war;[16] his prediction came true with a vengeance. On 10 October 1918, a 'National Council' set up in Fiume by its Italian inhabitants proclaimed the city's union with Italy.[17] The Italian interventionist and Nationalist press took up the cry for annexation, firing up the public's imagination. However, these groups demanded Fiume in addition to the territorial gains promised in the Treaty of London. Sonnino objected because he believed that the demand undermined the Treaty of London's sanctity. The more flexible Orlando entertained the idea of trading Dalmatian territory specified in the Treaty of London for Fiume, but agreed with Sonnino that acceptance of the London agreements by the Allies should be the starting point of negotiations. Eventually the Italian position as it emerged at the Conference was the Treaty of London (the Trentino and South Tyrol to the Brenner Pass; the Friuli-Julia area east to the watershed of the Julian Alps; Trieste and Istria and some islands of the Dalmatian coast; Valona and control of Albania; neutralization of the Dalmation coast) plus Fiume, with an attempt to square these demands with Wilson's Fourteen Points. Although this was obviously a negotiating position, it hurt the Italian case because the inflexible Wilson saw in it a cynical ploy that confirmed all his prejudices about Italians.

Foreseeing that the Italian attitude would lead to the isolation of Sonnino and Orlando at the Conference, the democratic interventionists sought to alter the basis of the delegation's negotiating position. At a cabinet meeting on 15 December 1918 Bissolati attempted to coax Orlando into supporting the principles behind Wilson's diplomacy. He presented a program according to which the Italian delegation would 'spontaneously and preemptively' give up demands to territory not prevalently inhabited by Italians, specifically the Austrian Tyrol, Dalmatia and the Greek-inhabited Dodecanese Islands (occupied during the Libyan War but for which Italy was seeking official recognition). The advantages Italy would gain from this move, according to Bissolati, would include: increased security for the territory it would gain; improved relations with the German Austrians and Slavs, blocking establishment of a possible anti-Italian coalition; greater independence of action for Italy which, if caught between Slavs and Germans, would be forced to rely more heavily on French support; increased Italian influence in the Mediterranean through friendlier relations with Greece, which chafed at French influence but was being pushed into depending on it by Italian claims. There would also be an increased possibility of championing 'Wilsonianism' at the Peace Conference against French and British imperialism, thus strengthening Italy which, as the poorest and weakest of the great powers, had an enormous stake in securing a peace that would lead to reduced expenditures for armaments; increased goodwill, providing the Italian delegation with an opportunity to request compensation in return for voluntarily giving up the more extreme Italian demands, for example, Fiume, which would become a free city under Italian protection; economic compensation, for example, mining rights in the upper Adriatic in exchange for the Dodecanese Islands; and closer relations with the United States that would benefit Italy in tangible ways.[18]

Bissolati's attempt to convince Orlando failed because the cabinet considered him too naïve. Only Francesco Saverio Nitti, whose government would later replace Orlando's, supported his position by emphasizing Italy's isolation,[19] but then pulled back. According to Bissolati, Sonnino dominated the meeting and threatened to resign, while Orlando wavered and then went along with him.[20] According to Orlando he was equidistant between Sonnino and Bissolati because he disagreed with Sonnino's methods but agreed with the substance of Bissolati's ideas. However, he rejected Bissolati's method of voluntarily renouncing gains without any understanding or compensation, and in the end concluded that Sonnino's method of proceeding was preferable.[21] On 26 December, Orlando and Diaz (who considered Dalmatia's military value minimal) raised the question of negotiating an exchange of Dalmatia for Fiume, but Sonnino argued against even raising the idea that part of the Treaty of London could be altered because it might threaten the validity of the entire Treaty. Orlando did not support Bissolati, and the democratic interventionist leader remarked, 'before this surrender by Orlando to Sonnino my duty was clear: to bring the question outside, to the country's conscience'. On 28 December, Bissolati made good a threat to resign. A cabinet reshuffle then practically eliminated democratic interventionist influence. After Bissolati died during an operation on 6 May 1920, the group faded into history, except as a punching bag for Nationalists and Fascists who, exploiting the fact that most of them were former Socialists, accused them of renouncing territory that others had fought and died for.

In the first week of January 1919, American President Woodrow Wilson visited Italy. The people acclaimed him, a welcome that caused Wilson to misinterpret popular feeling in the country. His popularity resulted from his being the representative of the power whose intervention had brought the war to a rapid and victorious end and from American propaganda efforts in Italy, rather than support for his peace program with regard to Italy. Moreover, since Italian officials kept him busy with official business, the President believed they were scheming to avoid scenes of popular acclaim for him. This belief made him suspicious and he concluded that a rift existed between the Italian people and their elected officials, who, he thought, epitomized the 'old' politics. Wilson adviser Ray Stannard Baker wrote that 'the best of Italy is not yet represented in its political control, and the leaders in Paris, Orlando and Sonnino, supported the crudest aims of the old order of national competition. ...'[22] Already during this trip, the President decided that dialogue with Italian officials was impossible, an attitude that contributed to the feeling, when the troubles at the Peace Conference began, that he could successfully appeal directly to the Italian people against their representatives.[23] As Orlando would point out, this was an unprecedented position to take toward a friendly power.

Yet even at this early date there were clear indications of the Italian public's opposition to Wilson's policy toward Italy. On 11 January 1919, Bissolati presented his program at an important speech at Milan's La Scala. A hostile crowd of Nationalists, Futurists, and other interventionists, including Benito Mussolini, shouted him down: 'For a few minutes Bissolati was allowed to go on, seemingly undisturbed by the confused murmur of the hall. Then at a given moment … the infernal symphony began. Squeaks, shrieks, whistles, grumbles, nearly human, and all the thinkable counterfeits of the wild pack's howling, made up the bulk of the sound wave; but a human, nay, a patriotic cry became distinguishable now and then and ruled the inarticulate mass with the rhythm of a brutal march. They said: "Croati no! Croati no!" meaning that they were not Croats, that they wanted no friendship with Croats or Yugoslavs; and they meant too that Bissolati was a Croat.'[24] Bissolati struggled on unable to be heard by the audience.[25] This incident symbolized the increasing fury against Italians who wished to compromise on the Adriatic question, now targeted as *rinunciatari* [renouncers], and was the beginning of the violent actions and demonstrations in Italy that ended with the rise of Fascism.

By 15 May 1919 the situation had deteriorated to such an extent that Orlando, in a prescient analysis, confided to a friend: *My gravest preoccupation, today, is our internal situation … .What really disturbs me is the state of disquiet that is spreading everywhere … . After so many sacrifices so heroically borne, after everything that it has given to the war, Italy had a right to expect a very different treatment. I understand the anxiousness and irritation of our people against the Allies, against its government, against me, against eve-rybody: but I must point out the danger because it is not a political agitation with ... some aims but a vortex of various tendencies that clash with and confuse each other.*[26] During the Peace Conference, Orlando continually cited the growing violence in Italy and pleaded with the American President to agree to some compromise that would defuse nationalist opinion, without result.

The dispute: the Adriatic, the Italian frontier and Yugoslavia

The Conference opened formally on 18 January 1919. Alongside Orlando, the Italian delegation was composed of Sonnino, Salandra, Radical politician Salvatore Bazilai, and former governor of Eritrea, Ambassador Giuseppe Salvago Raggi, with its headquarters at the Hotel Ourde. In effect, however, Orlando and Sonnino did almost all the negotiating. Disappointed because of his secondary role, former Prime Minister Salandra criticized Sonnino, accusing him of defending 'every comma' of the Treaty of London, and he soon resigned. The Italian delegation was rumoured to be split, and Orlando complained about having to make frequent trips to Rome to keep his fractious government together (see Chapter 8). With the dour Sonnino in his early seventies, and Orlando almost sixty with four grown sons who had fought in the war, the chief Italian delegates did not enjoy the Paris social scene much, and at night kept to their hotel.

Incredible complexity characterized the discussions at the Conference regarding territorial changes in areas of mixed ethnicity, into which category the Italian claims fell. Interminable discussions over small areas, competing experts, what the economic consequences of slight changes would be and the drawing of multiple detailed maps complicated the issue. Discussion of territorial claims, of history and of who lived where and what would happen if one country or another got a small slice of land or not has been fairly well covered in the literature.[27] The Italians made specific territorial claims in a memorandum on 7 February 1919 drafted by Barzilai. The document did not emphasize the Treaty of London, which the Americans refused to recognize because it was a secret treaty, and confronted the major issues directly. In the north, the frontier the Italians proposed was the one agreed to in the Treaty of London, with small increases. In this area the Italians also added an important railroad junction. Given the importance of Wilson's declaration to respect nationalities in this case as well as others, the Italians estimated the number of minorities that would be put into Italy, of course giving themselves the benefit of the doubt. The Italians justified the inclusion of minorities in Italy on the grounds of security and by arguing that if all the minorities in the territories they claimed were put into their country, Italy would still have the lowest number of minorities of any country, a claim few disputed. In the case of the northern frontier, the memorandum claimed that 180,000 Austrian Germans would come into Italy. On the eastern frontier, the line claimed by Italy enlarged the one drawn by the Treaty of London and would have added 411,000 Slavs and 482,000 Italians to the Kingdom. The argument here, besides security, was that by including all of Julian Venetia Italy would achieve its natural frontier; the Italians also claimed an historic and cultural prevalence in the area's urban centers, particularly in Trieste, Pola, Fiume, and Gorizia, that even the Slavs recognized. In Dalmatia, the Italians claimed the area awarded to it in the Treaty of London. Austrian statistics stated that only 12,000 in a population of 287,000 were Italians, but here the Italians emphasized security considerations and insisted that the coast and islands that it did not get would have to be neutralized. Finally, the most clamorous demand was for the city of Fiume, which had or did not have, an Italian majority, depending on the territory that was included in the city limits. Fiume had been excluded from the Treaty of London that the Italians had signed, but as the war dragged on was added to the list of demands. The issue had become an emotional one, and it was universally recognized that if the delegation did not bring home a satisfactory agreement, there would be major repercussions in Italy. Orlando was willing to make concessions in order to secure Fiume, and was eager to negotiate, while the Americans were not.[28] The Americans were willing to concede the Brenner Pass to the Italians and quickly did so, but held out against making concessions in the Adriatic till the end. The issue was complicated by Wilson's favouritism toward the Yugoslavs.

Two distinctive aspects of the Italian case have not been sufficiently emphasized. The first is that Italy, recognized as one of the Big Four and therefore having a voice in attempting to resolve the worldwide problems discussed at the Conference, laboured under the prejudices that have been noted in previous chapters. This condition handicapped Orlando's ability to exercise more authority than he did at the Conference on world problems. Moreover, the circumstance by which Italy's major enemy was Austria and not Germany, and that it focused on Adriatic affairs, irritated its allies and tended to marginalize the country's influence.

The second aspect in need of greater emphasis is the relationship between Italy and Yugoslavia. This connection has been analyzed with respect to the territorial disputes between the two countries, but Italian views of what were not yet facts in 1919 have not received their due and have been forgotten. The assumption that a unified South Slav state whose disunity was enshrined in its official title – The Kingdom of Serbs, Croats and Slovenes – would effectively coalesce was by no means a given, and the Italian emphasis on the tendency toward domination by a Serb 'police regime' were two interpretations by professional diplomats that had a great deal of truth.[29] Indeed, the term 'Jugoslav' itself was strange, and diplomats questioned exactly what it meant.

The other issue that has not been sufficiently emphasized is that the Allied, especially American, recognition of the South Slavs as allies disconcerted the Italians. The Slavs had fought for the Austro-Hungarian Empire, which kept the population's loyalty almost until the end of the conflict.[30] While this issue did not affect the Americans, who sent only a few troops to the Italian front, or even the British and French, it angered the Italians who had died fighting the South Slavs in the Austro-Hungarian armies. Nor should the historical element be ignored: during the years in which Austria occupied the Italian peninsula before the Risorgimento, part of the occupying army consisted of Slavic troops who oppressed the native population, an antipathy that lived on in Italian historical memory. However, at the Peace Conference the Yugoslavs demanded that they be treated 'with perfect equality' with regard to the Italians,[31] who resented official recognition of that status and who opposed considering them allied populations who had been oppressed by the Austrians. Orlando informed the American President as to this feeling, but Wilson ignored him.[32] Among the Italian population, Nationalists and Fascists easily manipulated this resentment to their advantage.

These attitudes made their appearance in the concrete negotiations regarding Italian claims at the Conference. The first issue to be considered was the one regarding Wilson's Fourteen Points. From the beginning the British and the French interpreted them as general principles and sought adjustments. The British, for example, took exception to Point II, which called for freedom of the seas, and presented a reservation to it during the pre-Conference discussions. Following the British example, Sonnino presented a reservation to Point IX calling for rectification of Italian frontiers 'along clearly recognizable lines of nationality', but Orlando withdrew it when he was told that it was irrelevant to the topic under discussion – the German armistice.[33] When the Italians later tried again to introduce their reservation, they were put off on technical grounds.[34]

It should be noted that relations between Italy and Yugoslavia remained very unfriendly during the inter-war period. Mussolini was convinced by the chafing of the Croats and Slovenes under Serb dominion and the new state's instability that Yugoslavia would fall apart. Making things worse, Italy's competitor in the Balkans, France, was Yugoslavia's protector. Poor Italo-Yugoslav relations were an important flashpoint during the interwar period.

As the negotiations continued, the American President kept hardening his attitude against the Italians, probably because he compromised his principles so often with regard to British and French demands, a position even his Italian supporters resented.[35] It should be noted that in discussing the future Peace Conference on 15 November 1918, Sonnino had remarked to Wilson's closest adviser and friend Colonel Edward House that the security and historical reasons, in addition to those of nationality and self-determination, that France had invoked regarding Alsace-Lorraine could not be limited only to French claims. House agreed, emphasizing that, in addition to France, Britain was

PRESIDENT WILSON'S FOURTEEN POINTS, 8 JANUARY 1918

The program of the world's peace, therefore, is our program; and that program, the only possible program, as we see it, is this:

I. Open covenants of peace, openly arrived at, after which there shall be no private international understandings of any kind but diplomacy shall proceed always frankly and in the public view.

II. Absolute freedom of navigation upon the seas, outside territorial waters, alike in peace and in war, except as the seas may be closed in whole or in part by international action for the enforcement of international covenants.

III. The removal, so far as possible, of all economic barriers and the establishment of an equality of trade conditions among all the nations consenting to the peace and associating themselves for its maintenance.

IV. Adequate guarantees given and taken that national armaments will be reduced to the lowest point consistent with domestic safety.

V. A free, open-minded, and absolutely impartial adjustment of all colonial claims, based upon a strict observance of the principle that in determining all such questions of sovereignty the interests of the populations concerned must have equal weight with the equitable claims of the government whose title is to be determined.

VI. The evacuation of all Russian territory and such a settlement of all questions affecting Russia as will secure the best and freest cooperation of the other nations of the world in obtaining for her an unhampered and unembarrassed opportunity for the independent determination of her own political development and national policy and assure her of a sincere welcome into the society of free nations under institutions of her own choosing; and, more than a welcome, assistance also of every kind that she may need and may herself desire. The treatment accorded Russia by her sister nations in the months to come will be the acid test of their good will, of their comprehension of her needs as distinguished from their own interests, and of their intelligent and unselfish sympathy.

VII. Belgium, the whole world will agree, must be evacuated and restored, without any attempt to limit the sovereignty which she enjoys in common with all other free nations. No other single act will serve as this will serve to restore confidence among the nations in the laws which they have themselves set and determined for the government of their relations with one another. Without this healing act the whole structure and validity of international law is forever impaired.

VIII. All French territory should be freed and the invaded portions restored, and the wrong done to France by Prussia in 1871 In the matter of Alsace-Lorraine, which has unsettled the peace of the world for nearly fifty years, should be righted, in order that peace may once more be made secure in the interest of all.

IX. A readjustment of the frontiers of Italy should be effected along clearly recognizable lines of nationality.

X. The peoples of Austria-Hungary, whose place among the nations we wish to see safeguarded and assured, should be accorded the freest opportunity to autonomous development.

XI. Rumania, Serbia, and Montenegro should be evacuated; occupied territories restored; Serbia accorded free and secure access to the sea; and the relations of the several Balkan states to one another determined by friendly counsel along historically established lines of allegiance and nationality; and international guarantees of the political and economic independence and territorial integrity of the several Balkan states should be entered into.

XII. The Turkish portion of the present Ottoman Empire should be assured a secure sovereignty, but the other nationalities which are now under Turkish rule should be assured an undoubted security of life and an absolutely unmolested opportunity of autonomous development, and the Dardanelles should be permanently opened as a free passage to the ships and commerce of all nations under international guarantees.

XIII. An independent Polish state should be erected which should include the territories inhabited by indisputably Polish populations, which should be assured a free and secure access to the sea, and whose political and economic independence and territorial integrity should be guaranteed by international covenant.

XIV. A general association of nations must be formed under specific covenants for the purpose of affording mutual guarantees of political independence and territorial integrity to great and small states alike.

invoking security in challenging the practical implementation of some of Wilson's points. 'He said that it would be advisable for us to allow others to expound their own reasons and motivations and then to cite the same reasons that they invoked.'[36] Thus this particular policy of the much-maligned Sonnino was suggested to him by House, although it was an obvious enough tactic given what was going on even before the Conference gathered. What Wilson allowed the British and the French to do, however, he refused to the Italians and, worse, his position on the Adriatic question emboldened Yugoslavia to resist a solution, occasioned a split among the American experts and caused an irreparable rift with House.[37] Meanwhile the British and French had to pay lip service to the London agreements because they bore their signatures, but they did not support the Treaty's terms with any conviction. The strong British pro-Yugoslav lobby and Lloyd George's desire to win Wilson's agreement for his colonial ambitions determined British policy while the French had their own ambitions in the Balkans.

Unlike the surface friendliness between the British and Italians, relations with France were characterized by open friction. The French still fumed because of the supposed Italian delay in launching a final offensive against the Austrians; but, more importantly, they viewed the Italians as competitors in the Balkans.[38] The dissolution of Austria-Hungary and French ideological hostility toward Bolshevik Russia produced a direct confrontation with Italy in the region. Concerned with possible German revival and the rise of Bolshevism, the French began building alliances with the medium-sized states of Central and Southeastern Europe, particularly with Yugoslavia, the central focus of French post-war foreign policy. The French saw Yugoslavia as a bulwark against the Communist regime of Béla Kun in Hungary and, after initial hesitation, helped it increase the size of its army.[39] This move came at a time when Italian and Yugoslav troops confronted each other militarily, when blood had been shed and when relations had been ruined by a series of unfriendly acts between the two countries.[40]

The Italian image was also being sullied by the charge that their occupation was inhumane, an attempt that Orlando got wind of as early as 3 November 1918 when he instructed the army to treat the Slavs in the occupied areas as well as possible under wartime conditions. *It is necessary*, he informed Diaz, *that we do everything honestly possible to allow people [in the occupied areas] to understand that we are arriving as liberators and not as oppressors.*[41] The Italians had difficulty supplying the large numbers of people in their occupation zones with food and necessities,[42] which led to charges that they were deliberately holding back supplies. The French accused the Italians of subordinating their policies to Germany – incredibly, charging them with lobbying for Austrian annexation to that country – and of aiding Béla Kun. The Italians resented these allegations and blamed the French for Wilson's unfriendliness toward them.[43] Combined with the French fear of Italian rivalry in the colonies,[44] hostility between the 'Latin sisters' was a constant theme of the Peace Conference.

With regard to the previously discussed memorandum of 7 February, Wilson agreed on giving the Brenner Pass to Italy, but Salvatore Barzilai argued that this boundary could be outflanked unless Italian requests were fulfilled in the Adriatic. Barzilai admitted that the requests would put a Slavic minority into Italy, but stated that if all the minorities in the territories claimed by Italy were put into the country, they would total only 3 per cent of the population, a smaller percentage than in other cases.[45] On 12 February 1919, the Yugoslavs rebutted Barzilai by demanding that they be given <u>all</u> of the Istrian peninsula, Dalmatia and Trieste, plus other territory and shrewdly asked Wilson to arbitrate between them and Italy. Sonnino refused to accept arbitration because of Wilson's well-known pro-Yugoslav bent: his belief that as successor states of Austria-Hungary Yugoslavia and Italy should be considered equals, and that as a consequence Yugoslav-inhabited areas should not go to Italy. Wilson then left for the United States for a month and, on his return, handed Orlando a memorandum on 14 April outlining his solution to the problem. This memorandum would have consigned much of Istria to Yugoslavia (the 'Wilson Line', worked out by American experts), along with all of Dalmatia and most of the islands under consideration. As for Fiume, it would have become a free city within the Yugoslav economic sphere.

Provoking the American President's ire, Orlando stuck to his guns, saying he could never accept such a solution, but maintaining he would not hold up the German Peace Treaty, a persistent rumor, and insisting that the Italian delegation would keep seeking a solution through Lloyd George's good offices.[46] The situation now became extremely complicated, with the British and the French threatening to look for ways to invalidate the Treaty of London, with Wilson contradicting himself, with Orlando wavering. All the statesmen's attempts to square the Italian circle failed, and in retaliation the Italians now supposedly threatened to hold up ratification of the German Treaty.[47] The press reported that the Italian delegation was planning to boycott the Peace Conference unless an emergency plan drafted by House resolved the Adriatic problem.[48] Convinced that the Italian people would listen to him rather than to their own representatives, President Wilson issued a 'manifesto' appealing to the Italian people over the heads of their delegation. This manifesto explained his principles as applied to Italy and the Adriatic but above all was an attempt 'to refurbish his prestige at home and abroad, for this had been badly tarnished before the Adriatic crisis came to a head by the countless concessions made to the Allies vis-à-vis former enemies'.[49] Whatever the background maneuverings and exactly what led to the public break, the consensus of serious historians is that Wilson's appeal was 'a capital error in judgment'.[50]

Orlando responded on 24 April. He kept to more practical matters, claiming that Wilson's manifesto appeared while the Italian delegation was discussing a proposal that might have resolved the issue. Orlando objected to Wilson's appeal to the Italian people against their representatives as an insult to Italy's democratic traditions, and rejected the President's implication that the Italian government did not represent its people. He restated the reasons in

> President Wilson himself has had the kindness to recognize, in the course of our conversations, that truth and justice are the monopoly of no one person, and that all men are subject to error, and I add that the error is all the easier as the problems to which the principles apply are more complex. Humanity is such an immense thing, the problems raised by the life of the people are so infinitely complex, that nobody can believe that he has found in a determined number of proposals as simple and sure a way to solve them as if it were a question of determining the dimensions, the volume and the weight of bodies with various units of measure.
>
> VITTORIO ORLANDO, 24 APRIL 1919

favor of granting Italy's requests, rebutting Wilson's contention that Italy had achieved a defensible frontier.

The dispute with Wilson now reached a climax. The Italian delegation left Paris in protest. Not surprisingly, the Italian people supported their representatives because of what it saw as unfair discrimination against an ally that had done its duty and suffered great human losses, temporarily united nationalists and neutralists and so bolstered the Orlando government that it asked for and received a vote of confidence. Wilson even alienated his Italian supporters, who emphasized his unequal treatment of the Italians as compared to the other Allies: 'Why does he want to impose what he considers absolute justice on the Italian people alone?' This statement by Italian historian Gaetano Salvemini, a democratic interventionist who had strongly supported the American President, illustrates the negative Italian reaction to the manifesto. Wilson managed to transform Orlando and even Sonnino into popular heroes, even if only briefly.[51]

The unity of former neutralists and interventionists stimulated by Wilson's manifesto strengthened Orlando's government only momentarily. The circumstances under which Italy was being denied what most Italians believed should be the just rewards of a costly and devastating conflict stimulated popular resentment because most Italians considered the treatment of their country dishonest. This feeling rapidly moved out of diplomatic circles to the population. The country's leaders understood this development and warned their allies against it. While Wilson argued in favour of his principles and tried to enforce them primarily on the weakest of his allies, Orlando admonished the American President not to forget that feelings of injustice constituted *the most likely cause of future wars*. As far as Italy was concerned, he warned, if the country did not receive Fiume the humiliation would provoke protest and hatreds so deep as to *cause violent conflicts in the more or less near future.* Moreover, denying Fiume to Italy would be *equally fatal* to Italian interests and world peace.[52]

In fact, Orlando received daily reports of increasing disorders in Italy.[53] The excitable Americans interpreted them as government-staged, alienating the Italian delegation even more. 'The Government made no attempt to curb the hostility to Wilson, ...' Baker wrote, 'in fact, instead of trying to bring about a calm consideration of the state of affairs, it did all in its power to inflame popular passions – by mendacious speeches and arguments, by "staged" demonstrations – in a way calculated to result in a mandate to stand out for the most extreme demands.'[54]

Italian documents starkly contradict this tendentious interpretation. A 23 May 1919 telegram from Gaspare Colosimo, Minister of the Interior and Vice President of the Council of Ministers, to the country's prefects states: 'With reference to my two circulars telegraphed to you yesterday N. 14666, I insist ... that in the public manifestations that may take place in your province that any words, phrases, speeches that in are any way directed against allied countries in general and against President Wilson and President Clemenceau in particular must be absolutely avoided stop I have no need to make your patriotism comprehend ... that the extremely delicate international situation that in this moment could be decisive for a solution to our problems imposes the most austere discipline and the maximum loyalty and correctness on our part without any verbal violence, which will be certainly exploited to damage us stop You must in all manner and in all forms inspire such a persuasion in all who may have direct contact

Gabriele D'Annunzio (1863–1938) was Italy's most famous poet and novelist, leading a dashing life filled with romance and political adventure. During the First World War, he served in the military with fanfare but with distinction. He took over Fiume in September 1919 and established a government that prefigured the future Fascist state and from which Mussolini took many of his rituals and ideas. It had a similar constitution, its militia wore similar uniforms, its followers shouted the same slogans, and D'Annunzio ruled as the *Duce* (Leader) and made speeches from a balcony to rapt crowds. It was during this occupation that he used the phrase '*vittoria mutilata*' claiming that the Italian victory had been 'mutilated' at the Conference. This slogan magnified popular anger and later proved effective in helping the Fascist drive for power. After the Fiume question was settled, D'Annunzio was chased out of the city, but he remained an important figure in Italian politics and a rival of Mussolini.

with the public; ... if ... some unpleasant incident should occur, you will be held personally responsible, and I would be forced ... to take adequate sanctions in the name of the government stop.' The telegram goes on to emphasize that the same measures applied to the press.[55] In free countries, however, it is difficult to stop expressions of popular rage. The Italian diplomats in Paris reported that Wilson took umbrage at the demonstrations, especially resenting a speech by the poet-warrior Gabriele D'Annunzio and attacks against his wife.[56]

In September 1919, D'Annunzio led an expedition to Fiume and took over the city, to popular acclaim. He hoped to force Italy to annex it, and when it did not, declared it an independent city. As Wilson reportedly threatened Italy with an economic blockade,[57] D'Annunzio instituted a laboratory for the future Fascist state in the city.[58]

The withdrawal of the Italian delegation from Paris was a tactical error, because it allowed Wilson and the Allies to conspire secretly against Italian interests in the defeated Ottoman Empire, and to connive together to settle important questions without Italian input.[59] During this period, Orlando kept in touch with developments at the Conference through detailed reports from Italian diplomats. These reports informed the Prime Minister of the opinions of the Allies and Wilson, in addition to Yugoslav developments. One attitude that is striking in them is the constant theme that Wilson would 'never' give in to Italian requests. One report cited French diplomat André Tardieu, an advocate of compromise, as quoting Wilson as saying that he would not give up at any cost. The same report noted that the American President, stung by support in the French press for the Italian position, blamed the Italian government and summoned his ablest 'agents' to Paris in order to rebut it.[60] According to Italian reports, Wilson would not agree to Italian demands because Italy would be forced to give in or 'face economic and financial ruin'.[61] This report stresses economics as a reason for American intransigence with regard to Italy and for its unwavering support for Yugoslavia. Citing a conversation with George B Ford, head of the Research Department of the American Red Cross in France, the report quotes him as saying:

America favors young populations that need capital, not to exploit these populations but to get a good return on American capital. Yugoslavia is the door to Central Europe and we Americans must possess that door. ... Italy interests us less than all the others from the viewpoint of economic and industrial utility [*sfruttamento*]. Don't forget that Wilson is for the new peoples.[62]

Orlando and Sonnino returned to Paris on 6 May because their boycott did not bring them any advantages and Britain and France threatened to use their walkout as a reason to abrogate the Treaty of London. *The very bitter return*, Orlando wrote on the timetable of the special train taking him back to Paris. Orlando had gained nothing as a result of his boycott but further weakened his bargaining position and his support in Italy. Negotiations dragged on over the Fiume question in Paris, but to no avail.[63] In June, with the Orlando government tottering, 'Wilsonian circles' were still insisting that Italy could not stand firm against the Americans for long because of its shortage of foodstuffs and raw materials,[64] for which it depended on the United States. The Americans were holding back an urgently needed $25 million credit.[65] This pressure was a major sore point for the Italians; the statement by Orlando when he returned from Paris that *If Italy knows hunger it does not know dishonour!*[66] drove the crowd wild.

Orlando's lack of success at the Paris Peace Conference led to the fall of his government on 19 June 1919. After his resignation, discussions on the Fiume question went on, but Wilson continued to block agreement, opposing a British and French solution to the problem that they had worked out with a new Italian government in early 1920. The depth of Wilson's intransigence against any concessions to Italy even after the Peace Conference and despite an Italian accord with the French and British is demonstrated by his threat to withdraw from Senate consideration *both* the Versailles Treaty, signed on 28 June 1919, and a treaty signed on the same day between the United States and France in which the Americans pledged to come to France's aid in case of unprovoked aggression by Germany.[67] Quite clearly, there could be no resolution of the Adriatic question while Wilson was in any way involved.

Agreement came through direct talks between the Italians and the Yugoslavs who negotiated the Treaty of Rapallo on 22 November 1920 with a new government headed by Francesco Saverio Nitti. This treaty defined the Italian border with Yugoslavia and made Fiume a free state, but if anything, it conveyed a greater impression of Italian weakness than previously. In January 1924, with Mussolini in power, Fiume was annexed to Italy.[68] This success enhanced the Duce's prestige, but it was not the final settlement. After the Second World War, Fiume's Italian population was driven out and the city became part of Yugoslavia and, after Yugoslavia finally fell apart, of an independent Croatia.

Although Orlando's government fell days before the signature of the Versailles Treaty, Orlando states that he deliberately did not sign it.[69] Sonnino, Guglielmo Imperiali and Silvio Crespi, members of the Italian delegation, signed for Italy on 28 June 1919, the fifth anniversary of Franz Ferdinand's assassination, in the Hall of Mirrors at the Versailles Palace – the ceremony hosted by Georges Clemenceau. It had been in the same hall that the German princes had proclaimed the German Empire on 18 January 1871. What was a joyful day for the French and a mournful one for the Germans could only have been sad for the Italians, given the baleful outcome of the Paris Peace Conference for them.

The Allies signed the Treaty of St Germain with the new Republic of Austria on 10 September 1919. This treaty dissolved the old Austro-Hungarian Empire, creating a series of 'successor states'. Italy gained the Brenner frontier, including Trent and the Trentino, a small piece of land that gave it control of one of the main railroads between Trieste and the Austrian frontier, and part of the Istrian peninsula. Ironically, its greatest gain from the First World War was the disappearance of Austria-Hungary and its replacement on the Italian borders by a series of weak states. However, the epic battle it waged in Paris against the most powerful country in the world masked that fact, and left the Italians with only resentment and a sense of frustration.

8
Italian Perspectives

Vittorio Emanuele Orlando attended the Peace Conference in Paris under more difficult circumstances than his Big Four counterparts. Ironically, he had to commute back and forth between Rome and Paris, a trip that required two days' travel time, a journalist who made the train trip with him on 8 January 1919 reported. He complained that he could not stay away from Rome for long because his government was always in a state of 'half crisis'. His main rival in the cabinet, Francesco Saverio Nitti, was the type of agitated person who continuously brought up problems, many of which were silly. He would leave the heroic atmosphere of Paris every week to get involved in insignificant disputes, he wrote – like a medieval knight participating in a discussion with a group of cheesemakers. Worse, Bissolati and Sonnino were polar opposites on how the Italians should conduct themselves at the Conference, with the first being too soft and the second being too inflexible, then shifting while Orlando struggled to keep the balance between them. As a result, the Italian delegation had no plan when the Conference opened and was unprepared to face the upcoming 'bitter struggle'.[1]

Austria-Hungary and the Balkans

An issue that the Italians were not ready to face was the fate of the Austro-Hungarian Empire. Sonnino had grown up with that empire and neither expected nor desired its breakup. As an old-time statesman, he feared the consequences if the Empire disappeared and was replaced with a series of successor states. Its disappearance created a new problem for Italy, that is, Austria's possible takeover by Germany. This possibility was a real one. During the period of German unification, the only reason that Austria was left out of Germany was because of its status as the centre of a great empire containing many disparate nationalities. When this impediment disappeared, as it did following the end of the First World War and when, in addition, Wilson argued that all national groups should be in the same nation-state, the union of Austria with Germany became a real possibility.

Even though it would soon seem unthinkable, it was still unclear at the time that Austria and Germany would not be joined, a possibility that increased Italian fears that it might face a vastly superior Germany on its borders and not a weak rump Austria. This was a powerful argument against Wilson's assertion that Italy was safe because Austria-Hungary no longer existed. It also strengthened the Italian view that, in addition to the Brenner Pass, Italy needed a secure eastern frontier on the Adriatic, which caused the explosive crisis with the Yugoslavs backed by the Americans. The Italians believed that if their northern frontier was secure because it would be protected by the mountains up to the Brenner Pass, a powerful Germany reinforced by Austria could easily come in through the 'back door' left open by their lack of a secure frontier. In other words, the problem for them was not to defend themselves against a weak Yugoslavia – as the

Americans saw the problem – but from an invasion by a possibly German-dominated Austria.[2] Interestingly, a strong *Anschluss* movement existed in Austria as well as Germany, and the attempted annexation of Austria in 1934, Adolf Hitler's success in 1938 and Germany's annexation after 1943 of the areas won by Italy during the First World War demonstrate that the Italian fear of Germany was real, even if Mussolini erred in allying with it during the Second World War.

Consequently, Sonnino's stubbornness in demanding everything he had bargained for in the Treaty of London had its logic, even if his inflexibility was misguided – not only because it alienated the Allies, but because it stimulated some of the divisions in Italy that contributed to the rise of Fascism, with all its deleterious consequences. Orlando demonstrated a knowledge of these consequences in January 1919 with an uncommon prescience. He noted Sonnino's inflexibility and said it hurt Italy in three ways: it prevented a dialogue with the Slavs; it fixated the Italians on the Adriatic problem while taking their focus off world problems of the first order which Italy had to face (the Adriatic issue, he suspected *might be indirectly stoked by one of our good allies in order to divert us from other problems*); and Sonnino's inaction on the Treaty of London resulted in continuous internal agitation *that could have even graver consequences because of the illusions it raises*.[3] Orlando feared the consequences of the Italian disorders and the other results from a failure to reach agreement with the Americans; if Wilson had met him halfway on the Adriatic question, he confided to a journalist, he would have broken with Sonnino.[4]

Orlando's views

It is indeed unfortunate that Orlando was distracted by
the Adriatic question and that historians have frequently
supplied us with a caricature of an intelligent and focused
person.[5] In fact, he was an astute observer of the people and
events around him.

With regard to the most controversial and important personage at the Peace Conference, it is interesting to compare
Orlando's views of Woodrow Wilson at the time with the
later ones described later in this chapter. Orlando defined
his future antagonist as an extraordinarily strong and cold
person who was in tune with the European masses. He opined
that if the European statesmen did not comport themselves
well, Wilson could launch an appeal to the people that would
shake their governments. In brief, Wilson was a new kind of
statesman challenging the old structure of world politics.
In discussing the Adriatic problems, Orlando reported a
conversation with the American President in which he said
that the Americans had no right to repudiate *secret treaties* of which they had never been a part. These were contracts between the parties that had signed them, the lawyer
in Orlando announced to the President; and while he could
renounce contracts on his own account, he could not do so
for his own country while allowing other countries to get
away with the *loot* they had gained from winning the war.
According to Orlando, Wilson answered, 'You're right.' He
told Wilson that his position against putting Slavic elements
into Italy while supporting putting Germans into Czechoslovakia or Poland was indefensible, but he concluded that
Wilson was unalterably biased in favour of the Yugoslavs. On
the other hand, the two men agreed on the importance of the
League of Nations, and Wilson appreciated Orlando's public

support for it. However, Orlando did not share the illusion of other European statesmen who hoped to get Wilson's aid for their goals by supporting the League. *The man is as hard as a boulder*, he exclaimed. *We are facing a conflict of two mentalities [between] tradition and that which is perhaps the future, and the conflict is rendered more dramatic because of the extraordinary personality of the man who is at its center. [A man] who is good, always cordial but exhibits a firmness in his ideas that is unknown to European statesmen.* On 28 January 1919, Orlando stated that he believed in Wilson's ideas but at the same time he could not compromise his country's interests or rights.[6] The stage was thus set for a dispute between two strong personalities who nevertheless had similar ideas.

Orlando's ideas with regard to the treatment of Germany were also important; and, ironically, years later historians and statesmen cited similar points to illustrate the errors made at the Peace Conference that may have contributed to the breakdown of the peace. He objected to the limiting of the German army to 100,000 soldiers. Switzerland and Holland could field 300,000, not to mention Poland and Czechoslovakia; imagine if such a fallen colossus still brimming with force and energy could be left at the mercy of any ruffian that came along, Orlando commented. He also criticized the abolition of the draft in Germany, which the British pushed through, and wondered how the French could have gone along with it. The other point Orlando subscribed to was the way in which the war ended, without a clear defeat of Germany. In the words of his interviewer, with whom Orlando agreed, 'it was necessary to march to Berlin and Vienna and impose in a brief time all the conditions of peace'.

Orlando also objected to the resolution of an issue that

would touch off the Second World War: the establishment of Danzig as a free city and the Polish Corridor. He said that the Allies objected to putting a small number of Slavs into Italy and then *they throw four million Germans into the new Polish state*. Orlando did not believe in free cities because they would always cause trouble, and distinguished between the cases of Danzig and Fiume. At the same time, Orlando defined as ridiculous the rumour that Italy would withhold its signature from the German peace treaty, demolishing the contention with the practice of a fourth-generation lawyer.[7] On reparations, he asked, *how can you force acceptance of an undetermined figure?* Finally, Orlando objected to the avidity of the British and the French, the French desire for revenge, the mistreatment of the Hungarians, placing Italy, an ally that had shed its blood for the victory against the Central Powers, on the same plane as the Poles, Slavs and Czechs who had not.[8] These elements doomed the peace.

Hungary suffered the most losses as a result of the First World War, losing two-thirds of its territory and its population. Millions of ethnic Hungarians were thrown into Romania, where they caused strife and the economy entered a drastic downturn. The result was a Communist revolution followed by a rightist dictatorship. In 1934, Fascist Italy, which had put itself at the head of a revisionist camp in an attempt to dismantle the Versailles settlement, signed the Rome Protocols with Hungary and Austria. This agreement contributed to the destabilization of the continent. Later Hungary came under the influence of Nazi Germany and fought on its side during the Second World War.

Unfortunately, the dispute with Wilson and the focus on Italy's Adriatic frontiers short-circuited the possibility of any real Italian influence in parts of the world where the country might have made a contribution to a peaceful resolution of problems and expanded its commercial interests. Orlando's papers are replete with reports of Italian diplomats on various issues that later developed into major problems for the post-war world and consistently complain about the efforts of their British, French, and American Allies to cut them out. For example, the Italians were very attentive to the Armenians, had a good rapport with them and were concerned with sending them humanitarian aid.[9] They also described British occupation of oil-rich Baku (in Russia; now in Azerbaijan) and their concern with petroleum, leaving the population to fend with greatly inflated prices for prime necessities.[10] The report of a Jewish commander in the Italian armed forces describes British 'divide and conquer' tactics, depicts the early rise of anti-Jewish Arab organizations in Palestine and gave a pessimistic assessment of the Jewish political and economic situation in the area.[11] In Egypt, the same officer ascribed recent disorders not only to distant historical causes but to British prohibition against allowing four Egyptian delegates to attend the Paris Peace Conference to present the requests of the 'nationalist party', exploitation by the British, poor administrators and the bad behaviour of Australian soldiers. The result was the strengthening of nationalist and Arab sentiment, with the sending of funds by Egyptians to Arabs in Palestine and Syria. This report also complains about British actions blocking Italian economic activities in the country, and claims they were jealous of Italian relations with Egyptian officials.[12]

Another report details the situation in Poland, emphasizes the commercial activities of the British, French and Americans and suggests the kind of actions the Italians could take that would produce fruitful commercial interchange between Italy and that country.[13] This activity demonstrates Italian interest in Eastern Europe, the Middle East and Africa[14] that might have given Italy a respectable economic and political role in those countries. These interests did not cease after the Peace Conference; they turned into revisionism led by the Duce, not a moderate foreign policy headed by a liberal democrat like Orlando.

Colonial issues

An important aspect of the Italian negotiations regarded colonial issues, in which Italy was supposed to be compensated in case of French and British gains. These were enshrined in the Treaty of London and included gaining full rights in the areas occupied during the Libyan War and removal of any rights the Turkish Sultan still retained in Libya itself. Potentially, Article IX of that treaty was the most important because it recognized Italy's interests in the Mediterranean Sea and promised it 'a just share' in the region around Adalia in the event of a partition of Turkey. In addition, it was assured 'just compensation' for any increase in British and French possessions at German expense. As previously noted, Sonnino was not much interested in colonial expansion, which explains the vagueness; and, given the difficulties Italy had with its allies, it turned out that Orlando could not devote much attention to the question either.[15]

With regard to the colonies, the negotiations in Paris failed. The French and British split up the colonies of the defeated countries, taking the lion's share under the thinly-veiled 'mandate' system and closely safeguarding their financial interests against any Italian competition.[16] Italian hopes for gains in Africa in areas such as Togo vanished and the mandates were all handed out without giving the Italians any or even taking them into consideration.[17] The Orlando papers contain a note from the Prime Minister to the Minister for the Colonies arguing that he could not overcome British and French opposition and Wilson's influence in the matter of colonial affairs: *the combat situation in which Italy has put itself out of necessity with President Wilson should have prepared us for complete lack of success. In colonial questions, France and Britain spontaneously have interests contradictory to ours; you can imagine how much President Wilson is disposed to support us against them!*[18] Orlando was already cognizant that the Allies would use mandates to escape from their commitment to give Italy compensation on 1 February 1919 and that the failure to make colonial gains would be harshly judged in Italy.[19]

As a result, Italy received no compensation in the colonies and the question was put off to a later time. This issue had crucial results, because Mussolini and French Premier Pierre Laval finally resolved the question with rectification of the borders of Libya in 1935. However, given the paucity of Italian gains then, the Duce only agreed because Laval secretly gave him a free hand to attack Ethiopia.[20] Thus a leftover problem from the Paris Peace Conference was at the origin of one of the most infamous incidents on the road to the Second World War.

Reflections on a Conference

The frustration with the outcome of the Paris Peace Conference for Italy emerged strongly in Orlando's memoirs, drafted between 1941 and 1945. The Italian Prime Minister's role in the Paris Peace Conference was not judged positively either by his people at the time or by historians later. Italians thought him weak because he could not obtain Fiume, while historians tend to view him as isolated, interested only in Italian affairs, and under the thumb of Sonnino.[21] However, since Orlando lived until 1952 and witnessed developments for three decades after the Conference ended, it is useful to summarize his views.[22]

Orlando's view of Wilson had changed radically. He argued that the Paris Peace Conference was not a conference at all but an 'arbitration proceeding' run by a judge (Wilson) in which there was no real dialogue. Wilson and the United States so completely dominated the proceedings because, unlike peace conferences after previous wars, no one besides the US had any power: not the defeated (despite Germany's explicit surrender on the basis of the Fourteen Points), nor the neutral countries, of which there were very few and they were weak, nor the completely exhausted victorious countries. The US dominated the world militarily, economically and financially, and Wilson had become its 'spiritual' leader. Thus, for Orlando, Wilson was the arbiter of the world's fate, in the worst sense of the word. In fact, Wilson always emphasized the independence of the United States from its allies, insisting that the country was an 'Associated' and not an 'Allied' power. The Yugoslav request to have Wilson 'arbitrate' the differences between them and Italy demonstrated that they were confident he would render a judgment favorable to them. This move illustrated as well the Conference's quality as a parody of arbitration, one in which the 'arbitrator' sits in judgment and is in a position to impose his will on the others, not an impartial person chosen by a third party to resolve a dispute.[23] It is interesting that this view is an early anticipation of later criticisms consistently made of US arrogance by other countries.

Orlando goes on to interpret the peace following the First World War as a complete failure because Wilson's personality did not allow him to implement his program: securing a peace that was as equitable as possible, one that did not cause bitterness or a desire for revenge among the defeated countries and one that secured their acceptance; his other aim was to create an international order that would prevent future aggressive war. The Fourteen Points were supposed to be the basis of the first part of his programme and the League of Nations the embodiment of the second. However, the 20 years between 1919 and 1939 proved Wilson's *disastrous failure* in achieving these aims: *never has a peace left behind it such a wake of resentment and hatred, not only of the defeated toward the victorious but of the victorious toward their victorious allies, and, even among the smaller nations created by the treaties, who are all ferocious toward one another and toward all the states to which they owe everything, beginning with their own existence! As for the League of Nations, after having demonstrated its perfect inability to achieve its essential aims, it ended up by being ridiculous.*[24]

Orlando claims that he and Wilson got along well at first and that it took him long months of discussion to understand that the President was what Orlando defined a *spontaneous hypocrite*. As noted earlier in this chapter, when he first met Wilson, Orlando defined him as *a man of extraordinary firmness and coldness* determined to exercise his power.[25] According to Orlando, hypocrisy was so ingrained in Wilson that *understanding and knowledge* of it did not even exist in his own mind but was second nature to him. Wilson enunciated the Fourteen Points, Orlando wrote, but then gave in on them, but only to certain countries; he condemned secret treaties on principle when Italy was involved as an excuse to reject Italian claims, then negotiated in secrecy when it suited him. Orlando is here referring to the deal by which Wilson hastily and secretly offered the Greeks occupation of Smyrna instead of giving it to the Italians to whom it was supposed to be allotted. 'Certainly this was a far cry from open covenants, openly arrived at,' commented the historian who studied Wilson's dispute with Italy in the most depth. Orlando himself cites Wilson's confidant Ray Stannard Baker as stating that this incident was the most shameful page of the entire Conference.[26] In his book, Baker indeed does reveal how the representatives of the Allied and Associated powers devoted to open negotiations surreptitiously met in 'Lloyd George's flat and took all precautions to keep the Italians from knowing what was under way'. Baker admits that it was a 'disreputable conspiracy', excused, of course, because 'it was only doing what the Italians were doing – playing the Italian game'.[27] Wilson thus joined in settling this particular question by the 'old method of secret diplomacy', which the Americans identified with Sonnino, instead of using 'new methods of impartial inquiry by experts' which they supposedly championed.[28] Orlando concluded that Wilson lived in an abstract, unreal world of his own making, akin to Calvin and other religious leaders of that ilk – fatal qualities when combined with the power of the United States.[29]

Besides his stormy relationship with Wilson, Orlando's association with his Foreign Minister remains a question mark. Sonnino's strong personality gave the Allies the impression that he and not Orlando determined Italian policy and caused the problems over the Adriatic that almost wrecked the Conference.[30] This interpretation raises the question of the relationship between Sonnino and the Prime Minister.

Orlando had the opportunity to address the question in his memoirs in a completely unobstructed manner, since Sonnino had died in 1922. Orlando defends Sonnino's actions very strongly, arguing that the Foreign Minister was concerned above all for Italy's security. In this context, Orlando upheld the Treaty of London – negotiated by Sonnino – and its secrecy, stating that national interest imposes secrecy in some matters and that Lloyd George acted in exactly the same manner.[31] He admits that he and Sonnino did not have the same views on everything and that they had some bitter disagreements, but he considers this normal and categorically denies that a split existed between the two. No doubt he was more flexible than the Tuscan Baron and this caused problems, but he states that sometimes the roles were reversed. The idea that he tried to put Sonnino aside and control the Italian delegation, Orlando declared *false; worse than false, grotesque*. Orlando then tells the story of a professor who visited him with the idea of writing a book arguing that Orlando at Paris did everything possible to assure a good outcome for Italy, but that Sonnino refused to cooperate and damaged his diplomacy. Orlando responded that if he wrote such a work, he, Orlando, would immediately publish a detailed response contradicting him and fighting the thesis *to the finish as erroneous and unjust at the same time*. In sum, Orlando undertook a spirited defense of the ever-unpopular Sonnino and cites Wilson and Clemenceau as examples of dictatorial personalities who did not cooperate with their Foreign Ministers, in contrast to himself.[32]

Interestingly, even at an early date, Orlando complained about being seen as vacillating compared with Sonnino. In a private conversation of 8 January 1919 with journalist Olindo Malagodi, Orlando said that Sonnino screamed in an official meeting that he would rather renounce Fiume than cede an inch on Dalmatia. Orlando, instead, believed that Fiume had an incomparably greater value for Italy because it would allow the country to exercise greater influence in Eastern Europe while Dalmatia had scarce economic value and was a political liability; he was open to trading Dalmatia for Fiume. However, in a meeting with the Allies Sonnino turned around and argued that Fiume was worth much more than Dalmatia because it was the key to penetrating the Balkans – the opposite of what he had previously insisted. Orlando lamented *and I, unfortunately, had to keep quiet*. Yet again, when the time came for a decision to be made on the question, 'he digs in his heels and it seems that he does not want to give up a stone in Dalmatia in return for Fiume'.[33]

In another conversation, Orlando contended that Italy had two disasters during the war, Sonnino and Boselli: *One was a stubborn little mind, the other represented governmental anarchy*. His proposed remedy in 1917 – replacing Sonnino with Salandra at the Foreign Ministry – hit a political stone wall because everybody hated Salandra. Orlando considered Salandra intellectually lazy and therefore that he could have dominated foreign policy himself, but against Sonnino's stubbornness nothing could have prevailed.[34] These harsh judgments are difficult to reconcile with Orlando's later unbridled defense of Sonnino.

In his portrait of Clemenceau at the Conference, Orlando argues that his duels with the French statesman never diminished his admiration for him. No one faced such a long list of crucial problems during the conflict as did Clemenceau, Orlando writes, but he succeeded by force of will in guiding his country out of mortal peril to victory. Only Joan of Arc compares to him in French history, '*the young saint … and the Freemason, the atheist from the Vendée: both united in the august title of saviors of the Fatherland*'.[35] Orlando recorded his recollections of David Lloyd George when he received news of his death in March 1945. The Englishman, and not Wilson, had towered over the Paris Peace Conference, a wistful Orlando wrote, praising his firmness and astuteness that reflected *the sense of wisdom, measure, and political equilibrium of the British people*.[36] These reflections demonstrate how Orlando

felt more at ease, and fitted in better with, his European colleagues than he did with the stiff American President.

A theme that emerges in the historiography regards
Orlando's supposed weakness and that he was too much of a
gentleman.[37] Orlando's failure to secure Fiume for Italy and
attacks by Nationalists certainly influenced the judgment of
his countrymen in this regard. Orlando's memoirs frequently
demonstrate the former Prime Minister's touchiness on this
question. Orlando reproduces a letter, dated 1 June 1939, in
which he responds to an article written by André Tardieu,
a major political figure of the Third Republic, portraying
him as a weak person surrounded by three men with characters of steel. Flashing the irony that he frequently employed,
Orlando answered that when France and Italy had attempted
to secure borders guaranteeing their security at the Conference, Wilson turned them down. What happened? The 'weak'
Italian resisted him and Clemenceau gave in. This weakness,
according to Orlando, put France in the dangerous situation
in which it found itself in 1939, while Italy had got Fiume
although Clemenceau had pledged it would never have it.
When Lloyd George came to see him after his *tempestuous*
meeting with Wilson of 14 April 1919, Orlando told him
that he could not accept Wilson's dictates *for the right and
honour of my country*. Orlando also pours out his resentment against Italy's allies for secretly conspiring against him
to assign Smyrna to Greece rather than to Italy.[38]

This letter has the undeniable quality of a man who considers himself wronged and is defending himself before
history, although it was lucky for Italy that Greece went into
Turkey, given the sound defeat the Greeks met. It is interesting, however, that some critics had afterthoughts about his
role. The Italian Ambassador to Britain, who joined the

chorus criticizing Orlando in his diary, stated in 1937 that he intended to modify his judgments on Orlando and Sonnino in a positive manner because he had come to believe that any errors committed at Paris by these men were minor, did not compromise Italy's position and were blown out of proportion by hatred. Such a re-evaluation especially of Orlando's role, Imperiali stated, 'was an "act of truth and loyalty" toward a political class that had been attacked for different and opposite reasons by neutralists, revolutionary leftists, and nationalists'; it had become a 'sacrificial lamb' offered to a public opinion manipulated and exasperated by nationalistic propaganda.[39] No doubt, opposition to the Fascist regime played a role in this reconsideration, as well it should have, but the excessively unkind views of Orlando have been unduly influenced by politics and should be reassessed.

While Orlando's memoirs portray well the heated atmosphere of the Conference and what he considers to have been the unholy alliance of the three most powerful nations in the world against a country that spilled its blood for the common victory, he frequently emphasizes the point Imperiali would later make. In his own country, anti-Nationalists and ultra-Nationalists regarded him with equal hatred, which not only spelled the end of his political career but would usher in a new and catastrophic era.[40] Orlando frequently cites this rage against him by extremists of all stripes as proof of his own strength and of devotion to his moderate policies under difficult circumstances. On balance, the failure of the Conference to resolve the Adriatic question – which caused such fury in Italy – owed more to Wilson's complex personality, prejudices and failure to prevail against the British and the French than to Sonnino's stubbornness or to Orlando's weakness.

Then there is this to consider: compared to the US, Italy's

weakness was an objective, not a subjective, fact. The United States presented itself on the world stage in a massive way for the first time. Lloyd George and Clemenceau had humiliated Wilson by inducing him to modify his Fourteen Points; could Wilson back off when confronted by an Italy whose performance during the First World War and whose military and diplomatic image had been undermined during the conflict itself and which had less than full support from its allies? Given the strength of the US, it could be argued that Orlando and Sonnino might have been better off surrendering to the new superpower instead of resisting it, but neither man would consider this solution. The issue of Italy at the Paris Peace Conference goes beyond the question of Orlando's supposed weakness, calls Wilson's judgment into question and stands as an object lesson for Americans. Orlando judged the peace so terrible that, had it been a private contract, the courts would have annulled it because it was based on the deceit that the Fourteen Points drove it.[41] The resentment against the events at the Conference contributed to Orlando's fall and to the chaos which would have disastrous domestic and international repercussions.[42]

Vittorio Orlando, the surviving member of the 'Big Four', receives a birthday kiss from his grand-daughter Maria Teresa in Rome, 19 May 1950

III

The Legacy

9
Fascism

Historians have long argued about the causes accounting for Fascism's rise to power in Italy. Several reasons coming together in the post-war world explain the Fascist phenomenon in Europe, but the First World War and its tempestuous aftermath, including the Paris Peace Conference, were major triggers that helped Benito Mussolini overthrow the Liberal State and jump-start Fascism's march through the 20th century. The Italian parliamentary system had faults before the conflict, as did others, but Italy had made major progress toward a fully democratic system. It had a functioning Parliament and its governments had to account for their actions in order to remain in power. Before the First World War, parliamentary responsibility was a major difference between Italy and Germany, Austria-Hungary and Russia, where the governments were responsible to the monarch. Parliament and popular opinion had a major voice in Italy, as they did in Britain and France, in affecting policy; the opposition of the Italian people to the Triple Alliance that made it impossible for any Italian government to go to war on Austria's side is just one example. One deficiency was that the Italian king had more power than his counterpart in Britain, but less than those in Germany, Austria-Hungary and Russia. In short, Italy was a 'democracy in the making' during the late 19th and early 20th centuries, and the results of the First World War constituted a major shift in the course of the country's history.[1]

Philosopher and historian Benedetto Croce attributed the rise of Mussolini and his Fascists in 1922 to that conflagration and its effects. The conflict created so great a moral, political and economic crisis that it knocked Italy off the democratic path on which it had been progressing and resulted in the rise of a dictatorship. Croce stated that between 1860 and 1922 Italy 'was one of the most democratic countries in Europe' and in a famous interpretation, labeled Fascism 'a sad parenthesis in its history'.[2] If Fascism was indeed a pernicious 'aside' in Italian history, the struggle at, and results of, the Paris Peace Conference made a major contribution to changing the course of Italy's history and, with Fascism's spread, that of Europe.

The 'Mutilated Victory'

After his cabinet's fall, Vittorio Emanuele Orlando never again held political power. However, he still had influence, on the one hand, as the 'President of the Victory', and, on the other, as a target of Nationalists and the supposed symbol of Italian weakness and failure. He also became President of the Chamber of Deputies on 2 December 1919. Along with other elder statesmen, during the Fascist regime Orlando remained a beacon of the old Liberal order's light and, after Mussolini's fall, represented the historical memory of a democratic tradition that inspired the new Italian Republic.

Orlando had been correct in highlighting, Cassandra-like,

the domestic effects of Italy's less than respectful treatment by the Allies at the Peace Conference. The idea that the Conference had transformed the heroic events of the First World War into the 'mutilated victory' rapidly gained currency in the country after the war. The dispute between 'intervention-ists' and 'neutralists', muted but never completely ended, returned transformed. The neu-tralists looked at the disappoint-ing results of the Conference and said, in effect, 'We told you so'. They had been correct, they argued, because the Italians had little to show for their part in the conflict except slight territo-rial gains and huge human and economic loses. This sentiment took hold immediately after the war, with Italians turning away in disgust from those who had advocated intervention and from the soldiers who had fought in the war. Numerous violent dem-

'We suffered the humiliation of seeing the banners of our glorious regiments returned to their homes without being saluted, without the warm cheer of sympathy owed to those who return from victorious war. Now, again, it seemed to me and my friends as if there was in everybody an instinct to finish the game of war not with the idea of real victory, but with content that he [sic] had lost as little as possible. ... Certainly the central government was no dike to prevent the flood of weakness.'
BENITO MUSSOLINI, 1928

onstrations took place, with red flags flying and participants 'cursing the war'.[3] Disappointment because of the war's results, the difficulty of transitioning from a wartime to a peacetime economy, high unemployment and inflation, and the influence of the Bolshevik Revolution produced the 'Red Biennium', the triumph of the extreme Left that brought the country to the edge of revolution.[4]

Former interventionists contested this view of the conflict. The neutralists had betrayed Italy by splitting Italian public opinion by renouncing the fruits of victory, by hamstringing the Italian delegation to the Peace Conference and by encouraging Wilson in his anti-Italian crusade, convincing him that he had strong support in Italy itself. They blamed the Socialists for having scuttled the country's efforts to reap the rewards of its sacrifices, lumping the democratic interventionists and Liberals such as Orlando and Giolitti in with them. After attempting to sabotage the war effort, the 'renouncers' repudiated colonialism and nationalism and the just Italian claims to Fiume and to Dalmatia. The interventionists quickly turned to violence against their enemies, the first, clamorous example of which was the demonstration against Bissolati during his speech attempting to explain his views at La Scala on 11 January 1919. Benito Mussolini became the leader of the interventionist groups, which included influential Futurist intellectuals.[5] Futurism was a political movement dedicated to violence as much as it was an artistic phenomenon, and now it linked up with nascent Fascism. This alliance combined with another event of prime importance. After the war returning soldiers felt stronger ties with the nation because of their sacrifices, but did not identify with the Liberal State. This development helped turn the battle between interventionists and neutralists 'into episodes of civil war'.[6]

Journalist Francesco Coppola, an interventionist and influential Nationalist, expressed strongly the conventional view of the Paris Peace Conference as the 'mutilated victory' and laid the responsibility for this on the Italian government led by Orlando.[7] The devotion of the Allies to Wilson's new ideas of justice and open negotiations was a farce, Coppola wrote, citing the incident by which they surreptitiously

'My action was at first tied to the urgent duty to fight against one important and dark treason. These Italians were actually setting themselves against the Mother Country. Dalmatia, Italian in its origins, ardent as a saint in its faith, had been recognized to be ours by the Treaty of London. Dalmatia had waited for the victorious war with years of passion, and, holding in its bosom still the remains of Venice and of Rome, was now lopped off from our unity. The politics of renunciation, helped by foreigners, galloped forward. Wilson was the distiller or supporter of theoretical formulas. He could not comprehend Italian life or history. By his unconscious aid this treason to us was nourished. Fiume, the sacrificed town, whose people called desperately for Italy in its manifestations on the public squares, who sent pleasing missions to our military chiefs, was occupied by corps of international troops. ...

'I said then that never in the life of any nation on the day after victory had there been a more odious tragedy than that of this silly renunciation.'

BENITO MUSSOLINI, 1928

handed Smyrna over to Greece despite their having promised it to Italy. Noting Greece's dubious entrance into the war, he claimed that Greece had lost one one-thousandth of the soldiers lost by Italy and did not deserve Smyrna.[8] Italy, Coppola maintained, had saved the Entente at least four times. He emphasized the withdrawal of Russia, which allowed the Austro-Germans to pour troops into the battle against Italy; Italians believed that had their country collapsed at this point, the Central Powers would have been able to deploy millions of Austrian troops to fight the Allies on the Western

Front and win the war. Yet the Allies denigrated the Italian war effort and instituted a new 'Triple Alliance' against it, Coppola wrote, spearheaded by the Anglo-Saxon powers that aimed to control Constantinople and all the world's strategic seaways.[9] Because Italy was not small enough to be a vassal or client state and 'not yet' great enough to instill fear into them, the Allies could throw everything against it, 'and everything was systematically and cynically used' because they could not understand anything that did not serve their immediate interests. Coppola then listed the characteristics of the different Allies that explained this inability: America's 'gross and bigoted intellectual puerility'; Britain's 'immediate materialistic egoism'; France's 'triumphalistic, egocentric pride'.[10]

Coppola continued his tirade against the Italian negotiators who he felt had betrayed Italy through their ineffectiveness both during the war and at the Paris Peace Conference. He listed ten critical errors made by Italian governments during the conflict, ranging from not having negotiated more generous terms for Italian entrance into the war to having failed to increase territorial demands when Russia withdrew from the war, from having allowed Britain to claim the lion's share of colonies to not including Fiume in the Treaty of London. Most importantly, Coppola criticized the government for having failed to create a war aims ideology based on the nationality principle – the same one that the Allies violated and cynically used only against Italy. With regard to the Peace Conference, Coppola listed egregious errors: having agreed to a premature armistice that cut short military action; having done nothing between December 1918 and January 1919 while the Allies wheeled and dealed. But the most serious blunder was to have followed a policy that was not global, as befitted a great power, but one that was 'narrow-mindedly local, small, miserable ...' and acting as if islands in the Adriatic were important. The person responsible for these errors: Vittorio Emanuele Orlando. 'Impotent in any struggle, he obstinately continues to delude himself and to delude [others] that he can face and fight the terrible political battle for existence that is fought here and for the future of peoples and for world domination.'[11]

Fascism's victory stifled Orlando's response, but he reacted immediately after its fall. Orlando pronounced the *mutilated victory* a legend that the Fascists cleverly utilized to achieve power, first by blaming the Italian representatives and later by accusing the Allies of betrayal. True, Italy was mistreated because it dared to challenge *the will of the arbiter of the world* and then, in effect, was *excluded* from the Conference: the famous boycott he believed was forced on the delegation. The Allies utilized this absence by making crucial decisions that Italy opposed and, in any case, without the country's input. However, he argued, Italy made sufficient gains worthy of its sacrifices during the war, but they came as a result of negotiations subsequent to the Paris Peace Conference. The important point for Orlando was the humiliating manner in which Italy was treated by its allies at the Conference and which deeply offended the country. He could well understand and justify the resentment of the Italian people, but, he concluded, in their drive for power, political parties extended the legend from *its form to its substance*, wrongly claiming that Italy was unjustly and violently deprived of the fruits of victory. *The New York Times* reported Orlando as saying that the war changed character with the intervention of the United States and Italy had to compromise, but that it nevertheless achieved its essential aims.[12] A Fascist philippic against him during the death throes of Mussolini's regime demonstrated the emotional force of the '*vittoria mutilata*' concept and its capacity to inflame Italian passions even after many years.[13]

However, when Orlando argued that concrete gains came to Italy after the Peace Conference, he made a weak argument that reduced his own role. In fact, the major security benefit for Italy was probably its attainment of the Brenner Pass frontier. Orlando is correct, however, in emphasizing the dreadful manner in which the Allies treated Italy at Paris. This treatment contributed to the rise of Fascism and the desire to overthrow the post-war settlement established in Paris, and alienated Italy from its traditional allies during the inter-war period. Italy became the champion of revising the Paris settlement and in so doing opened the road to Hitler and the Second World War.

Informed modern scholarship has tended to confirm Orlando's opinions during the Conference itself. After 90 years, the passions of the time have faded to such a point that it is difficult to understand them. In the 1920s, however, an Italy that considered itself – rightly so – as having contributed much to victory could not understand, and considered vicious, the decisions of the Peace Conference with regard to its desires after the war, and this feeling powerfully contributed to the idea of the 'mutilated victory' that negatively influenced Italian history, even among non-Fascists. 'What-ifs' do not make history, but some questions beg to be asked. Given the generally-accepted negative effects on world history of the Paris Peace Conference, it is reasonable to wonder what might have been the effect of less rigidity toward Italian aspirations on the collective destiny of the world. If the myths at the Peace Conference had had less force, if the Allies had been more flexible toward a country that had suffered as much as they had and if Wilson had been less intransigent, would Italy have split off from the wartime alliance and its traditional allies? Had Wilson followed through on negotiations to which the Italians were open, would this have prevented Italy from adopting the revisionist policy, even under Mussolini, that contributed so importantly to the outbreak of the Second World War?[14]

The Fascist period

During the conservative reaction that followed the 'Red Biennium', Orlando re-entered the political game, living with his wife in a small villa in Rome (one picture, undated, has him surrounded by three grandchildren and a handwritten dedication, 'One of the four Vittorio Emanuele Orlando'). As a survivor of the embattled Liberal regime, he was an outsider, living politics only in a tangential manner. As a Liberal and a patriot, he strongly opposed the looming possibility of a leftist revolution but he certainly did not favor a rightist dictatorship. Like other Liberals, Orlando at first was taken in by the possibility that Mussolini and his Fascists might restore stability and be induced to accept the parliamentary system that the wartime statesman considered the most ideal. During the crisis that produced a Mussolini cabinet at the end of 1922, Orlando was mentioned as the possible head of a 'pacification' government with the Socialists that would restore peace and defend liberty. Giolitti, apparently, blocked this solution that might have prevented Mussolini from seizing power.[15] On 16 November 1922, after the 'March on Rome' of 28 October during which the Fascists claimed the government, Mussolini won a vote of confidence and formed a government. Orlando commented on these dramatic events in a private letter: *What can I say? My soul is mournful. I am like the healthy part of a body while*

a surgical operation is taking place cutting out and cauter-
izing the gangrenous part. The healthy part suffers just as
much, and can even die.[16]

Orlando's doubts about how to act can be explained by
recalling that Italy was the first country that faced Fascism,
and that many elder statesmen had hopes and perplexities
similar to those of Orlando. Mussolini received a vote of confidence in 1922 because the Liberals and most other parties
believed that the Chamber of Deputies could always vote him
out of power. At the time, the Fascists constituted only a slim
minority in the Chamber of Deputies (35 deputies out of
535). More importantly, however, the Duce's squads controlled the country and this fact allowed Mussolini to consolidate
his power over the next three years, including over parliament.
The Fascists proposed legislation that would help them win
a majority, and they succeeded with the help of their squads
and their governmental posts, particularly Mussolini's
control of the Interior Ministry. Most Liberals, Catholics,
and democrats, unused to the idea that a dictatorship could
be consolidated in a Western liberal democratic state, under-
estimated the possibility. The Fascists cleverly helped their
cause by targeting proportional representation, established
in 1919 and deemed by most politicians as the leading cause
of governmental instability that had plagued Italy since the
conflict. Proportional representation as it worked in practice
during this period favored the election of small groups with
little support in the country, increasing fragmentation in the
Chamber of Deputies and making it difficult for any cabinet
to win a stable majority. In February 1923, as a response to
this attitude, the government proposed the 'Acerbo Law'
that modified proportional representation by stating that
the party that received a plurality of the votes in an election

(provided it was 25 per cent) would receive two-thirds of the seats in the Chamber, while the other seats would be divided proportionately. The non-Fascist majority in the Chamber voted for the law under the assumption that the new mechanism would stabilize the country. They did not anticipate that the Fascists would employ widespread violence in order to win the elections.

With a national election scheduled for 6 April 1924, Mussolini aimed to win the two-thirds representation outright. In the preparation for the balloting, he hoped to establish an electoral list that would include the country's most important politicians with recognizable names in all the different Italian regions (the *listone* or 'big list') allied to the Fascists. The widespread use of intimidation and violence was the major factor in his winning of two-thirds of the vote anyway, but the clever technique of the allied list gave him respectability and helped his cause.

On 30 May, when the newly-elected Chamber of Deputies met, a Socialist deputy named Giacomo Matteotti denounced the violence, argued that it had invalidated the voting and called for new elections. On 10 June Matteotti was kidnapped and murdered. Although his body was discovered only in August, the country blamed Mussolini and a crisis began that seemed to signal the end of his regime. The opposition initiated a boycott of Parliament known as the 'Aventine Secession'. It hoped that Vittorio Emanuele III would fire Mussolini or take other action against him, but the King merely reshuffled the cabinet because he believed that the only alternative to the Duce was a Socialist government. As the crisis dragged on, Mussolini was finally convinced by his more radical followers to end it by consolidating his dictatorship. He began the process with a famous speech to Parliament – from which the opposition was absent – on 3 January 1925, in which he claimed moral responsibility for Matteotti's murder, challenged the opposition to move against him and reshuffled his cabinet to appoint new Fascist ministers who had the monarch's support.

Orlando had been re-elected to the Chamber of Deputies in 1919 and again in 1921, and chaired the Foreign Affairs Committee, but he did not have a crucial political role during those chaotic years. He wrote articles for an Argentine newspaper and in 1922 was appointed extraordinary Ambassador to Brazil. He banded together with other old Liberals, including Salandra, and a local Liberal group in Sicily in order to defend Liberal ideals. Orlando voted for the first Mussolini cabinet, which did not have a Fascist majority, in the belief that some elements in the Fascist Party that favored a return to the parliamentary system would win out, as well as the Acerbo Law in February 1923, which had the declared aim of restoring stability. Mussolini considered Orlando's support important to a good electoral showing in Sicily in 1924 and skillfully courted him. Orlando tried to hold off a firm commitment while he attempted to set conditions favoring a return to normal parliamentary functioning. The Fascists outmaneuvered him with the help of the Mafia, who considered it important to put off a showdown with Mussolini. The Mafia was influential in Sicilian politics and its support was necessary for any side that hoped to win elections in the island. As a result of these conditions and Orlando's inability to match government maneuvering, the Fascists succeeded in adding him to the *listone* flanking the Fascists without, of course, committing themselves to restoring parliamentary government.[17] This list won 38 out of 57 seats.

In a private letter, Orlando poured out the doubts plaguing

him about what action to take with regard to the list and to the elections; his thoughts reflect the quandary that confronted the old Liberals in the confusing situation that followed the First World War: *When I received your telegraphed message my anguish was so great that I think I have never experienced anything like it in my life, even though it has been so stormy. ... my interior perplexities about knowing what conforms with (or clashes least with [o meno difforme]) my duties toward myself and my country are immense. Even now I still do not know whether I did well or not! In my life I have always drawn my force from the tranquility of my conscience. This time, tranquility is lacking and, as I have told you, I have almost made an illness out of my decision. It is true that my conscience assures me that I have acted for the best, but this comfort is not enough should an event reveal that a goal that is good has not been attained.*[18]

Given the violence perpetrated by the government during the elections and Matteotti's murder, Orlando turned resolutely against Mussolini, labeled Fascism a counter-revolution and renewed his Liberal faith. His opposition to Fascism rose to a crescendo. In a speech to the Chamber of Deputies on 22 November 1924 he presented a motion calling for the 'reestablishment of constitutional normality'. On 16 January 1925, two weeks after the Duce began constructing a totalitarian state, Orlando denounced a bill restricting the right to vote. In August, he headed a list opposing the Fascists in the Palermo city elections; his list received 12,000 votes despite government interference but lost to the Fascists who received 26,000. But the 65-year-old Orlando wondered: *'how does one win against legal violence, ballot swindles and voting frauds?'*[19] On 18 November he resigned from the Chamber of Deputies. In his letter of resignation he cited the experience of the Sicilian local elections, writing, *the belief that I can in some way usefully serve my country would be worse than an illusion; it would be a deceit that could no longer be excused by the righteousness of my intentions.*[20] In the meantime, a new book proposed a revival once again of Orlando's early writings on jurisprudence, claiming that they showed how without liberty citizens are simply instruments of governments.[21]

During the next four years, Orlando lectured on administrative law at the University of Buenos Aires and resumed his academic career at the University of Rome. In March 1929, immediately following the Lateran Accords between the Catholic Church and Italy that strengthened Mussolini's image, especially in the US, Orlando published an article in the *Saturday Evening Post* telling the story of how he had worked out the main outlines of the agreement with the Church at his hotel in Paris during the Paris Peace Conference. Only the fall of his government had blocked an agreement with the Church ten years before the Mussolini government achieved it.[22] Orlando's revelation could be seen as an attempt to diminish Mussolini's prestige in the foreign country where he was most popular. In fact, the Lateran Accords had a long diplomatic history even though the Duce took sole credit for the agreements, and Orlando's negotiations were an important part of the story. In 1931, Orlando traveled to the United States and in a further act of defiance against Mussolini refused to take a required loyalty oath to the Fascist regime and resigned his position at the University of Rome.

Orlando would have a brief flirtation with the regime during the Ethiopian War, when the League of Nations imposed sanctions against Italy, as did other prominent opposition Italians, but with Orlando there was an interesting twist. He sent Mussolini a letter offering him his support. After consulting the King, the Duce considered appointing Orlando as the President of the Senate. Had this appointment come off, it would have added luster to the Duce's image, but the attempt failed because Orlando reportedly posed unacceptable conditions for his acceptance, including dissolution of the Fascist militia and reconstitution of the opposition parties disbanded in January 1925.[23]

Fascist revisionism

Besides being able to use the unsatisfactory results of the Paris Peace Conference for Italy in his drive for power, the baleful Italian experience there encouraged Mussolini to pursue an aggressive foreign policy. Even if the Duce had never come to power, however, the problems hanging fire would have posed formidable challenges for any Italian leader. The unsatisfactory international situation created by the Peace Conference was less than favourable to Italian interests. Italy had always been concerned with expanding its influence in the Balkans, in close proximity to the peninsula, and had been in competition with Austria-Hungary in the area for years. Although it dominated Albania after the war, Italy now faced a continual challenge from Yugoslavia, exacerbating the already bad relations between the two countries.[24] France, however, represented the real challenge to Italian interests. The post-war settlement had resulted in a great increase of French influence in Eastern Europe and the Balkans, strong French support for Yugoslavia, establishment of a 'Little Entente' (Yugoslavia, Czechoslovakia and Romania), whose members had gained the most territory as a result of the war and French economic penetration of the region. In these circumstances the Italians dismissed the argument generally cited in criticizing their quest for gains – that they had incorporated some minorities into their country – as a red herring designed to deny them the territory they had won. They argued that this number paled in comparison to the Slavs, Hungarians and Germans that the victorious Allies had allowed Czechoslovakia, Romania and Poland to incorporate. In Mussolini's mind, the fiasco of the entire post-war settlement symbolized by the unfair treaties following the First World War justified revision of the entire post-war settlement.[25]

Mussolini had criticized the post-war settlement before he came to power, and after he became Prime Minister he made a famous remark that treaties were not 'eternal'. The Italians claimed to be particularly moved by the outrageous treatment of the Hungarians by the Allies after the First World War and argued that Mussolini's initial revisionism was simply an attempt to make the post-war treaties fairer and more work-able.[26] In the face of Italian dissatisfaction, French policy wavered. With Hitler's rise to power in 1933, the French craved Italian support against Germany but 'also pursued French interests in south, central and eastern Europe and colonial policies in the Mediterranean that conflicted with Italy'. A four-power pact with Britain, France and Germany pushed by Mussolini failed to solve the German problem. The French fluttered between making a deal with Italy and neglecting it, ultimately coming to no lasting agreement.[27]

Another legacy of the war and the Peace Conference was the Austrian problem. The Treaty of St Germain permanently prohibited the union of Austria and Germany, but the Ital-ians had been extremely worried about just such a possibility since the First World War because it would put a strength-ened Germany on their borders; this fear had accounted for Sonnino's desire that Austria-Hungary remain intact and that

Italy have defensible borders on the Adriatic even after the Empire's dissolution, policies that Wilson opposed. Mussolini was necessarily attentive to the same threat; and, paradoxically, the Austrian crises of the 1930s became intertwined with another legacy of Paris: Italy's failure to make colonial gains.

The Italian invasion of Ethiopia is generally linked to a desire for revenge for the defeat at Adowa in 1896, but the problem is more complex. Italy's inability to make colonial gains at the Paris Peace Conference put off the issue of compensation specified in the Treaty of London until an unspecified later date. Watching the British and French split up the German and Turkish colonies while they received nothing rankled with the Italians, and Mussolini was determined to move in this area. The groundwork for the Ethiopian invasion had already been set by previous agreements with the Allies that had not been fulfilled, including a claim to British Jubaland in East Africa and parts of the former Ottoman Empire. Turkish revival had vitiated the Italian claims in Turkey but Mustafa Kemal ('Atatürk')'s abandonment of old Ottoman lands allowed the British and

In 1934, an attempted Nazi coup d'etat occurred in Austria; Mussolini sent troops to the border with Austria, forcing Hitler to back down. The French and the British did nothing, while the Americans were out of the picture. The Allies got used to the idea that it should be the Italians' job to stop any attempt at *Anschluss* because they had the most to lose. The Duce, however, wished concessions in the colonies in return for his action against Hitler, which benefited all the wartime Allies. When they refused, he concluded that the British and French wanted him to guard the Austrian borders forever, preventing Italy from making colonial gains while they strengthened their own colonial empires. Consequently, after 1934 Mussolini tried to exploit the renewed balance-of-power situation in Europe occasioned by German revival by playing off Germany and France, which meant that he would become powerless to prevent a German takeover of Austria in 1938. Hitler's success damaged not only Italy but Britain and France as well.

French to hold onto the colonies seized in the Middle East, leaving Italy nothing. In a quest to fulfill the terms of the Treaty of London, Mussolini claimed a share of British and French economic privileges in their spheres and coveted Iraq.[28]

When these hopes fell through and France needed Italian support against Hitler's Germany, on 7 January 1935 the new French government under Pierre Laval struck a deal with Mussolini. The French gave up some territory bordering the Italian colonies of Libya and Eritrea in return for Italy's relinquishing the special rights it had over Italians living in Tunisia, then a French colony. This was an uneven exchange, explained only by the 'free hand' Laval secretly gave Mussolini in Ethiopia. The ambiguities over this arrangement have been argued over ever since, but while Laval tried to minimize his acquiescence regarding an Italian takeover of the only independent African nation, claiming that he meant economic rights and a policy of gradually increasing Italian control over Ethiopia, Mussolini interpreted the 'free hand' to mean that France would not interfere with an Italian conquest. Otherwise, he asked, why would he have relinquished '100,000 Italians in Tunis and received in return half a dozen palm trees in one place and a strip of desert which did not even contain a sheep in another'?[29] On 5 December 1934, a border clash between the Italians and the Ethiopians at Wal-Wal escalated tensions between the two and war appeared imminent.

When Mussolini turned to securing a British agreement for a free hand in Ethiopia, the African issue became entangled with the European one. Hitler repudiated the disarmament clauses of the Versailles Treaty on 16 March 1935, leading to a meeting of the three wartime allies at a conference held in Stresa. At that meeting, the Italians tried to get the British and French to take a strong stance against Hitler, which they refused to do. Instead, the British interpreted Stresa as an agreement making Italy the watchdog against any German attempt to annex Austria, thus preventing the Italians from moving troops from the Austrian border to fight in Africa. When it became clear to the French that Britain would remain passive before German aggression, they reached a deal with Italy in which they transferred troops to the German border, freeing up Italian soldiers to invade Ethiopia.[30] No doubt the Duce's aggressiveness was primarily responsible for the Italian invasion of Ethiopia in October 1935, but the scene had been set in Paris 16 years earlier, as had the premise for the enormous popular support he received in response to his defiance of the Allies. On 7 May 1936 Italy annexed Ethiopia. Two days later King Vittorio Emanuele III was proclaimed Emperor of Ethiopia and the Italians united Ethiopia, Eritrea and Italian Somaliland into the colony of Italian East Africa.

The origins of Italian policy towards Yugoslavia might also be traced back to the Peace Conference. Fiume had become a free city under the Treaty of Rapallo between Italy and Yugoslavia signed on 12 November 1920, to which Orlando gave his blessing as Chair of the Foreign Relations Committee of the Chamber of Deputies. The thorny question seemed finally resolved, but the Nationalists still demanded that the city become Italian and Mussolini agreed. 'In Italy, still palpitating and open,' Mussolini wrote, 'was the wound of the Rapallo Treaty with Jugoslavia. I wanted to medicate that and heal it.'[31] In 1923 he proposed that the Yugoslavs accept Italian annexation of Fiume, and after they stalled, he cut the Gordian knot on 16 September. An Italian military commander seized control of the city, and the Yugoslavs, failing to get French support on this issue, acquiesced; on 27 January 1924 the two countries signed the Treaty of Rome recognizing

Italian annexation of Fiume.[32] This agreement hardly resolved the hostility between the two countries and they continued their duel in Albania. In 1926, Mussolini mobilized 20 divisions because of a suspected Serb attack with French complicity.[33] Enraged at French support, he aimed at Yugoslavia's breakup throughout the inter-war period and supported Croatian terrorists who opposed the government.

Clearly the Duce's aggressiveness toward Yugoslavia and ideological factors played an important role in Italo-Yugoslav relations. However, the bad relations between the two countries, complete with insults, dated back to the period of the Paris Peace Conference. Ever since then the Yugoslav press had continued its habit of denigrating the Italian performance in the First World War, and the Italians their habit of demeaning Slavic culture as inferior to Italian. The Italians denounced French support of Yugoslavia, without which that country could not have competed with the Italians in their back yard or challenged them for control of Albania. In brief, fights similar to those waged at the Paris Peace Conference between both countries continued to be fought long afterward – continually fanned by increasing Italian resentment, Fascist ideology and Serb obstinacy.

Italian revisionism between the wars was not, however, confined to Yugoslavia or to Ethiopia. Italy also favoured the reintegration of Germany into the European diplomatic system and its recognition as a great power. In theory, the idea was a reasonable one because the Italians argued that as long as Germany was not treated as an equal the threat of a violent explosion would always be present; but the Italians also aimed to reestablish a second camp in Europe that Mussolini could exploit diplomatically to change the post-war *status quo* in Europe and in the colonies. Despite his ambivalent attitude toward Hitler, rightly fearing that Germany might become dangerous for his country, Italy's actions favoured *de facto* revisionism of the Versailles Treaty. Hitler took advantage of the Ethiopian crisis, for example, to remilitarize the Rhineland in 1936. Italy kept revisionism of the post-war settlement on the front burner throughout the inter-war period. In 1938 Hitler made a state visit to Rome, and Italy maintained cordial relations with Germany until the outbreak of the Second World War. Italy then entered the Second World War on the side of Nazi Germany. Although in history nothing is inevitable and nations must share responsibility for outcomes, historical events are interconnected. Unfortunately, part of the Paris Peace Conference's legacy to Italy was Fascism and the Nazi alliance.

10
End of the Legacy

Italy remained neutral when the Second World War began on 1 September 1939 with Hitler's invasion of Poland. Despite appearances, any resemblance to Italian neutrality and intervention in 1915 was purely coincidental. While the Italians had justifiable war aims that had induced them to enter the First World War, which for them as well as the other Allies became a war for the defense of democracy, they did not have legitimate aims in the Second World War. There was no Irredenta, no Italian minority being abused and no threat on its borders, except from its German ally which had absorbed Austria in 1938 and which after 1943 annexed the areas Italy had won between 1915 and 1919. Mussolini coldly calculated that if he were on the winning side of the conflict he could control the Mediterranean and make enormous gains in the colonies without having to fight very much. That was another distinction that must be made from the First World War, when the Italians believed they could make a difference and end the conflict earlier, perhaps overestimating their strength, but staying the course till the end. Mussolini entered the war knowing that Italian intervention would not win it, but assuming he would make gains from Hitler's victory. He vacillated until he was convinced Germany would win, but with all doubt in his mind removed brought Italy into the conflict on 10 June 1940.

As in the First World War, Italy was unprepared for a major war, but the Duce assumed that the conflict was over anyway. This opinion turned out to be a monumental miscalculation, not only because his guidance of the war was so inept but because the basis on which he had entered it precluded any appeal for national unity on legitimate grounds, such as the defense of freedom that Orlando had used to rally the country in 1917. Had they had the choice in 1940, the Italian people would not have fought on the German side; for most of them, it was the 'wrong war'. Unlike the situation before the First World War, when a liberal democratic system had made it possible for them to make clear to their government that they would never fight on the side of the Austrians, they had no say in the selection of allies in the Second World War. The Italian armed forces fought on the Nazi side only reluctantly, and this feeling contributed to their poor performance during the conflict. They fought badly, unlike in the First World War, and became dependent on their German allies for military support.

On 10 July 1943, the Anglo-Americans landed in Sicily. This threat to the homeland stunned the country. Widespread strikes had already taken place in March 1943, the only ones that occurred in Axis or Axis-occupied Europe. The disorders affected war production negatively and alienated big business and Fascist hierarchs from the Duce. The Sicilian landing convinced important Fascist leaders that there was no choice other than overthrowing Mussolini and seeking to withdraw from the war. They plotted to dislodge Mussolini with the

King's support because he was still the supreme constitutional authority and he retained the support of the army. At a dramatic meeting of the Fascist Grand Council that lasted from 5.25 p.m. on 24 July until 2.40 a.m. the next morning, a majority of the Fascist hierarchs called on the Duce to surrender his powers to the King for the country's sake. Mussolini kept an appointment at 5.00 p.m. on 25 July to work out a compromise with the King, but Vittorio Emanuele III had finally made the choice to get rid of the Duce. At 11.00 a.m. the monarch had already requested Marshal Pietro Badoglio to head a military government and had Mussolini arrested after their meeting.

Italy's disastrous participation in the Second World War and its aftermath brought the legacy of the Paris Peace Conference to an end. Following Mussolini's overthrow, Fascism collapsed, and before the final Allied victory, the Nazis occupied Italy and the country was split into two with the puppet Italian Social Republic set up in the north. With the gripping developments that took place between 25 July 1943 and the Allied victory in Italy on 25 April 1945, the Italian domestic situation changed radically and a referendum held on 2 June 1946 established a republic. The Italian Peace Treaty signed on 10 February 1947 settled the borders with Yugoslavia that had caused so many problems after the First World War by removing Italian gains while the Yugoslav Communists murdered or expelled the Italian population in those regions.

When these developments occurred Orlando was in his eighties, but he played a final role in his country's history that mirrored its most dramatic events. During preparations for Mussolini's removal Vittorio Emanuele III requested a consultation with Orlando as the country's elder statesman. Orlando advised the King to get rid of Mussolini himself instead of leaving it up to the Fascist Grand Council, and to install a government composed of the surviving leaders of liberal democratic Italy. This advice was in line with Orlando's post-war policy emphasizing the country's continuity with Liberal Italy and demonstrating that Fascism was an aberration. He participated in the talks that resulted in Mussolini's overthrow while struggling to interpret political developments as fitting into the mechanisms of the Liberal constitutional order – the Duce's government had fallen merely to be replaced by a new one. Orlando had the support of important factions in this endeavour, from the royal house to Vatican interests to dissident Fascists like Dino Grandi who hoped he could repeat the feat of 1917 by rallying the country in a wave of national enthusiasm against the invaders. But the premise of a democratic Italy fighting for its survival against repressive forces that had worked after Caporetto, made such a policy fanciful – and Vittorio Emanuele was not one to take bold action. He reacted to Orlando's suggestion for the formation of a national unity government by remarking in his Piedmontese dialect that the old Liberal leaders were 'ghosts'. In the end, the King left the task of liquidating the Duce to the Fascists and appointed the retired Marshal Pietro Badoglio to run a military government.[1] This move alienated the British, who favored former Ambassador to Britain Dino Grandi as Mussolini's replacement and who distrusted Badoglio.[2] In addition to his advice, Orlando wrote drafts of addresses to the nation to be presented by the King and by Badoglio. Vittorio Emanuele did not use Orlando's text and Badoglio used a soon-to-become infamous phrase in a manner contrary to Orlando's intentions.[3]

History of a phrase

The Duce's overthrow brought out no defenders and Fascism rapidly dissolved. Badoglio's government did away with many of the regime's restrictive measures but stopped short of establishing a democratic order. The major problem facing Badoglio was how to disengage from the Germans with as few negative repercussions as possible. In order to accomplish this task, Badoglio addressed the nation explaining the latest developments but announced that 'the war continues'. As generally interpreted, this phrase was designed to trick the Germans into believing that Italy would honour its alliance with them while Badoglio negotiated with the Allies. In fact, Badoglio did not fool Hitler, who ordered the peninsula occupied during the 45 days of his government, and did not convince the suspicious Allies that he would not stick with the Germans. The Badoglio government proved incapable of negotiating an effective armistice to save the country from Nazi occupation and, in addition, contributed to the image of Italian disloyalty by negotiating two. He bungled the armistice talks with the Allies and a planned Allied landing in Rome. He left the army without orders to resist the German takeover, which led to the fall of Rome and to its collapse. While the army disbanded, Badoglio and the monarch fled ignominiously to Brindisi in the South seeking Allied protection.[4]

Badoglio tried to exculpate himself by placing responsibility for the phrase on Orlando. This contention produced a polite exchange between Orlando and Ivanoe Bonomi, former democratic interventionist and Prime Minister after Badoglio following Rome's liberation in June 1944.

Orlando wrote a letter objecting to Bonomi's acceptance at face value of Badoglio's attempt at denying blame for his disastrous performance by attributing 'the war continues' phrase to Orlando. Orlando explained that he had indeed coined the phrase, but had intended it differently. *How could it have been otherwise?*, Orlando asked. *It was a question of honour that was more important than all the political interests and all the dangers that we feared*. It was also a technical question, given the impossibility of an immediate separation of two armies that had fought together and were still collaborating. 'The war continues', therefore, was supposed to signal the first, brief phase in the separation, to last only 24 hours. A second phase was supposed to have followed in which the Italians would have informed the German Ambassador that *Italy is in no condition to go on; Italy has to ask for an armistice. It will request it for you, not for itself, sacrificing itself if need be to be faithful to the alliance it agreed to. How? By asking the Allies to allow the technically necessary time for the German troops to retreat*. In Orlando's intention, 'the war continues' was supposed to set into motion a rapid but clearly reasoned Italian disengagement from the German alliance on the basis of radically changed conditions, not the ambiguous collaboration that Badoglio dragged on for 45 days. This error confused the army, allowed the Germans to pour in troops into Italy, gave the Allies a mistaken impression of Italian intentions and fed into the myth of Italian duplicity. *It would be good for future history that light be thrown on this point*, Orlando wrote.[5]

> Towards the ends of their lives, there was a cordial, leftist oriented, political 'understanding' among three former prime ministers of the Liberal era who had once been competitors: Vittorio Emanuele Orlando, Francesco Saverio Nitti and Ivanoe Bonomi. All were either over eighty like Orlando, or in their late seventies, and became jocularly known as the O.N.B. These had been the initials of the Fascist youth organization, the *Opera Nazionale Balilla*.

Orlando's solution might not have worked, but it might have saved the country's honour by stimulating more resistance to the Nazis and enabling them to organize Allied aid effectively at a crucial time when the Germans had fewer troops on the spot, instead of allowing them time to pour in soldiers on the pretext that the Italian alliance continued.

Prime Minister Orlando?

In German-occupied Rome Orlando was the object of a manhunt conducted by both Nazis and Fascists, and fled to the Vatican. With the liberation of Rome, he reappeared at the centre of political activity. On 8 June 1944, he was present for the swearing-in ceremony when Ivanoe Bonomi took over the government from Badoglio. The next day, Vittorio Emanuele III's son Umberto, now officially ruling as 'Lieutenant General of the Realm' received him. In an effort to emphasize continuity with Liberal Italy, Bonomi resurrected the Chamber of Deputies with Orlando as the only living former speaker of that house 'presiding'. This 'Chamber' had no members and the Communist-dominated Resistance forces refused to let it take on any content, especially under such a symbolic head. However, this position and his membership in the 'Consulta Nazionale' instituted because of the impossibility of having elections, gave Orlando a certain weight in the affairs that produced the birth of the Republic.[6]

The rage against Fascism and its collaborator Vittorio Emanuele III raised the question of whether Italy should do away with the monarchy. Resistance leaders advocated this solution, but the country remained divided. The Communists and Socialists hoped for a revolution that would sweep aside the old order and set up Soviet-style rule, while Christian Democrats and Liberals sought a return to liberal democracy.

Among the occupation forces, the British favoured retaining the monarchy, and at first the Americans deferred to their allies where Italian policy was concerned. In January 1944, the left-wing Communist, Socialist and Action parties formally proposed the monarchy's abolition and ran into the predictable Christian Democratic objections. The Left compromised by asking for Vittorio Emanuele's abdication followed by establishment of an anti-Fascist government, but the King refused. On 14 March, the Soviet Union suddenly forced a change of course on the Communists. It recognized the Badoglio government. The Italian Communist leader Palmiro Togliatti returned from his Moscow exile and announced postponement of the 'institutional question'. Instead of attempting a revolution, the Communists would try to achieve power legally by working within the constitutional system. This dramatic turn became known as the *svolta di Salerno*, from the city where Togliatti announced the new policy.[7]

Since Orlando favored a return to Liberal government and was considered pro-monarchy, the Crown and its moderate supporters looked to him as a possible prime minister to replace Badoglio. Orlando's credentials were in order because he had participated in the ousting of Mussolini and in the later moves to rid Italy of Fascism. The botched negotiations with the Allies and developments following the Nazi occupation of the peninsula after the armistice of 8 September 1943 ended Orlando's chances.[8] With the *svolta di Salerno*, however, the political situation became fluid once again. On 14 August 1944, negotiations for a 'national concentration' cabinet headed by the 84-year-old Orlando were reported to be 'far advanced'. Pushing for this solution, it was said, was a group of important Britons with significant behind-the-scenes clout who wished to see the monarchy represented in the cabinet. The refusal of Communists and Socialists to enter the cabinet and Orlando's pledge not to lead a new government unless he had the consent of all major parties presented a stumbling block, but their decision was considered a bargaining tactic.[9]

On 4 November 1944, the anniversary of the Austro-Italian armistice that ended the First World War on the Italian front, Orlando 'came out of his retirement of twenty-five years … and delivered one of the greatest speeches of his career to appeal for Italian unity'. The speech kept old and young 'spellbound', according to *The New York Times* correspondent Herbert L Matthews, and was so effective that 'He has returned to the present with so much authority that many are now speaking of him as a possible active political force representing unity'. However, Orlando's appeals fell on deaf ears, as monarchists in the large audience began raining down leaflets and fighting with advocates of a republic.[10] By this time, Vittorio Emanuele III had surrendered his powers to his son Umberto. Debate occurred over who wielded sovereign power legitimately – Umberto or the committees formed within the Resistance movement.[11] In November 1945, the Ferruccio Parri government, an emanation of the radical Northern Resistance, resigned as the result of Liberal Party and Christian Democratic opposition. 'What they want is a governmental shift to the right under the presidency of Orlando and the ousting of the left from the Interior Ministry and the offices of the presidency [of the Council of Ministers],' noted Socialist leader Pietro Nenni in his diary.[12] Orlando, however, was given the lead to become Prime Minister in talks with the Lieutenant General. Both Liberals and Christian Democrats favored him and he might have been accepted by the Left, including Nenni, 'although certainly not with enthusiasm'.

Two factors worked against Orlando: his age and the opposition of American officials who 'deplore the possibility of a throwback to the days before Fascism'.[13] The crisis ended with the formation of a government by Christian Democratic leader Alcide De Gasperi. Although Orlando tried to form another government when the De Gasperi cabinet fell in 1947, the now 87-year-old statesman failed again to do so.[14]

On 2 June 1946 a referendum abolished the monarchy and established a republic. The Christian Democrats proposed Orlando for provisional president, but the Socialists opposed him.[15] In the end the political parties accepted a compromise worked out by Togliatti whereby all the candidates for the Constituent Assembly elected on 2 June 1946 were excluded from consideration, and a famous jurist of the Giolittian period, Enrico De Nicola, received the post. Orlando, however, became the leading candidate for election as Italy's first regularly-elected president until he alienated the Christian Democrats over a question that harked back to the Paris Peace Conference of 1919. He could not suppress his memories of the First World War and the Peace Settlement, and they became important factors for him with regard to the Peace Treaty ending the Second World War negotiated by the De Gasperi government. The Treaty of Paris, signed on 10 February 1947, renounced the Adriatic areas won by Italy after the First World War and for which Orlando had negotiated so hard among myriad difficulties: Trieste, Fiume, Zara, the Istrian peninsula, Dalmatia and other areas. In the discussions on ratification of this treaty, Orlando spoke against it and warned that the delegates would have to answer for their 'abjectness stemming from an excess of servility [*cupidigia*].' When after the 18 April 1948 elections the Chamber of Deputies and the Senate met to elect the President, the Christian

Democrats abandoned Orlando; he became the candidate of the Left and lost the presidential election to economist Luigi Einaudi. Orlando's criticism of the treaty ending the Second World War had cost him the honour of becoming the Republic's first regularly-elected chief executive, as his troubles with the treaty ending the First World War had cost him his political career.[16]

The elections of 18 April 1948 were probably the most important of post-war Italy. The Constitution of the new republic had officially come into effect on 1 January 1948. These first elections held under that document pitted the 'Popular Front', a longtime leftist alliance of Communists and Socialists, against the Christian Democrats and their allies. The Popular Front confidently expected victory because of its role in the Resistance and its enjoyment of Soviet financial support, while the Americans and the Catholic Church supported its opponents. The Americans asked Italian-Americans to write letters to their relatives in Italy, gave financial aid to the anti-Communists and threatened to cut off aid to Italy if the Front won. Both sides resorted to wild charges against the other. The elections resulted in a big victory for Alcide De Gasperi's Christian Democrats. De Gasperi could have ruled alone following these elections but wisely brought his small, secular party allies into the ruling coalition.

The Constituent Assembly

On the same day that Italy held a referendum on whether the country should become a republic, it elected a Constituent Assembly that also served as a parliament until a new constitution could be drafted and come into effect. Orlando won election to this body as an independent candidate, and played a prominent role in the debates. As the Dean of the new body, he presided over the first two meetings on 25 and 26 June until its president could be elected. The Assembly chose a committee of 75 to draft a new constitution and to present it to the whole body for discussion and a vote. Orlando was not part of this committee, but he participated vigorously in the discussions on the draft.

In his considerations on the draft constitution, Orlando

returned to his first love: jurisprudence. In a series of highly technical interventions, Orlando discussed the role of juris-prudence in the life of a country, emphasizing Italy's links not only with the Italian but with the European Liberal order. In addition to intervening on specific questions such as the role of the President of the Republic and convincing the del-egates to eliminate the 'National Assembly' (the Chamber of Deputies plus the Senate) as a formal standing institution, limiting it to meeting only in certain circumstances, Orlando concentrated on general issues.[17] He defended Italy's demo-cratic tradition preceding Fascism, attacked by leftist poli-ticians, and stressed the continuity of these traditions. His opinions as expressed in the Constituent Assembly debates and at talks at the University of Rome (his chair had been restored in April 1947) emphasized that Italy and the world had crossed over into a new era that could be considered revo-lutionary. The recognition of mass parties, labour and social issues by modern constitutions characterized this new period. He both recognized and accepted the change. At 87 years of age, this opinion gained him the esteem of the Left. Com-munist Party Secretary Palmiro Togliatti publicly recognized Orlando as a 'maestro': 'I feel respect and more than respect,' Togliatti informed his Constituent Assembly colleagues, 'for the men who sit in this Hall who belong to groups that were an integral part of this old ruling class.'[18] In his diary entry when Orlando died, Socialist Party Secretary Pietro Nenni wrote: 'In the last years he was very close to us, and certainly it was our error (although not mine) not to have understood the useful function that he could have served at the head of the government or of the State.'[19]

Orlando's ideas regarding acceptance of the 'social ques-tion' in the juridical and political structures of the 'new age' state and his foreign policy views were what made him sympathetic to the Left. Influenced by his memories of the debates at the Paris Peace Conference and by his disapproval of the 1947 Peace Treaty negotiated by the Christian Democratic government, Orlando strenuously opposed Italian entrance into NATO. Not surprisingly, the dissension with the Americans at the Paris Peace Conference predisposed him to suspect them, as did his memory of the non-participation of the United States in the League of Nations that had contributed to the outbreak of the Second World War. These views dovetailed with those of the Communists and Socialists who vigorously opposed ratification of the NATO alliance. Orlando, however, staunchly opposed 'Russian tyranny'.[20]

Orlando often objected to Christian Democratic Premier Alcide De Gasperi's policies, but frequently consulted with him because of his long-standing links with the Catholics that made the elder statesman a trusted confidant of the Vatican. De Gasperi needed his advice because of the crisis situation that faced Italy during the immediate post-war period. For example, Orlando had been made a Senator for life in 1948 according to a formula applied to prominent anti-Fascists and to persons who had held high office during the Liberal regime. The elections of 18 April 1948 had given the Christian Democrats a majority in the Chamber of Deputies, but the formula added 107 life members to the other 243 elected Senators. This situation meant that De Gasperi did not enjoy an automatic majority in that body, which under the new Constitution was co-equal with the Chamber. As a result, De Gasperi cultivated close ties with Orlando, utilizing the young future Prime Minister Giulio Andreotti as a go-between. Andreotti has recalled the fascinating discussions and battles he witnessed between the great men of Italy's Liberal past

– Orlando, Nitti and Croce – and has described how Orlando contributed to the resolution of important questions of the era. The Vatican particularly respected this senior politician who had worked for decades to reconcile Church and State. When Cardinal Giovanni Battista Montini, the future Pope Paul VI, torpedoed an international plan to protect the Holy See, Orlando expressed his great pleasure 'as an Italian'. Here one hears the distant echoes of the First World War. Because of Italian fears of international interference in Italian-Church affairs, Sonnino had insisted on inserting a provision in the Treaty of London that denied the Church representation at any future peace conference once the war ended; this stipulation had stimulated vociferous Vatican protests when the news became known, and had touched off one of the more important crises at the Paris Peace Conference. The Vatican never failed to congratulate Orlando for his continued activities, and particularly appreciated an article he wrote expressing his joy at the beatification of his old friend Pius X, subsequently made a saint. When Orlando died, the Vatican newspaper *L'Osservatore Romano* published a long article on its first page paying tribute to Orlando as a statesman, as an Italian and as a Catholic.[21]

In his last years, Orlando never ceased writing and publishing, especially on jurisprudence. From 1946 to his death in 1952, he served as President of the Dante Alighieri Society. Inspired by Nobel Prizewinner Giosuè Carducci and founded in 1889, this organization had the task of disseminating Italian language and culture throughout the world. During the Fascist period it had come under government control, and Orlando carried out the job of restructuring it in Italy and abroad so as to readapt it to its original cultural mission. He successfully completed his last assignment before dying, and the organization pledged to follow the 'shining path' he had traced for it.[22]

On 1 December 1952 Vittorio Emanuele Orlando died aged 92 of a cerebral hemorrhage. 'With him,' commented an old friend, 'his, our, Italy has descended into the tomb' – Liberal Italy of the Risorgimento.[23] Orlando was buried alongside other First World War heroes, including Armando Diaz, in the ancient Church of Santa Maria degli Angeli in Rome, carved out of Diocletian's Baths. The strains of the '*Canzone del Piave*', a famous patriotic song describing how the Italians broke the back of the Austrian offensive in 1918, followed him to his tomb.[24] The song is still commonly heard, especially on the anniversary of the Republic, 2 June.

'Il Presidente della Vittoria'

Vittorio Emanuele Orlando was an eminent jurist and liberal democrat who was a prominent legal theorist, deputy and governmental leader. During his tenure as Justice and Interior Minister, he pioneered the reconciliation between Church and State that troubled the history of modern Italy. In another achievement that redounds to his credit, during the First World War he resolutely and successfully defended civil rights against Nationalist leaders who would have curtailed them in the name of national security. His battle against Luigi Cadorna, powerful commander of the Italian armed forces during the first two years of Italy's war, is particularly noteworthy, because Orlando blocked Cadorna's strong effort to crack down on anti-war opponents and opposition parties, and prevented what may have developed into a serious attempt at a military takeover. Had these endeavors not been curbed, Italian democracy would have been at risk and its will to fight sapped.

In what was the greatest achievement of his career, Orlando took over the country after the disastrous defeat of Caporetto, rallied it and led it to victory. 'Only those who experienced the anguish of those days can fully evaluate the merit of President Orlando,' stated the *Popolo del Veneto* when he died.[25] In this situation he played a similar role to that of Clemenceau in France. Unlike Clemenceau, however, Orlando's crucial role – and that of the Italian war effort in the First World War and the sacrifices of its soldiers and people – still has not been recognized. The Italians, at very high cost, tied down enormous numbers of enemy troops in the most difficult front of the conflict and prevented them from being thrown into the battle against the British and the French on the Western Front. The situation became particularly critical after the collapse of Russia encouraged the Austro-Germans to launch an offensive that they believed would deliver a knockout blow against Italy and that would allow them to concentrate more troops in the West. Orlando's leadership prevented that scenario from becoming reality and preventing disaster for the Allies.

Following the war, Orlando's conflict with President Wilson is what is most remembered about him. He has been criticized for being too much of a gentleman (it is true that Wilson and Clemenceau were not), of being weak and for the walkout of the Italian delegation during the Paris Peace Conference. His supposed weakness cannot be reconciled with his ability to keep Italy together and fighting in its darkest hour. The boycott is generally seen as an error because the Allies made important decisions in Italy's absence. However, Wilson's manifesto made it necessary and it is doubtful that the Italians would have achieved much more had they remained in Paris; the betrayal perpetrated by the Allies in their absence clearly demonstrated that the Allies were capable of as much perfidy as anyone else. American intervention did not alter the diplomatic criteria that had existed before the conflict. In a situation in which Italy was the weakest of the Big Four, the Italian delegation considered it important to stand up against what it considered American arrogance, as exhibited by its President, and the high-handedness of the French.

A crucial aspect of the Paris Peace Conference was that neither the Italian war effort nor Orlando were treated with respect, an attitude that persists in current Anglo-American historiography.[26] The Allies shrugged off Orlando's warnings that if the Italian delegation returned home without more to show for Italy's war effort than what it had already been granted, and if the population was left with the impression that the country had not been treated with respect, *there will arise in the Italian people so violent a reaction of protest and hatred that it will cause violent conflicts in the more or less near future* – but he was correct.[27] In the end, it was not only Italy that paid the price of Allied inflexibility, through the rise of Fascism and Italy's revisionist inter-war foreign policy, but also France, Britain and Europe. If the post-war settlement bears a great deal of the blame in the rise of Nazism in Germany and the outbreak of the Second World War, the same argument holds with regard to the rise of Fascism in Italy and its problematic foreign policy in the years between the wars.

It is not surprising that Orlando's government fell even before the Versailles Treaty was signed, done in by the rigidity of Wilson and Clemenceau. However, Orlando remained as a symbol of the Liberal State during the Fascist period and beyond. Clemenceau and Wilson suffered a similar fate, but Orlando resembled to a greater degree British Prime

Minister Lloyd George whom he admired and respected. Had Orlando come out of the war and the peace process with honour instead of disgrace, the history of Italy might have been very different. The country might have continued on its course toward democracy instead of passing through the Fascist 'parenthesis'. Orlando played a role in Italy after the Fascist period, but conditions in the country had completely changed. Fascism had destroyed its liberal democratic tradition and had instilled a 'Fascist' mentality in the younger generation, even in the anti-Fascist youth.[28]

Orlando's political life was thus tragically cut short, even if his physical one lasted until the age of 92. Scholars seeking books or scholarly articles on Orlando in English outside the context of the Paris Peace Conference will be sorely disappointed. Even in Italian, books on him are rare, unlike Wilson, Clemenceau and Lloyd George. If historians have consigned him to oblivion, however, in Italy's popular consciousness he will always be 'The President of the Victory'.

> Last night in the theater where I was, an unknown person in the gallery shouted: Long Live the President of the Piave! and the numerous members of the audience rose to their feet applauding. Real people do not forget, and this more than compensates for the oblivion of the official ceremonies.
>
> VITTORIO ORLANDO, 23 JANUARY 1925

Notes

1: Less than Great

1. Spencer M. Di Scala, *Italy: From Revolution to Republic, 1700 to the Present*, 4th ed (Westview Press, Boulder: 2009) pp xi–xx; hereafter Di Scala, *Italy*.

2. The literature on the Italian Risorgimento is vast. See the discussion in the bibliographical essay in Di Scala, *Italy*. In Italian, a classic source is Giorgio Candeloro, *Storia dell'Italia moderna*, Vol V (Feltrinelli, Milan: 1970) hereafter Candeloro, *Storia dell'Italia*.

3. See Richard Drake, *Byzantium for Rome: The Politics of Nostalgia in Umbertian Italy, 1878–1900* (The University of North Carolina Press, Chapel Hill: 1980).

4. See John Whittam, *The Politics of the Italian Army, 1861–1918* (Croom Helm, London: 1977).

5. See Alexander De Grand's biography, *The Hunchback's Tailor* (Praeger, Westport: 2001).

6. On the Socialists, see Spencer M. Di Scala, *Dilemmas of Italian Socialism: The Politics of Filippo Turati* (University of Massachusetts Press, Amherst: 1980), hereafter Di Scala, *Dilemmas*.

7. On these points, see A. William Salomone, *Italy in the Giolittian Era: Italian Democracy in the Making* (University of Pennsylvania Press, Philadelphia: 1960) hereafter Salomone, *Giolittian Era*. On the Nationalists, see Alexander J. De Grand, *The Italian Nationalist Association and the Rise of Fascism in Italy* (The University of Nebraska Press, Lincoln: 1978).

8. Giulio Cianferotti's *Il pensiero di V.E. Orlando e la giuspubblicistica italiana fra ottocento e novecento* (A. Giuffrè, Milan: 1980) discusses Orlando's juridical thought.

9. Marcello Pera, 'Un liberale senza tempo', *Vittorio Emanuele Orlando: lo scienziato, il politico e lo statista* (Rubettino, Rome: 2002) p vii.

2: European Alliances and the Path to War

1. For a general discussion of Italian affairs immediately after unification, see Di Scala, *Italy*, pp 125–34.

2. For Visconti Venosta's foreign policy, see Francesco Cataluccio, *La politica estera di E. Visconti Venosta* (Marzocco, Florence: 1940), republished in 1990 in microform.

3. Candeloro, *Storia dell'Italia*, VI, pp 154–61.

4. Arturo Labriola, *Storia di dieci anni* (Il Viandante, Milan: 1910) pp 25–7, 40.

5. *Atti Parlamentari (Camera), XXI Leg., 1a sess.,* 7 March 1901, 3: 2238–44.

6. In case the French attacked the Germans the Triple Alliance obliged the Italians to send half their army to help the Germans, thus making a reduction in the armed forces impossible. See the memoirs of General and former Prime Minister Luigi Pelloux,

Quelques souvenirs de ma vie (Istituto per la storia del Risorgimento italiano, Rome: 1967) p xxi, hereafter Pelloux, *Ma vie*. See also Filippo Turati, 'Militaristi senza saperlo', *Critica Sociale*, 1 May 1909.

7. 'Il convegno italo-austriaco a Trieste', *Il Tempo*, 13 April 1905 and 'Dissolvere, non risolvere', *Il Tempo*, 6 May 1905.

8. Filippo Turati, 'Le spese militari': Lettera aperta a Leonida Bissolati, *Critica Sociale*, 16 April 1909; Leonida Bissolati, 'Le spese militari e il Parito socialista: Risposta a Filippo Turati', *Avanti!*, 6 May 1909.

9. Leonida Bissolati, *La politica estera dell'Italia dal 1897 al 1920* (Treves, Milan: 1923) pp 160–3.

10. Di Scala, *Dilemmas*, pp 128–9.

11. Di Scala, *Dilemmas*, pp 135–9.

12. Di Scala, *Dilemmas*, pp 129–31.

13. On the Socialists, see Di Scala, *Dilemmas*.

14. Spencer M. Di Scala, '"Red Week" 1914: Prelude to War and Revolution' in Frank J. Coppa (ed), *Studies in Modern Italian History from the Risorgimento to the Republic* (Peter Lang, New York: 1986).

15. Partito Socialista Italiano, *Resoconto stenografico del XIII congresso nazionale* (Unione Arti Grafiche, Città di Castello: 1913) pp 69–72.

16. Luigi Lotti, *La settimana rossa* (Le Monnier, Florence: 1965) pp 36–8; *Avanti!*, 9 June 1914 hereafter Lotti, *La Settimana*.

17. Lotti, *La Settimana*, pp 259–63.

18. Lotti, *La Settimana*, p viii.

19. Vittorio Emanuele Orlando, *Miei rapporti di governo con la S. Sede* (Forni, N.p: 1980) pp 15–31; hereafter Orlando, *rapporti*.

20. Massimo Ganci, *Vittorio Emanuele Orlando* (La Navicella, Rome: 1991) pp 84–8 hereafter Ganci, *Orlando*.

21. See Christopher Seton-Watson, *Italy From Liberalism to Fascism 1870–1925* (Methuen, London: 1967) p 216 hereafter Seton-Watson, *Italy*.

22. William C. Askew, 'The Austro-Italian Antagonism, 1896–1914' in Lillian Parker Wallace and William C. Askew (eds), *Power, Public Opinion, and Diplomacy* (Duke University Press, Raleigh: 1968), hereafter Askew, 'Austro-Italian Antagonism'.

23. Askew, 'Austro-Italian Antagonism', p 180.

24. Walter Littlefield, 'England Key to Italy's Attitude Toward Triple Alliance', *The New York Times*, 30 August 1914, hereafter Littlefield, 'England Key'.

25. Askew, 'Austro-Italian Antagonism', pp 183–4.

26. René Albrecht-Carrié, *A Diplomatic History of Europe Since the Congress of Vienna* (Harper, New York: 1958) p 268.

27. See Luigi Albertini, *The Origins of the War of 1914* (Oxford University Press, London: 1965) I, pp 174–184.

28. Askew, 'Austro-Italian Antagonism', pp 217–19.

3: Neutralists versus Interventionists

1. See Giolitti's direct testimony on this issue in Giovanni Giolitti, *Memorie della mia vita* (Garzanti, Milan: 1967) pp. 311–12, 316–17, hereafter Giolitti, *Memorie*.

2. Candeloro, *Storia dell'Italia*, VIII, pp 26–9; Seton-Watson, p 396.

3. Olindo Malagodi, *Conversazioni della guerra 1914–1919* (Ricciardi, Milan-Naples: 1960) 1, pp 85–6, hereafter Malagodi, *Conversazioni*.

4. Littlefield, 'England Key'.

5. Mark Thompson, in *The White War: Life and Death on the Italian Front 1915–1918* (Basic Books, New York: 2008) p 20, hereafter Thompson, *White War*, describes how the Germanic powers hid their intentions and did not reveal to the Italians that they would send an ultimatum to Serbia but produces the startingly weak conclusion: 'This violated the letter of the Triple Alliance.' Unfortunately, this attitude is too typical in British historiography, where supposed violation of the Treaty by the Italians is given great play while gross violations by the Germans and Austrians are consistently downplayed.

6. Candeloro, *Storia dell'Italia*, VIII, pp 31–2.

7. San Giuliano's summary is in Antonio Salandra, *La neutralità italiana 1914–1915* (Mondadori, Milan: 1928) pp 76–78; hereafter Salandra, *neutralità*.

8. Littlefield, 'England Key'.

9. Salandra, *neutralità*, pp 83–93.

10. See Salandra's letter to Sonnino in Sidney Sonnino, *Carteggio 1914/1916* (Laterza, Rome-Bari: 1974) p. 39; hereafter Sonnino, *Carteggio*. For an account of San Giuliano's death, see 'San Giuliano Dead; Peace Policy Stays', *The New York Times*, 17 October 1914.

11. Giolitti, *Memorie*, pp 321–4.

12. The most complete treatment of the PSI during this period is Leo Valiani, *Il partito socialista italiano nel periodo della neutralità 1914–1915* (Feltrinelli, Milan: 1963).

13. See Di Scala, '"Red Week" 1914: Prelude to War and Revolution'.

14. Benito Mussolini, 'Dalla neutralità assoluta alla neutralità attiva ed operante', *Avanti!*, 18 October 1914, hereafter Mussolini, *Neutralità*.

15. Renzo De Felice, *Mussolini il rivoluzionario* (Einaudi, Turin: 1965) pp 269–83; in these pages, De Felice also discusses the charge that Mussolini 'betrayed' the movement.

16. Both groups made major contributions to Italian Fascism's 'Corporate State'. For a brief discussion, see Di Scala, *Italy*, pp 254–5.

17. Gaetano Salvemini, 'La guerra e la pace', *L'Unità*, 28 August 1914.

18. Ugoberto Alfassio Grimaldi and Gherardo Bozzetti, *Bissolati* (Rizzoli, Milan: 1983) pp 149–162. The Bissolati quotation cited in the text is on p 150.

19. Candeloro, *Storia dell'Italia*, VIII, pp 18–19.

20. The various negotiations, from the official Italian viewpoint, can be followed in Antonio Salandra, *L'Intervento [1915]. Ricordi e Pensieri* (Mondadori, Milan: 1930); hereafter Salandra, *L'Intervento*. The Sonnino, *Carteggio* is also fundamental for the negotiations.

21. See the letters in Sonnino, *Carteggio*, pp 46–51.

22. Richard Bosworth's characterization of the mistakes made by both these men is in *Italy and the Approach of the First World War* (MacMillan, London: 1983) pp 133–6.

23. Guglielmo Imperiali, *Diario (1915–1919)* (Rubbettino, Catanzaro: 2006) pp 131–2 hereafter Imperiali, *Diario*.

24. Imperiali, *Diario*, p 143.

25. See Imperiali, *Diario*, pp 132–50.

26. See the letter of former Foreign Minister and Ambassador to France Tommaso Tittoni to Sonnino in which he states that Sonnino accepted both too much and too little; Tittoni wrote, among other things: 'It is up to us to see whether it is in our interests to take into our house two hotbeds of irredentism, one German and one Slovene that quickly becoming pretexts for future wars will oblige us to undertake a policy of continual armaments'. Sonnino, *Carteggio*, pp 318–21.

27. René Albrecht-Carrié, 'The Present Significance of the Treaty of London of 1915', *The Political Science Quarterly* 54, N. 3 (September 1939) p 366.

28. Leo Valiani, 'Documenti francesi sull'Italia e il movimento Yugoslavo', *Rivista Storica Italiana* 80, N. 2 (1968) pp 351–64.

29. H. James Burgwyn, *The Legend of the Mutilated Victory: Italy, the Great War, and the Paris Peace Conference, 1915–1919* (Greenwood Press, Westport: 1993) p 23, hereafter Burgwyn, *Legend*.

30. Istituto Giangiacomo Feltrinelli, *Dalle carte di Giovanni Giolitti. Quarant'anni di politica italiana. III: Dai podromi della grande guerra al fascismo 1910–1928* (Feltrinelli, Milan: 1962) pp 170–2.

31. On 8 January 1916 Giolitti espoused the argument in a private conversation that the Treaty of London was not binding if Parliament had rejected it. Giolitti argued in this discussion that he had been lied to by Salandra, who had continuously assured him that he hoped to avoid war and resolve Italy's problems through diplomatic means. See Malagodi, *Conversazioni*, pp 83–85.

32. Spencer M. Di Scala, 'Parliamentary Socialists, the *Statuto* and the Giolittian System', *The Australian*

Journal of Politics and History, 25, N. 2 (August 1979)
pp 155–68.

33. Vittorio Emanuele Orlando, *Memorie (1915–1919)*
(Rizzoli, Milan: 1960) pp 34–42; hereafter Orlando,
Memorie.

34. Salandra, *L'Intervento*, pp 65–6.

4: Fighting the War

1. Ganci, *Orlando*, pp 141–43.

2. Candeloro, *Storia dell'Italia*, VIII, pp 163–73.

3. Antonio Salandra, *Memorie politiche, 1916–1925*
(Garzanti, Milan: 1951) pp 1–11.

4. 'Prime Minister' in Italy was not a post. The formal
name of the head of the government was 'President
of the Council of Ministers', and he usually was also
Minister of the Interior (as was the case, for example,
for Salandra). Only when the Prime Minister was weak
and considered a kind of caretaker was he not named
Interior Minister; an example was the case of Giuseppe
Zanardelli in 1901, when the Interior Ministry went to
Giovanni Giolitti, but there were other examples as well.

5. Orlando, *Memorie*, p 47.

6. Both were French Radicals who opposed the war or
who advocated a negotiated peace. After Georges
Clemenceau became Prime Minister, he attacked their
patriotism and both were tried in what became famous
wartime cases.

7. Named for the Minister of Justice during the period,
the old Liberal Ettore Sacchi, these decrees published
persons convicted of 'depressing the spirit of the public'
were primarily directed at the main war opponents, the
Socialists, seem to have been applied mainly to Socialists

opposing the conflict; see Candeloro, *Storia dell'Italia*, VIII, p 198. Thompson, *White War*, pp 273, 333, exaggerates their import, given that they were a normal reaction during the war effort and after a major military disaster.

8. Orlando, *Memorie*, pp 48–55.

9. Ottorino Fragola, *V.E. Orlando* (Istituto Editoriale Italiano, Rome: 1920) pp 22–4 hereafter Fragola, *Orlando*.

10. Orlando, *Memorie*, pp 56–7.

11. Emilio Lussu's brilliant novel/memoir, *Un anno sull'altiplano* (Einaudi, Turin: 2005) accurately describes the fighting on the Italian front and the practice of 'decimation'. This book is one of the most remarkable to have emerged from the First World War experience and, although there is an English translation, *Sardinian Brigade,* it is not well known among English-speaking readers.

12. Cadorna's letters of 6 and 13 June to Boselli and the attached report of the military tribunals, 'OSSERVAZIONI del Reparto Disciplina, Avanzamento e Giustizia Militare sui processi penali espletati dai Tribunali militari di guerra o speciali dal 1 al 31 maggio 1917' are in Archivio Centrale dello Stato, *Carte Orlando*, busta 67; hereafter ACS 67. The 13 June letter is published in Orlando, *Memorie*, pp 58–9.

13. 'CIRCOLARE. OGGETTO: Sospensione delle licenze per la Sicilia', signed by Army Deputy Chief of Staff C. Porro. ACS 67.

14. 'COMMANDO DELLA 3a ARMATA. STATO MAGGIORE. N. 3747-L di prot.'. 7 May 1917. ACS 67.

15. 'CIRCOLARE. N. 101758 di prot. OGGETTO: Licenze per la Sicilia', 25 May 1917, signed by C. Porro, and 'COMMANDO DELLA 3° ARMATA Stato Maggiore, N. 4339 di prot. L.', 29 May 1917. ACS 67.

16. IL PRESIDENTE DEL CONSIGLIO DEI MINISTRI, 'A S.E. il prof. Avv. V.E. ORLANDO Ministro dell'Interno', 17 June 1917. ACS 67.

17. An interesting sidelight on this point is that after the War 370,000 Italians living abroad went to the Italian Consulates to take advantage of an amnesty and to regularize their situation with regard to the draft in Italy: 300,000 Italian-Americans, of which 90,000 were born in Italy, served in the United States Army.

18. Orlando's letter is reproduced in his *Memorie*, pp 59–61 and is preserved in his papers at the ACS 67.

19. The entire phrase is quoted in Quotation 6 and may be found in Orlando, *Memorie*, p 52. Unfortunately, Orlando does not elaborate any further, but the incident and the entire context of the dispute between the Interior Minister and the General accounts for the rumors of a possible coup d'etat, led by Cadorna, that circulated at this time.

20. In France 1917 was the year of mutinies. Thirty thousand soldiers left their trenches and walked home and at one point half the French army refused to obey its commanders, leading to mass arrests, the trial of 24,000 men, and the issuing of 400 death sentences, most commuted to prison terms. This phenomenon far exceeded what happened in Italy.

21. Orlando's response and attachment is in his *Memorie*, pp 62–3. The response, including earlier drafts and corrections, are also found in ACS 67.

22. Orlando, *Memorie*, pp 63–7.

23. Malagodi, *Conversazioni*, 1, pp 166–7.

24. Whether or not Cadorna was planning a coup will be discussed later; however, at the current state of historical research, it is impossible to know with certainty. The insinuation in Thompson, *White War*, that the incident was somehow linked to Fascism through his analysis of the word 'Duce'(p 233), and how it was used in Italy reveals that he is unfamiliar with the usage of the term, since it simply meant 'Leader' and was also employed at times for leftist leaders including Socialists.

25. Orlando, *rapporti*, pp 37–45.

26. Orlando's explanation of events and the legal basis for the expropriation is in *rapporti*, pp 75–86. Cardinal Gasparri's letter, 'PRO-MEMORIA', 6 October 1916, is in ACS 50.

27. Orlando, *rapporti*, p 65.

28. Orlando, *rapporti*, p 66.

29. Candeloro, *Storia dell'Italia*, VIII, pp 178–9.

5: Military Affairs

1. A taste of this attitude, and its perpetuation in the historical literature, may be seen in Margaret MacMillan's best-selling *Paris 1919: Six Months that Changed the World* (Random House, New York: 2003) hereafter Macmillan, *Paris*, p 283, where she writes: 'The British and French felt, rightly or wrongly, that Italy had not contributed much to the Allied victory. Italy's armies had delayed their attack on Austria-Hungary, and then made a mess of it. Italian ships had rarely ventured out of port, despite repeated promises to patrol the Mediterranean and Adriatic. The Italian

government had squeezed resources out of its hard-pressed allies which it had then refused to use in the war effort.'

2. Di Scala, *Dilemmas*, p 63; Pelloux, *Ma vie*, p xxi.

3. At the time, the exchange rate was about 5 Italian lire to the American dollar.

4. Nicola Tranfaglia, *La prima guerra mondiale e il fascismo. Storia d'Italia dall'Unità alla fine della Prima Repubblica* (TEA, Milan: 1995) p 61, hereafter Tranfaglia, *La prima guerra mondiale*.

5. Seton-Watson, *Italy*, p 63.

6. For Britain and France and their imperialistic activities during and after the First World War, see David Fromkin, *A Peace to End All Peace* (Owl Books, New York: 1989).

7. Russia, the largest country on earth, had aims on the Mediterranean by taking the Dardanelles and increasing its power through its influence on Serbia.

8. See Fritz Fischer, *Germany's Aims in World War I* (Norton, New York: 1961).

9. By its infamous ultimatum, Austria-Hungary wanted to make Serbia a vassal state and dominate the Balkan Peninsula.

10. S L A Marshall, *World War I* (Mariner, Boston-New York: 2000) pp 169–70 hereafter Marshall, *WWI*.

11. Marshall, *WWI*, p 170.

12. 'War on Austria; not on Turkey or Bulgaria', *The New York Times*, 7 December 1917.

13. Here is some relevant documentation: 'Mission Board Told of Turkish Horrors', *The New York Times,* 17 September 1915; 'Armenians' Own Fault, Bernstorff Now Says', *The New York Times,* 29 September 1915;

'Turkey Not Dying, Says Morgenthau', *The New York Times*, 2 June 1916; 'Outrage by Turks May Presage War', *The New York Times*, 20 June 1918.

14. See Tranfaglia, *La prima guerra mondiale*, p 64.

15. John Keegan, *The First World War* (Vintage Books, New York: 2000) p 344, hereafter Keegan, *WWI*.

16. Mario Silvestri, *Isonzo 1917* (Einaudi, Turin: 1965) p 466, hereafter Silvestri, *Isonzo*.

17. See the discussion of this issue in Chapter 6.

18. Keegan, *WWI*, p 345.

19. See Gaetano Salvemini, *The Origins of Fascism in Italy* (Harper and Row, New York: 1973) p 2, point 2; hereafter Salvemini, *Origins*.

20. John R. Schindler, *Isonzo: The Forgotten Sacrifice of the Great War* (Pager, Westport: 2001) is the most objective military history of the Italian front in English.

21. The Serbs feared Italian plans for expansion in the Balkans. For the Italian reaction to their moves, see Sonnino, *Carteggio*, pp 500–6. The Romanians were asking for too much territory, which aroused Sonnino's fears they would break up the Austro-Hungarian Empire, which he did not favour; and in any event the Russians were opposed. Some Italian officials argued that if the Romanians did not enter the War, the Treaty of London did not oblige them to do so either. The Romanians did not intervene at this time because of these issues and because of the altered military situation. See Sonnino, *Carteggio*, pp 442–3, 454–6 and 481–4.

22. Sonnino, *Carteggio*, p 517; I have quoted part of the letter above.

23. Piero Pieri, *L'Italia nella Prima Guerra Mondiale* (Einaudi, Turin: 1965), hereafter Pieri, *Prima Guerra Mondiale*, p 83.

24. Schindler, *Isonzo*, pp 43–44.

25. Cadorna certainly understood his task in this way. See Generale Luigi Cadorna, *La guerra alla fronte italiana, fino all'arresto sulla linea del Piave e del Grappa* [Volume 2 of his memoirs] (Treves, Milan: 1921) p 268.

26. More is probably known about the incompetence of the French and British generals, but see also the book by the Chief of the German General Staff on the errors of the German war effort: General [Max] Von Hoffman, *The War of Lost Opportunities* (Kegan Paul, Trench, Trubner & Co Ltd, London: 1924) hereafter Von Hoffman, *Lost Opportunities*.

27. Schindler is good in describing the military aspects of these campaigns from both the Italian and Austrian sides; see pp 41–242; the *Strafexpedition* is described on pp 144–50.

28. David Lloyd George, *War Memoirs of David Lloyd George 1917* (Little, Brown and Company, Boston: 1934) p 434.

29. See Orlando, *Memorie*, p 106.

30. Von Hoffman, *Lost Opportunities*, p 193.

31. See the documents cited in Chapter 6.

32. See Gaetano Salvemini's enumeration of similar defeats and disasters suffered by the Allies in World War I and the attempts of official historians to cover them up; *Origins*, pp 13–18.

33. Malagodi, *Conversazioni*, 1, pp 171–2.

34. Imperiali, *Diario*, p 447. In his earlier entries, Imperiali had referred with admiration to the comportment of troops from the South.

6: Prime Minister

1. Cadorna apart, this problem was unusual in Italy, where the army was loyal to the King who respected parliamentary decisions. The French Third Republic never fully resolved the problem of civilian control, and fights between British Prime Minister Lloyd George and military commanders were frequent and serious.

2. John Keegan's term.

3. Sidney Sonnino, *Diario 1916–1922* (Laterza, Bari-Rome: 1972) 3, pp 206–7; hereafter Sonnino, *Diario*. For an example of the simplistic treatment of this issue by some English-speaking historians, see the discussion in footnote 7.

4. Orlando, *Memorie*, p 228; Candeloro, *Storia dell'Italia*, VIII, pp 192–4.

5. Orlando, *Memorie*, pp 72, 73.

6. Cadorna held the post for only two months, after which he was recalled, edged out, and forced to retire.

7. See Orlando's telegram to the King, 9 November 1917, in which he displays considerable irritation at Cadorna's dragging his feet in leaving; and the King's telegram to Orlando, dated 10 November 1917 (marked '10[sic]-11–1917' in the original), in which he announces Cadorna's departure the day before, both in ACS 67.

8. Fragola, *Orlando*, p 32.

9. Fragola, *Orlando*, pp 32–35.

10. Telegram from Orlando to Diaz, 9 November 1917, in ACS 67.

11. Orlando's telegram to the King, 9 November 1917.

12. 'Allied Forces Close to Italian Front. British Correspondent Says They Are a Powerful Factor in Reserve', *The New York Times*, 27 November 1917.

13. From General Cittadini, 10 November 1917, marked 'Urgenza-Precedenza delle precedenze', ACS 67.

14. Second telegram, dated 10 November 1917, ACS 67.

15. Mario A. Morselli, *Caporetto: Victory or Defeat* (Cass, London: 2001) pp 106–23, hereafter Morselli, *Caporetto*, has an excellent, well-documented, discussion on the issue of Allied intervention.

16. Malagodi, *Conversazioni*, 1, p 195.

17. Orlando's telegram to Diaz, 9 November 1917, in ACS 67.

18. There is a debate over Orlando's naming of Badoglio to the post because of his responsibilities for the Caporetto defeat. Silvestri is good on this, pp 469–70. Orlando himself kept above the fray in his memoirs, pp 76–7, saying that Badoglio's role in the defeat was unknown at the time.

19. Pieri, *Prima Guerra Mondiale*, p 177.

20. See Silvestri, *Isonzo*, pp 467–70 on Bissolati's alarmist proclamations and his change of heart, which came only in January 1918. For Bissolati's own view of the reasons for the Caporetto disaster and his assessment of the military situation, see Malagodi, 1, pp 190–6.

21. Orlando, *Memorie*, pp 238–9.

22. Telegram from Orlando to Bissolati, dated 3 November 1917, in ACS 67.

23. Imperiali's communication from London, dated 28 October 1917, ACS 60.

24. Cadorna's note to Orlando, dated 31 October 1917, with attached deliberation signed by Generals Robertson and Foch and marked 'Treviso 31-X-1917', ACS 60.

25. Morselli, *Caporetto*, pp 110–11.

26. Malagodi, *Conversazioni*, pp 206–07.

27. See the reports of the Ambassadors to France (5 September 1917), to the United States (6 December 1917) and to Sweden (6 December 1917) in ACS 60.

28. Pieri, *Prima Guerra Mondiale*, p 170.

29. Silvestri, *Isonzo*, pp 467, 470. Part of the report is printed in English in Shepard B. Clough and Salvatore Saladino, *A History of Modern Italy: Documents, Readings & Commentary* (Columbia University Press, New York: 1968) pp 336–43.

30. 'Fascicolo C.-Proclama del Re per Caporetto-10 novembre 1917 (?) [sic]' and telegram from Vittorio Emanuele III to Orlando, 'Fascicolo C.-Tel. Da Villa Italia-1° [sic]-11–1917 part. 1° [sic], 5 arr. 11.' ACS 67.

31. Orlando, *Memorie*, pp 77–80. In the following pages, Orlando blames the Fascists for re-igniting the disputes between the two factions.

32. 'Fascicolo C.-Proclama del Re per Caporetto'.

33. Morselli, *Caporetto*, p 124.

34. Schindler, *Isonza*, p 276 and Pieri, *Prima Guerra Mondiale*, p 177. See also Fragola, pp 77–80.

35. 'Italian Troops in Foch's Reserve. Washington Hears That Large Contingents of Them Are Behind the Western Front', *The New York Times*, 6 April 1918.

36. 'Italians Form Right Wing. Orlando Stirs Deputies to Enthusiasm by the Official Announcement', *The New York Times*, 20 April 1918.

37. G.H. Perris, 'Italians at Bligny Again Whip Teutons. Night Assault of Crown Prince's Troops Southwest of Rheims is Severely Repulsed', *The New York Times*, 25 June 1918; Pieri, *Prima Guerra Mondiale*, p 186.

38. Ambassador Imperiali's telegram to Orlando dated 8 December 1917, ACS 60.

39. Ambassador Cellere's telegram to Orlando dated 12 December 1917, ACS 60.

40. For an account of this Conference in all its details, see the letters of Gaetano Salvemini in Enzo Tagliacozzo (ed), *Gaetano Salvemini. Carteggio 1914–1920* (Laterza, Rome-Bari: 1984) pp 372–82 hereafter Tagliacozzo, *Cartegio*.

41. Tagliacozzo, *Cartegio*, p 415.

42. Tagliacozzo, *Cartegio*, pp 410–13.

43. Malagodi, *Conversazioni*, 2, p 372.

44. Tagliacozzo, *Cartegio*, p 415.

45. Orlando, *Memorie*, p 382.

46. 'A S.E. il Presidente del Consiglio dei Ministri. Roma,' marked <u>RISERVATISIMO PERSONALE</u>, 3 November 1917, ACS 67.

47. Pieri, *Prima Guerra Mondiale*, pp 176–9; Morselli, *Caporetto*, pp 126–7; Schindler, pp 276–8.

48. Diaz to Foch, 14 May 1918, in ACS 60.

49. Fragola, pp 33–4, 84–7.

50. This battle is also known as the 'Battle of the Solstice'.

51. Schindler, *Isonzo*, pp 282–87; Pieri, *Prima Guerra Mondiale*, pp 180–6.

52. Salvemini, *Origins*, pp 15–16.

53. Diaz to Foch, 6 July 1918, ACS 60.

54. Fragola, *Orlando*, p 91.

55. Orlando, *Memorie*, p 106.

56. 'SUPREME WAR COUNCIL AMERICAN SECTION VERSAILLES', 17 July 1918, with attached 'ALLIED PLAN OF CAMPAIGN FOR AUTUMN AND WINTER OF 1918, AND SUMMER OF 1919', dated 15 July 1918, point 3. ACS 60.

57. It should be noted with reference to this point that three American divisions on the Italian front had been reduced to ten battalions in August because of the War plan elaborated in July and 'considering the fact that pressure is being put upon us by Marshall Foch to collect all possible troops for operations in France …'. See 'From: – War Office, To: General Delme Radcliffe. Comando Supremo, Italy. Despatched at 6:30 p.m. 8.9.18.' in ACS 60.

58. Orlando telegram to Diaz, undated but with the notation '[1918 set 14]', ACS 67.

59. Sonnino, *Diario*, 3, p 300.

60. 'LE MARECHAL FOCH, COMMANDANT EN CHEF LES ARMÉES ALLIÉES, à Son Excellence M. ORLANDO, PRÉSIDENT DU CONSEIL. ROME', 28 September 1918, in ACS 60.

61. 'dal Signor Orlando Presidente del Consiglo d'Italia al Signor Maresciallo Foch Comandante in Capo degli Eserciti Alleati', 1 October 1919, in ACS 60.

62. Orlando telegram to Diaz, dated 14 October 1918, ACS 67.

63. Diaz telegram to Orlando, 19 October 1918, ACS 67; see also the telegram from Diaz to Orlando on 18 October 1918.

64. Schindler, *Isonzo*, pp 289–311, gives an account of the final battles from both the Austrian and Italian

perspectives; the account in Pieri, *Prima Guerra Mondiale*, is more succinct but very good.

65. Telegram, Diaz to Orlando, 2 [A.M.], 30 October 1918, ACS 67.
66. Telegram, Diaz to Orlando, 12:45 [P.M.], 30 October, ACS 67.
67. Telegrams, Orlando to Diaz and to 'Comm. Petrozziello', dated 28 and 29 October 1918 in ACS 67.
68. Joel Blatt, 'France and the Franco-Italian Entente, 1918–1923', *Storia delle relazioni internazionali*, 6 (1990/2) p 175.
69. MacMillan, *Paris*, p 283.

7: Italy at the Paris Peace Conference

1. The estimate was given to Orlando's chef de cabinet. See 'Fonogramma da Parigi, 16=2=1919 [sic], ore 14. Al Comm. PETROZZIELLO', ACS 81.
2. Malagodi, 1, p 198.
3. G. A. Borgese, *Goliath. The March of Fascism* (Viking, New York: 1937) p 149, hereafter Borgese, *Goliath*.
4. Ray Stannard Baker, *Woodrow Wilson and World Settlement. Written From His Unpublished and Personal Material*, 2 vols. (Peter Smith, Gloucester: 1960) 2, p 130, hereafter Baker, *Woodrow Wilson*.
5. Nick Salvatore, *Eugene V. Debs: Citizen and Socialist* (University of Illinois Press, Urbana and Chicago: 1982) pp 290–8.
6. The vast literature on this period in American history that produced the Sacco-Vanzetti case along with many other sorry events continues to be produced. See, for example, Kevin Baker's review of Beverly Gage's *The Day Wall Street Exploded*, 'Blood on the Street', *The*

New York Times Book Review, 22 February 2009, p 12. For Wilson's attitude on labor unions, see 'Woodrow Wilson Hits Labor Unions. They Give the Least Possible for Wages, He Tells Princeton Graduates', *The New York Times*, 14 June 1909.

7. Woodrow Wilson, *A History of the American People. Vol. V. Reunion and Rationalization* (Harper Brothers, New York and London: 1902) p 212.

8. Baker, *Woodrow Wilson*, 2, p 139.

9. MacMillan, *Paris*, p 287.

10. 'BOLLETTINO N. 110. CONFIDENZIALE. NOTIZIE SULLA CONFERENZA', Paris, 11 May 1919, in ACS 81.

11. Malagodi, *Conversazioni*, 1, p 201.

12. Wilson would agree to extending Italian borders to the Brenner Pass, which put an Austrian German minority in Italy, for the sake of security. He would agree to the inclusion of large minorities in the victorious states in other cases as well for security's sake, but he did not abide by this principle (which violated several of his Fourteen Points) with regard to Italy's Adriatic borders.

13. 'Wilson to Back Claims of Italy to Large Extent', *The New York Times*, 11 January 1919.

14. MacMillan, *Paris*, p 287.

15. Malagodi, *Conversazioni*, 2, p 475.

16. Imperiali, *Diario*, p 131.

17. The Italians were probably a bare majority of the city's inhabitants but were by far the most politically active. During the discussions at the Peace Conference, the ethnic majority of Fiume depended on which areas were included.

18. Raeffale Colapietra, *Leonida Bissolati* (Feltrinelli, Milan: 1958) pp 267–8, hereafter Colapietra, *Bissolati*. There is a briefer discussion of Bissolati's points (which also appeared in the English *Morning Post*) in René Albrecht-Carrié, *Italy at the Paris Peace Conference* (Archon Books, Hamden: 1966) pp 71–2; hereafter Albrecht-Carrié, *Italy*. Sonnino's Diary has a very brief account of this meeting, 3, pp 318–19.
19. Sonnino, *Diario*, 3, pp 319–20.
20. Colapietra, *Bissolati*, p 270.
21. Malagodi, *Conversazioni*, 2, p 473.
22. Baker, *Woodrow Wilson*, p 138.
23. Daniella Rossini, *Woodrow Wilson and the American Myth in Italy* (Harvard University Press, Cambridge: 2008) p 136.
24. Borgese, *Goliath*, p 143.
25. An account of the incident is in Colapietra, pp 272–9.
26. Malagodi, *Conversazioni*, 2, p 649.
27. In this sense, the previously-cited *Italy at the Paris Peace Conference* by Rene Albrecht-Carrié, originally published in 1938, has not been surpassed. This book is also valuable for the documents, translated into English, published in its appendix.
28. Albrecht-Carrié, *Italy*, pp 96–9.
29. 'NOTIZIARIO JUGOSLAVO', undated, but late April 1919, and unsigned report, ACS 81.
30. See, for example, Schindler, *Isonzo*, pp 291–2 and Albrecht-Carrié, *Italy*, pp 112 and 122–3.
31. Sonnino, *Diario*, 3, p. 330.
32. See Orlando's letter to Wilson, dated 3 April 1919, reproduced in Baker, *Woodrow Wilson*, 2, pp 148 and 137.

33. See Sonnino, *Carteggio*, pp 514–15.

34. Albrecht-Carrié, *Italy*, pp 62–6.

35. Candeloro, VIII, p 253.

36. Sonnino, *Diario*, 3, p 314.

37. Paul Birdsall, *Versailles Twenty Years After* (Reynal and Hitchcock, New York: 1941) pp 269–88.

38. Albrecht-Carrié, *Italy*, p 113.

39. Joel Blatt, 'France and Italy at the Paris Peace Conference', *The International History Review*, 8, n. 1 (February 1986) p 29.

40. 'Last Warning Given to Fighting Allies', *The New York Times*, 26 January 1919; 'Slav Decree Bans All Trade With Italy. Rome's Lifting of Adriatic Blockade Is Nullified in Large Part by Belgrade's Action', *The New York Times*, 28 March 1919. See also Burgwyn, *Legend*, pp 270–3.

41. Orlando to Diaz, from Paris, 3 November 1918, ACS 67.

42. Fragola, *Orlando*, pp 106–9. Fragola estimates the number of people in those areas at five million.

43. 'Italians Disturbed by Paris Criticism', *The New York Times*, 23 June 1919; see also 'Base Conflicts on the 14 "Points"', *The New York Times*, 28 March 1919.

44. Blatt, 'France and the Franco-Italian Entente', p 175.

45. 'Claims Which Italy Presented at Paris', *The New York Times*, 26 April 1919.

46. Orlando's account of the meeting, in which he emphasizes his refusal to give anything up, is in Malagodi, *Conversazioni*, 2, pp 629–34; Fragola, *Orlando*, pp 134–5.

47. A full account of these negotiations may be found in Albrecht-Carrié, *Italy*, pp 86–140.

48. 'Acute Crisis Over Adriatic', *The New York Times,* 22 March 1919; 'Fiume Decision Left to Wilson', *The New York Times*, 23 March 1919; 'Declares All Italy Backs Fiume Claim', *The New York Times*, 6 April 1919.
49. Burgwyn, *Legend*, p 279.
50. See the balanced discussion of Albrecht-Carrié, *Italy*, pp 141–4; Wilson's manifesto is reproduced on pp 498–500.
51. Albrecht-Carrié does a good job in analyzing Orlando's statement and summarizing Italian reaction in *Italy*, pp 144–9. The quote is from an article by Gaetano Salvemini, cited at length by Albrecht-Carrié. See also 'Orlando Enters Rome, Acclaimed as National Hero', *The New York Times*, 27 April 1919.
52. See the quotes in Albrecht-Carrié, *Italy*, pp 471 and 473–4.
53. See the telegram marked 'Riservata-Personale' to the Minister of War, General Enrico Caviglia, 3 May 1919, and the telegram dated 25 May 1919, in ACS 50.
54. Baker, *Woodrow Wilson*, 2, p 175.
55. Telegram from Colosimo to the prefects signed 'ON BEHALF OF THE PRESIDENT OF THE COUNCIL OF MINISTERS' 23 May 1919, ACS 50.
56. 'Bollettino No 112. Confidenziale. NOTIZIE SULLA CONFERENZA', ACS 81.
57. 'Hear President Threatens Italy With Blockade', *The New York Times*, 26 September 1919.
58. Michael Ledeen, *The First Duce* (The Johns Hopkins University Press, Baltimore: 1977).
59. See the details later in this chapter.

60. 'Bollettino No 96. Confidenziale. NOTIZIE SULLA CONFERENZA', 27 April 1919, ACS 81. These numerous 'bulletins' are in this folder.
61. 'Bolletino No. 110. Confidenziale. NOTIZIE SULLA CONFERENZA', Paris, 11 May 1919, ACS 81.
62. Ibid., p 6. This paragraph is marked in hand in the original.
63. The maneuverings and the details of the negotiations can be followed in Albrecht-Carrié, *Italy*, pp 156–200.
64. 'Bollettino No. 142. Confidenziale. NOTIZIE SULLA CONFERENZA', Paris 16 June 1919, ACS 81; see p 3 of this report.
65. MacMillan, *Paris*, p 300.
66. Fragola, *Orlando*, p 142.
67. The relevant documentation regarding these negotiations is in Paris Peace Conference, 1919. Supreme Council. Senate Document No. 237, *The Adriatic Question* (Government Printing Office, Washington: 1920). Wilson's threat is contained in a note of February 10, reprinted on p 18. The Senate refused to ratify both documents anyway.
68. The details may be found in Albrecht-Carrié, *Italy*, pp 293–309.
69. Orlando, *Memorie*, p 482.

8: Italian Perspectives
1. Malagodi, *Conversazioni*, 2, pp 469–74.
2. On this issue, note the American argument in Albrecht-Carrié, *Italy*, p 99.
3. Malagodi, *Conversazioni*, 2, p 473.
4. Malagodi, *Conversazioni*, 2, pp 482–3, 663–4.
5. See, for example, MacMillan, Paris, pp 279, 298.

NOTES

6. Malagodi, *Conversazioni*, 2, pp 475–6, 477–80, 481, 495, 497–9.

7. Malagodi, *Conversazioni*, 2, pp 569–72, 573, 591, 592, 665–6.

8. Malagodi, *Conversazioni*, 2, pp 481, 576, 592, 666.

9. Undated 'NOTIZIARIO CAUCASIO', 'Il nostro informatore si recò ieri dal Dottor M. Ohandjanian …'ACS 81.

10. Second undated 'NOTIZIARIO CAUCASIO', 'Persona giunta ha riferito che il Governo Repubblicano è stato sciolto ….' ACS 81.

11. Undated 'NOTIZIE VARIE', 'Il Commandante Levi Bianchini riferisce quanto segue circa le agitazioni Arabe in Palestina ….' ACS 81.

12. Second undated 'NOTIZIE VARIE', 'Il Commandante Levi Bianchini che ha lasciato l'Egitto pochi giorni fa ha raccontato quanto segue sopra i disordini colà avvenuti in questi ultimi tre mesi ….' ACS 81.

13. Undated NOTIZIARIO POLACCO', 'Le condizioni della Polonia e la nostra futura penetrazione commerciale e militare in quella Regione,' ACS 81.

14. See undated 'NOTIZIARIO COLONIALE', 'Notizie sulla ferrovia di GIBUTI-ADDIS.ABABA-' ACS 81.

15. See Albrecht-Carrié, *Italy*, pp 201–2 and Burgwyn, *Legend*, pp 296–8. For more information on colonial issues, see Albrecht-Carrié's articles 'Italian Colonial Problems in 1919', *Political Science Quarterly*, vol. 58, n.4 (Dec., 1943) pp 562–80 and 'Italian Colonial Policy', *The Journal of Modern History*, vol. 18, n. 2 (Jun., 1946) pp 123–47.

16. 'Bollettino No. 115 Confidenziale. NOTIZIE SULLA CONFERENZA', Paris, 16 May 1919 and

'Bollettino No. 143 Confidenziale. NOTIZIE SULLA CONFERENZA', Paris, 17 June 1919, in ACS 81, p 3.

17. The relevant documents in the ACS 81 include the telegrams of the Minister for Colonies, either incoming or outgoing, numbers 5491, 3673, and 1660, all dated 16 May, 6 June 1919 and one dated 'Parigi –VI-1919'; and the documents 'RELAZIONE DELLA COMMISSIONE COLONIALE PROGETTO FRANCESE 3–6-19', and ' A. S. E. l'On CRESPI commissario Italiano nella Commissione per l'applicazione dell'art. 13 del Patto di Londra'. Albrecht-Carrié has good sections on the colonial issue, *Italy*, pp 201–30 and pp 310–26.

18. 'Sua Eccellenza Colosimo Presidenza del Consliglio. Rome', 25 May 1919, ACS 81.

19. Malagodi, *Conversazioni*, 2, pp 519–21.

20. Laval denied this interpretation, but historians generally credit Mussolini's version of the deal as being accurate. See, for example, G. Bruce Strang, 'Imperial Dreams: The Mussolini-Laval Accords of January 1935', *The Historical Journal* 44:3 (2001) pp 799–801.

21. See MacMillan, *Paris*, pp 287–302.

22. Orlando never completed his memoirs. He kept notes and writings in files of different colors and tied them together in a package. His son Ambrogio, who was familiar with the circumstances surrounding their creation, aided Rodolfo Mosca and Mario Toscano, diplomatic historians who edited the fragmentary writings. They were published in 1960.

23. Orlando, *Memorie*, pp 413–44.

24. Orlando, *Memorie*, p 449.

25. Malagodi, *Conversazioni*, 2, p 475.

26. Albrecht-Carrié, *Italy*, p 218–19, 158; Orlando, *Memorie*, pp 343, 398.
27. Baker, *Woodrow Wilson*, 2, p 192.
28. See Baker, *Woodrow Wilson*, 2, p 140.
29. Orlando, *Memorie*, pp 353–4.
30. MacMillan, *Paris*, p 281. MacMillan's portrait of Sonnino and of the Italian situation in this chapter is not entirely accurate.
31. Orlando, *Memorie*, pp 337–46.
32. Orlando, *Memorie*, pp 377, 381–9.
33. Malagodi, *Conversazioni*, 2, pp 474–5.
34. Malagodi, *Conversazioni*, 2, p 251.
35. The portrait of Clemenceau is in Orlando, *Memorie*, pp 359–73.
36. See Orlando, *Memorie*, pp 355–8.
37. See Baker, *Woodrow Wilson*, 2, pp 138–9.
38. The letter is in Orlando, *Memorie*, pp 397–400.
39. Imperiali, *Diario*, p viii.
40. Orlando, *Memorie*, p 359.
41. Orlando, *Memorie*, p 482.
42. The news from Italy reported increasing unrest at the time the Orlando government was falling. See, for example, 'Italian Strikes Sap Vitality of Nation', *The New York Times*, 16 June 1919.

9: Fascism

1. The classic work on this topic is Salomone, *Giolittian Era*.
2. Benedetto Croce, *Scritti e discorsi politici (1943–1947)*, (Laterza, Bari: 1963), 2, p 199 and Benedetto Croce, *Storia d'Italia dal 1871 al 1915* (Laterza, Bari: 1962), Introduction to the 9th edition, March 1947, p viii.

3. Benito Mussolini, *My Autobiography* (Hutchinson & Co, London: n.d.[originally published, 1928]) p 69.

4. For the details of this troubled period, see Di Scala, *Italy*, pp 211–17.

5. Emilio Gentile, '*La nostra sfida alle stelle*': *Futuristi in politica* (Laterza, Rome: 2009) pp 87–94.

6. Emilio Gentile, *La Grande Italia: The Myth of the Nation in the 20th Century* (The University of Wisconsin Press, Madison: 2009) pp 74, 80.

7. Coppola was a founder of the Italian Nationalist Association in 1910 and the journal *L'Idea Nazionale* in 1911. He strongly advocated Italian intervention in the conflict in 1914–15 and fought in the War in 1916. In 1917 and 1918, he traveled abroad on fact-finding and diplomatic missions and was in Paris during the Peace Conference. He was associated with Mussolini and Fascism since 1919.

8. Francesco Coppola, *La pace democratica* (Zanichelli, Bologna: 1921) pp 212–15, hereafter Coppola, *La pace*. Greece bargained with the Entente for entrance into the war, but King Constantine kept the country out of the conflict because he favored the Central Powers. The Allies forced the country into the war on their side in July 1917.

9. Coppola, *La pace*, pp 216–17.

10. Coppola, *La pace*, pp 231–33.

11. Coppola, *La pace*, pp 238–43

12. Orlando's views on the 'vittoria mutilata' can be found in Croce-Orlando-Sforza, *Per la pace d'Italia e d'Europa* (Il Filo di Arianna, Rome: 1946) pp 43–56 (reproductions of articles that appeared in the *Corriere di Roma*, 1944); Orlando, *Memorie*, pp 543–4; and

'Orlando Backs Acts in Peace Settlement', *The New York Times*, 20 November 1944.

13. Giacomo Etna, *Le menzogne di Orlando* (edizione erre, Venice-Milan: 1944). I thank the Rare Book, Manuscript and Special Collections Library, Duke University, for sending me a copy of this pamphlet.

14. See Carlo Ghisalberti, 'Il mito della vittoria mutilata', in Antonio Scottà, *Conferenza di pace tra ieri e domani (1919–1920)* (Rubbettino, Catanzaro: 2003) pp 125–39, especially his conclusions on pp 138–9. It might be recalled that Hitler wrote in *Mein Kampf* that a major objective of German foreign policy should be to detach Italy from the wartime alliance.

15. Adrian Lyttelton, *The Seizure of Power: Fascism in Italy 1919–1922* (Charles Scribner's Sons, New York: 1973) pp 80–1.

16. Letter to Umberto Galeota, dated 27 November 1922, in Umberto Galeota, *V.E. Orlando* (D'Agostino, Naples: 1958) p 44, hereafter Galeota, *Orlando*.

17. Galeota, *Orlando*, pp 138–40.

18. Letter to Galeota dated 7 March 1924, in Galeota, *Orlando*, p 47.

19. Letter to Galeota dated 8 April 1925 in Galeota, *Orlando*, p 48.

20. Ganci, *Orlando*, pp 198–202.

21. Sabino Alloggio, *Vittorio Emanuele Orlando* (Casa Editrice Sabina, Naples: 1928) p 134. Orlando included the Soviet Union in his critique.

22. Orlando, *rapporti*, pp 123–4 and Giulio Andreotti, 'Orlando visto da vicino', in Senato della Repubblica, *Vittorio Emanuele Orlando: Lo scienziato, il politico e*

lo statista (Rubbettino, Catanzaro: 2002) p 12; hereafter Senato, *Orlando*.

23. Ganci, *Orlando*, pp 197–98.

24. H. James Burgwyn, *Italian Foreign Policy in the Interwar Period 1918–1940* (Praeger, Westport: 1997) pp 26–7; hereafter Burgwyn, *Foreign Policy*. This is the best book in English on Italian diplomacy between the wars.

25. Giulio Caprin, *Sistema e revisione di Versaglia nel pensiero e nell'azione di Mussolini* (Istituto per gli Studi di Politica Internazionale, Milan: 1940) pp 32–40, hereafter Caprin, *Sistema e revisione*.

26. Caprin, *Sistema e revisione*, pp 44–49.

27. Blatt, 'France and the Franco-Italian Entente', pp 183–96; the quotation is on p 189.

28. Burgwyn, *Foreign Policy*, pp 21–2.

29. Burgwyn, *Foreign Policy*, p 110.

30. The details are in Burgwyn, *Foreign Policy*, pp 110–121.

31. Mussolini, *Neutralità*, p 230.

32. Burgwyn, *Foreign Policy*, pp 24–5.

33. Burgwyn, *Foreign Policy*, pp 41–8.

10: End of the Legacy

1. Paolo Pombeni, 'L'ultimo Orlando: il Costitutente', in Senato, pp 36–7.

2. Andreotti, 'Orlando visto da vicino', Senato, p 3–4.

3. Senato, *Orlando*, p 37.

4. The story is told in Elena Agarossi, *A Nation Collapses: The Italian Surrender of September 1943* (Cambridge University Press, Cambridge: 2000).

5. Letter from Bonomi to Orlando dated 5 May 1949; letter from Bonomi to Orlando dated 6 May 1949, ACS 4, fasc. 173.

6. Senato, *Orlando*, p 38.

7. The complicated political maneuverings during this period can be followed in Spencer M. Di Scala, *Renewing Italian Socialism: Nenni to Craxi* (Oxford University Press, New York: 1988) pp 24–27; hereafter Di Scala, *Renewing*. For American policy, see James Edward Miller, *The United States and Italy, 1940–1950* (The University of North Carolina Press, Chapel Hill: 1986) and John Lamberton Harper, *America and the Reconstruction of Italy, 1945–1948* (Cambridge University Press, Cambridge: 1986).

8. Ganci, *Orlando*, pp 210–11. Orlando denied the rumors, but apparently he did draft the King's address, which was not used.

9. 'Shift to Orlando Speeded in Italy', *The New York Times*, 15 August 1944.

10. Herbert L. Matthews, 'Orlando Appeals for Italian Unity', *The New York Times*, 5 November 1944.

11. For discussions of the maneuvers in light of this complex question and the position of the different parties, see Di Scala, *Renewing*, pp 27–30.

12. Pietro Nenni, *Tempo di guerra fredda. Diari 1943–1956* (SugrarCo, Milan: 1981) pp 155–6 hereafter Nenni, *Diari*.

13. 'Orlando in Lead for Rule of Italy', *The New York Times*, 27 November 1945.

14. 'Orlando Abandons Attempts in Italy', *The New York Times*, 23 May 1947.

15. Nenni wrote in his diary that Socialist opposition to him was a mistake; see Nenni, *Diari*, p 555.

16. Ganci, *Orlando*, pp 222–24; Nenni, *Diari*, p 555.

17. See Ganci, *Orlando*, pp 213–22.

18. See Pombeni in Senato, *Orlando*, p 54. Pombeni's essay is excellent on Orlando's role in the Constituent Assembly.

19. Nenni, *Diari*, p 555.

20. Andreotti in Senato, *Orlando*, p 14.

21. Andreotti in Senato, *Orlando*, pp 12–14.

22. Letter published by the central administration of the Dante Alighieri Society (Rome) on the occasion of Orlando's death, 30 December 1952.

23. *Il Gazzettino di Lecce*, 2, n. 2, p 2.

24. The following link will bring readers to the song: http://www.youtube.com/watch?v=STRD20k5rYM. (accessed 9 April 2009).

25. *Il Popolo del Veneto*, 8, n. 31, p 3.

26. See, for example, the strange depiction of Orlando by Margaret MacMillan, *Paris*, p 279 and p 298, who seems to consider his fits of weeping important.

27. Albrecht-Carrié, *Italy*, Document 41, p 471. The statement was made on Easter Sunday, 20 April 1919 at a meeting of the Council of Four. Orlando was specifically referring to Fiume; but he obviously, in general, referred to the way Italy was being treated.

28. See the citation in Pombeni, Senato, *Orlando*, p 36.

Chronology

YEAR	AGE	THE LIFE AND THE LAND
1860		11 May: Giuseppe Garibaldi lands on Sicily (at Marsala).
		19 May: Vittorio Emanuele Orlando born into family of lawyers.
1861	1	17 Mar: Kingdom of Italy proclaimed.
		6 Jun: Camillo Benso, Count of Cavour, dies.
1866	6	Prussia defeats Austria in Seven Weeks' War.
		Italy gains Venetia.
1868	8	Church issues *Non expedit* ordering Italian Catholics to boycott national political elections.
1870	10	20 Sep: Rome becomes capital of Italy.
		Papal infallibility proclaimed by Vatican Council.
		Pope encourages Catholic powers to restore temporal power in Italy.
1874	14	12 Jun: Foundation of *Opera dei Congressi*, guides Catholic intransigent political action against government.
1876	16	Government of 'Right' falls; 'Left' takes over under Agostino Depretis.
1877	17	Orlando enters University of Palermo Law School.
1878	18	King Vittorio Emanule II and Pope Pius IX, Risorgimento protagonists, die.
		Orlando publishes first literary work, on Aeschylus.
1881	21	Orlando graduates with honours from Law School; writes *Della riforma elettorale*.

YEAR	HISTORY	CULTURE
1860	Second Maori War in New Zealand begins. Abraham Lincoln elected US President.	Wilkie Collins, *The Woman in White*.
1861	Confederate States of America formed: US Civil War begins.	Royal Academy of Music, London, founded.
1866	Revolts in Crete against Turkish rule.	Fyodor Dostoevsky, *Crime and Punishment*.
1868	British Abyssinian expedition. Meiji Restoration in Japan.	Wilkie Collins, *The Moonstone*.
1870	Greece agrees to leave Crete. Red River Rebellion begins in Canada. Opening of Suez Canal.	Mark Twain, *The Innocents Abroad*. Richard Wagner, *Rheingold*.
1874	Risings in Bosnia and Herzegovina against Turkish rule.	W S Gilbert and Arthur Sullivan, *Trial by Jury*.
1876	Serbia and Montenegro declare war on Ottoman Empire.	Auguste Renoir, *Le Moulin de la Galette*.
1877	Russo-Turkish War begins.	Henry James, *The American*.
1878	Russo-Turkish War: Ottoman Empire seeks armistice, British fleet arrives off Constantinople, armistice signed.	Thomas Hardy, *The Return of the Native*.
1881	First Boer War.	Jacques Offenbach, *Les Contes d'Hoffmann*.

YEAR	AGE	THE LIFE AND THE LAND
1882	22	Triple Alliance (Germany, Austria-Hungary, Italy) signed.
		Orlando becomes *Docente* of Constitutional Law, youngest in Italy, at University of Modena.
1885	25	Orlando becomes *Docente* of Constitutional Law at University of Messina, then Director of Administration, University of Palermo.
1887	27	29 Jul: Depretis dies; Francesco Crispi becomes Premier.
1890	30	New, more liberal law code drafted by Giuseppe Zanardelli implemented.
		Orlando founds public law journal, *Rivista di Diritto Pubblico*.
		9 Dec: Orlando marries Ida Castellano.
1891	31	Pope Leo XIII publishes *Rerum Novarum* calling for social justice.
1892	32	Oct: Filippo Turati and Anna Kuliscioff found Italian Socialist Party.
		Liberal Giovanni Giolitti government, friendly to workers, takes office.
1893	33	Spring: *Fasci siciliani* revolts in Sicily; period of crisis for Liberal State begins.
1896	36	1 Mar: Italians defeated at Battle of Adowa, Ethiopia.
1897	37	Orlando elected to Chamber of Deputies from Partinico, agricultural center in Palermo area.
1898	38	Two-year political crisis threatening survival of Parliament follows major disorders that shake country.
		Catholic Social Movement begins.

YEAR	HISTORY	CULTURE
1882	British occupy Cairo. Hiram Maxim patents his machine gun.	Leslie Stephen, *Science of Ethics*. Richard Wagner, *Parsifal*. Peter Tchaikovsky, *1812 Overture*.
1885	General Charles G Gordon killed in fall of Khartoum to the Mahdi.	H Rider Haggard, *King Solomon's Mines*.
1887	First Colonial Conference in London.	Giuseppe Verdi, *Otello*.
1890	Germany's Kaiser Wilhelm II dismisses Otto von Bismarck. First general election in Japan.	Oscar Wilde, *The Picture of Dorian Gray*. Pietro Mascagni, *Cavelleria Rusticana*.
1891	Triple Alliance renewed for 12 years.	Gustav Mahler, *Symphony No 1*.
1892	Britain and Germany agree on Cameroon. Pan-Slav Conference in Cracow.	George Bernard Shaw, *Mrs Warren's Profession*. Peter Tchaikovsky, *The Nutcracker*.
1893	Franco-Russian alliance signed.	Giacomo Puccini, *Manon Lescaut*.
1896	Jameson Raid fails in Transvaal.	Giacomo Puccini, *La Bohème*.
1897	Britain's Queen Victoria celebrates Diamond Jubilee.	Edmond Rostand, *Cyrano de Bergerac*.
1898	Horatio H Kitchener defeats Mahdists at Omdurman. Spanish-American War.	Thomas Hardy, *Wessex Poems*. Henry James, *The Turn of the Screw*.

YEAR	AGE	THE LIFE AND THE LAND
1900	40	29 Jul: King Umberto II assassinated at Monza; succeeded by son Vittorio Emanuele III.
		Catholic reconciliation with state begins.
1901	41	Jun: Liberal government headed by Giuseppe Zanardelli and Giovanni Giolitti as Interior Minister becomes first Italian Cabinet to receive Socialist votes; 'Liberal Springtide' government begins favouring workers, lasts until 1903.
		Orlando named *Docente* of Constitutional Law at University of Rome.
		Orlando named to special chair of Public Law at University of Rome.
1903	43	9 Aug: Pius X crowned Pope, centralizes Papal control of Catholic politics in Italy.
		Nov: Liberal Giovanni Giolitti becomes Prime Minister, continues long term domination of Italian political scene, ending only with First World War.
		3 Nov: Orlando begins tenure as Education Minister.
1904	44	15 Sep: Italy's first general strike begins; lasts four days.
		Non expedit loosened; Catholic cooperation with Liberals in elections, won by Giolitti; *Opera dei Congressi* dissolved.
1905	45	27 Mar: Orlando resigns as Education Minister.
1907	47	14 Mar: Orlando named Justice Minister in Giolitti's 'long government'.
		Pope Pius X condemns Modernism.

YEAR	HISTORY	CULTURE
1900	Second Boer War; Relief of Mafeking. Boxer Rising in China.	Giacomo Puccini, *Tosca*. Anton Chekhov, *Uncle Vanya*.
1901	Britain's Queen Victoria dies: Edward VII becomes King. US President William McKinley assassinated: Theodore Roosevelt succeeds him. Negotiations for Anglo-German alliance end without agreement. First transatlantic radio signal transmitted.	Thomas Mann, *Die Buddenbrooks*. August Strindberg, *Dance of Death*. Rudyard Kipling, *Kim*. Pablo Picasso's 'Blue Period' begins.
1903	King Alexander I of Serbia murdered. Russian Social Democratic Party splits into Mensheviks and Bolsheviks (led by Lenin and Trotsky) at its London Congress.	Henry James, *The Ambassadors*. G E Moore, *Principia Ethica*. George Bernard Shaw, *Man and Superman*. Anton Bruckner, *Symphony No. 9*.
1904	Entente Cordiale settles British-French colonial differences. Russo-Japanese War begins. Theodore Roosevelt elected US President.	Anton Chekhov, *The Cherry Orchard*. Henri Rousseau, *The Wedding*.
1905	Russo-Japanese War ends.	Claude Debussy, *La Mer*.
1907	Peace Conference held in the Hague.	Pablo Picasso, *Les Demoiselles D'Avignon*. Maxim Gorky, *Mother*.

YEAR	AGE	THE LIFE AND THE LAND
1909	49	20 Feb: First Futurist manifesto appears in *Le Figaro.* 10 Dec: Orlando resigns as Justice Minister after passing important reforms. Further loosening of *Non expedit* allowing more Catholics to vote in 1909 national elections.
1911	51	29 Sep: Libyan War with Turkey begins.
1912	52	18 Oct: Libyan War ends. Quasi-universal manhood suffrage passed (no literacy requirement).
1914	54	7–14 Jun: 'Red Week', leftist revolt in Emilia-Romagna region. 2 Aug: Italy formally declares neutrality. 12 Aug: Orlando becomes part of commission studying statistics and legislation. 20 Aug: Pius X dies; succeeded by Benedict XV. 5 Nov: Orlando joins Antonio Salandra Cabinet as Justice Minister.
1915	55	26 Apr: Treaty of London signed committing Italy to enter war on Allied side. 3 May: Italy denounces Triple Alliance. 23 May: Italy declares war against Austria-Hungary.
1916	56	20 May: Orlando named member of Permanent Court of Arbitration, the Hague. 27 Aug: Italy declares war against Germany. 19 Jun: Orlando named Interior Minister in Paolo Bosselli government.

YEAR	HISTORY	CULTURE
1909	Britain's Edward VII makes state visits to Berlin and Rome. Anglo-German discussions on control of Baghdad railway. Turkish nationalists force Kiamil Pasha, Grand Vizier of Turkey, to resign.	H G Wells, *Tono-Bungay*. Richard Strauss, *Elektra*. Frederick Delius, *A Mass of Life*. Henri Matisse, *The Dance*.
1911	Agadir crisis.	Rupert Brooke, *Poems*.
1912	First Balkan War begins. Woodrow Wilson elected US President.	C G Jung, *The Theory of Psychoanalysis*.
1914	Archduke Franz Ferdinand of Austria-Hungary and wife assassinated in Sarajevo. First World War begins: Battles of Mons, the Marne and First Ypres; trench warfare on Western Front.	James Joyce, *Dubliners*. Theodore Dreiser, *The Titan*. Gustav Holst, *The Planets*. Matisse, *The Red Studio*. Georges Braque, *Music*. Film: Charlie Chaplin in *Making a Living*.
1915	First World War: Battles of Neuve Chapelle and Loos, Gallipoli campaign. Germans sink British liner *Lusitania*, killing 1,198.	Pablo Picasso, *Harlequin*. Marc Chagall, *The Birthday*. Max Reger, *Mozart Variations*.
1916	First World War: Battles of Verdun, the Somme and Jutland. Woodrow Wilson re-elected. David Lloyd George becomes British Prime Minister.	James Joyce, *Portrait of an Artist as a Young Man*. Claude Monet, *Waterlilies*.

YEAR	AGE	THE LIFE AND THE LAND
1917	57	24 Oct: Battle of Caporetto, major Italian defeat, begins.
		31 Oct: Orlando becomes Prime Minister, rallies country, remains interim Interior Minister.
		Nov: (First) Battle of the Piave; Italians stop Austro-German advance begun at Caporetto with aim of knocking Italy out of war.
		Dec: Peace negotiations between Central Powers and Russia open, sanctions Russian defeat in First World War and official abandonment of war effort.
1918	58	Influenza epidemic begins.
		8 Jan: Woodrow Wilson publishes Fourteen Points.
		15–23 Jun: (Second) Battle of the Piave; Italian forces stop Austria-Hungary's last great offensive.
		Commission on Caporetto defeat formed, with Orlando as a member.
		8 August: Allied counteroffensive begins on Western Front.
		27 September: Allies on Western Front break through Hindenburg Line.
		24 October: Battle of Vittorio Veneto destroys Austro-Hungarian Army.
		4 November: Armistice ends war on Italian Front.

YEAR	HISTORY	CULTURE
1917	First World War: Battle of Passchendaele (Third Ypres); British and Commonwealth forces take Jerusalem; USA declares war on Germany; China declares war on Germany and Russia. February Revolution in Russia.	T S Eliot, *Prufrock and Other Observations*. Leon Feuchtwanger, *Jud Suess*. Sergei Prokofiev, *Classical Symphony*.
1918	First World War: Peace Treaty of Brest-Litovsk signed between Russia and Central Powers; German Spring offensives on Western Front fail; Romania signs Peace of Bucharest with Germany and Austria-Hungary. Ex-Tsar Nicholas II and family executed. Kaiser Wilhelm II of Germany abdicates.	Luigi Pirandello, *Six Characters in Search of an Author*. Giacomo Puccini, *Il Trittico*. Edvard Munch, *Bathing Man*.

YEAR	AGE	THE LIFE AND THE LAND
1919	59	18 Jan: Paris Peace Conference opens; Catholic Partito Popolare Italiano oriented toward social reform founded by Catholic priest Don Luigi Sturzo.
		24 Apr: Italian delegation boycotts Conference, leaves Paris.
		6 May: Italian delegation returns to Conference.
		10 Jun: Orlando leaves Paris definitively.
		15 Jun: Government crisis; Orlando resigns.
		Demonstrations against developments at Conference; massive strikes.
		Beginning of 'Red Biennium', fear of Communist revolution.
		12 Sep: D'Annunzio's expedition occupies Fiume.
		Oct: Radicals take over Italian Socialist Party.
		16 Nov: general elections; Socialist Party becomes largest party; Popular Party second largest; parliamentary paralysis begins.
		2 Dec: Orlando elected Chamber of Deputies President.
1920	60	26 Jun: Orlando resigns as Chamber of Deputies President.
		Sep: Factory occupations.
		End of 'Red Biennium'; Benito Mussolini's rise to power begins.
		22 Nov: Treaty of Rapallo.
1921	61	Jan: Communist Party of Italy founded after Communist faction splits from Socialists.
		6 Feb: Orlando begins collaboration with *La Nacion* (Buenos Aires).
		Fascist violence increases.
		15 May: General elections; Fascists win 35 seats (33 in alliance with Liberals).

YEAR	HISTORY	CULTURE
1919	Communist Revolt in Berlin. US Senate vetoes ratification of Versailles Treaty leaving US outside League of Nations. Irish War of Independence begins.	Wassily Kandinsky, *Dreamy Improvisation.* Edward Elgar, *Concerto in E Minor for Cello.* Manuel de Falla, *The Three-Cornered Hat.*
1920	League of Nations comes into existence. The Hague selected as seat of International Court of Justice. League of Nations headquarters moves to Geneva.	F Scott Fitzgerald, *This Side of Paradise.* Franz Kafka, *The Country Doctor.* Katherine Mansfield, *Bliss.*
1921	Paris Conference of wartime allies fixes Germany's reparation payments. Irish Free State established. Peace treaty signed between Russia and Germany. Washington Naval Treaty.	Aldous Huxley, *Chrome Yellow.* D H Lawrence, *Women in Love.* John Dos Passos, *Three Soldiers.*

YEAR	AGE	THE LIFE AND THE LAND
1922	62	Orlando named extraordinary Ambassador to Brazil.
		Oct: Socialist Party splits again.
		28 Oct: March on Rome.
		Nov: Mussolini becomes Prime Minister.
1923	63	Jun: Acerbo Law modifying proportional representation passed.
		31 Aug: Italians occupy Corfu after dispute with Greece, giving hint of Mussolini's future aggressive foreign policy.
1924	64	27 Jan: Treaty of Rome between Yugoslavia and Italy recognizes annexing of Fiume.
		Apr: General elections give Fascists and allies majority.
		Orlando heads allied list in Sicily.
		10 Jun–Dec: Matteotti assassination threatens Mussolini's rule.
		Orlando lectures at University of Buenos Aires.
1925	65	Jan: Fascist regime begins construction and consolidation.
		Nov: Orlando resigns in protest from Chamber of Deputies.
1926	66	Fascist regime completes consolidation.
		Lira revalued at high rate.
1927	67	Orlando gives course on Administrative Law at University of Buenos Aires.
		21 Apr: Fascist government issues 'Labour Charter'.
		Fascist Grand Council alters method of electing Chamber of Deputies, merges Party and State institutions.
		Italy signs pact with Hungary.

YEAR	HISTORY	CULTURE
1922	Chanak crisis.	T S Eliot, *The Waste Land.*
	League of Nations Council approves British Mandate in Palestine.	James Joyce, *Ulysses.*
		BBC founded: first radio broadcasts.
1923	French and Belgian troops occupy the Ruhr when Germany fails to make reparation payments.	Sigmund Freud, *The Ego and the Id.*
		George Gershwin, *Rhapsody in Blue.*
1924	Lenin dies.	E M Forster, *A Passage to India.*
	Dawes Plan published.	Thomas Mann, *The Magic Mountain.*
	Greece proclaimed republic.	
	German Nazi Party enters Reichstag with 32 seats for first time after elections.	Fernand Leger, *Ballet Mecanique.*
	Calvin Coolidge elected US President.	
1925	Paul von Hindenburg elected President of Germany.	Franz Kafka, *The Trial.*
	Locarno Treaty signed in London.	Ferruccio Busconi, *Doctor Faust.*
1926	General Strike in Britain.	Giacomo Puccini, *Turandot.*
1927	German president Paul von Hindenburg repudiates Germany's responsibility for First World War.	Marcel Proust, *Le Temps Retrouvé.*
		Hermann Hesse, *Steppenwolf.*
	Britain recognises Iraq's independence; promises to support its League of Nations membership application .	Adolf Hitler, *Mein Kampf.*
		Virginia Woolf, *To the Lighthouse.*

YEAR	AGE	THE LIFE AND THE LAND
1928	68	Jan: Large Italian arms shipment to Hungary discovered.
		21 Feb: Fascist militia absorbed into Italian army, ends long-standing dispute.
		2 Aug: Italo-Ethiopian Friendship treaty.
		1 Sep: Italian-influenced Ahmad Zogu proclaimed King in Albania.
1929	69	Libyan rebellion ends.
		11 Feb: Lateran Accords with Catholic Church.
		24 Mar: Fascists receive 99 per cent of vote in general election.
1930	70	Ruralization policy aims to keep Italians on land.
		6 Feb: Italo-Austrian Friendship treaty.
		30 Apr: Italy launches major naval program after failure to achieve internationally-recognized parity with France.
		24 May: Mussolini publicly calls for revision of Versailles Treaty, initiates official policy to revise post-war order.
1931	71	Vast public works policy to combat Depression begins.
		31 Oct: Government acts to save banks.
		Nov: Istituto Mobiliare Italiano (IMI) created to make loans to ailing companies.
		Orlando travels to United States.
		Orlando refuses to take required loyalty oath to Fascist regime, gives up position as Professor at University of Rome.
1932	72	25 May: Italo-Turkish Non-Aggression Pact renewed.
		14 Sep: Germany leaves Disarmament Conference, Geneva; Italy had favored reducing German military inequality.
		4 Oct: Closer Italo-Hungarian relations as Gyula Gombos becomes Prime Minister.

YEAR	HISTORY	CULTURE
1928	Kellogg-Briand Pact outlawing war and providing for peaceful settlement of disputes signed. Herbert Hoover elected US President. Alexander Fleming discovers penicillin.	Henri Matisse, *Seated Odalisque.* George Gershwin, *An American in Paris.* Kurt Weill, *The Threepenny Opera.*
1929	Germany accepts Young Plan at Reparations Conference: Allies agree to evacuate Rhineland. Wall Street Crash.	Erich Maria Remarque, *All Quiet on the Western Front.*
1930	Britain, France, Italy, Japan and US sign London Naval Treaty regulating naval expansion. German Nazi Party gains 107 seats.	Igor Stravinsky, *Symphony of Psalms.* W H Auden, *Poems.* Max Beckmann, *Self-portrait with a Saxophone.*
1931	Austrian Credit-Anstalt bankruptcy begins Central Europe's financial collapse. Britain abandons Gold Standard. Bankruptcy of German Danatbank leads to closure of all German banks.	Salvador Dali, *The Persistence of Memory.* Noel Coward, *Cavalcade.* William Faulkner, *Sanctuary.*
1932	Franklin D Roosevelt wins US Presidential election. Britain, France, Germany and Italy make 'No Force Declaration' renouncing use of force for settling differences.	Aldous Huxley, *Brave New World.* Pablo Picasso, *Head of a Woman.* Sergei Prokofiev, *Piano Concerto NO.5 in G major Op. 55.*

YEAR	AGE	THE LIFE AND THE LAND
1933	73	Jan: Istituto per la Ricostruzione Industriale (IRI) created as state holding company to fight Depression; new Hitler government sworn in, raises possibility of Italo-German cooperation; Italian arms shipment to Hungary intercepted.
		14–16 Feb: Little Entente strengthens organization.
		19 Mar: Mussolini calls for Four-Power Pact uniting Italy, Britain, France, Germany to ensure international security.
		11–19 Apr: High level German officials visit Rome, agree to join Four-Power Pact.
		Jul: Hungarian Premier visits Rome asking support for country's claims for return of Hungarian speaking territories lost after First World War.
		15 Jul: Diluted version of Mussolini's Four-Power Pact signed.
1934	74	Jan: Libya reorganized.
		5 Feb: Law creates 'Corporate State'.
		17 Mar: Rome Protocols concluded by Italy, Hungary, Austria to contest Little Entente, establish anti-French Danubian bloc under Italian leadership.
		14–15 Jun: Hitler visits Italy.
		23 Jun: Italy strengthens control over Albania after blockade.
		20 Jul: Italy and Britain define border between Libya and Anglo-Egyptian Sudan.
		25 Jul: Mussolini mobilizes four divisions to protect Austria from Nazi takeover.
		5 Dec: Wal-Wal incident in East Africa presages Italian invasion of Ethiopia.

YEAR	HISTORY	CULTURE
1933	Fire destroys Reichstag in Berlin.	George Orwell, *Down and Out in Paris and London.*
	Japan announces it will leave League of Nations.	Henri Matisse, *The Dance.*
	Geneva Disarmament Conference collapses.	All modernist German art suppressed in favour of superficial realism.
	Start of official persecution of Jews in Germany.	
	Germany withdraws from League of Nations and Disarmament Conference.	
1934	Anglo-Russian trade agreement.	Nobel Prize in Literature: Luigi Pirandello (Italy).
	General strike staged in France.	F Scott Fitzgerald, *Tender Is the Night.*
	Germany: 'Night of the Long Knives'; role of German President and Chancellor merged, Hitler becomes *Führer* after German President Paul von Hindenburg dies.	Robert Graves, *I, Claudius.*
	USSR admitted to League of Nations.	

YEAR	AGE	THE LIFE AND THE LAND
1935	75	3 Jan: Ethiopia appeals to League of Nations after Wal-Wal incident.
		7 Jan: Agreement between Mussolini and Laval on Italian colonial borders in Africa, granting Italy free hand in Ethiopia.
		11–14 Apr: Stresa Conference among Italy, France, Britain in response to German rearmament.
		May: Italy agrees to arbitration of Ethiopian question.
		3 Oct: Italy invades Ethiopia.
		3 Oct: Orlando writes to Mussolini suggesting cooperation.
		6 Oct: Italians occupy Adowa, avenging 1896 defeat.
		7 Oct: League declares Italy aggressor.
		11 Oct: League imposes sanctions on Italy; war fears.
		9–18 Dec: Hoare-Laval proposals to stop Italian invasion fail.

YEAR	HISTORY	CULTURE
1935	Saarland incorporated into Germany following plebiscite.	Richard Strauss, *Die Schweigsame Frau*.
	Hitler announces anti-Jewish 'Nuremberg Laws'; Swastika becomes Germany's official flag.	T S Eliot, *Murder in the Cathedral*. Films: *The 39 Steps. Top Hat.*

YEAR	AGE	THE LIFE AND THE LAND
1936	76	12 Jan: Orlando's wife, Ida Castellano, dies.
		Feb: League abandons attempt to impose oil sanctions on Italy.
		19 Mar: Economic agreements with Albania strengthen Italian control.
		23 Mar: Italy, Austria, Hungary sign Three-Power Pact to counterbalance Germany in Eastern Europe.
		5 May: Italy occupies Addis Ababa, Ethiopian capital.
		9 May: Italy annexes Ethiopia, combines it with Eritrea and Italian Somaliland to create Italian East Africa; declares Empire.
		4 Jul: League sanctions against Italy end.
		18 Jul: Spanish Civil War begins; Italy sides with insurgents, sends 'volunteers'.
		5 Oct: Italian lira devalued.
		25 Oct: Italo-German agreement produces 'Axis' against Britain and France establishing formal revisionist camp.
		26 Oct: Because of tensions over Ethiopia with Britain and France, Italy gives Germany 'free hand' in Austria, Germany recognizes Italian conquest of Ethiopia.
		18 Nov: Italy recognizes Nationalist Spanish government.
		25 Nov: Italy, Germany and Japan sign Anti-Comintern Pact to combat communism.

YEAR	HISTORY	CULTURE
1936	German troops occupy Rhineland, violating Treaty of Versailles.	J M Keynes, *General Theory of Employment, Interest and Money.*
	Franklin D Roosevelt re-elected US President.	Sergei Prokofiev, *Peter and the Wolf.*
	British King George V dies: succeeded by Edward VIII, who abdicates at end of year to marry Wallis Simpson; succeeded by George VI.	Berlin Olympics.

YEAR	AGE	THE LIFE AND THE LAND
1937	77	2 Jan: Anglo-Italian Mediterranean Treaty seeks rapprochement between the two countries.
		25 Mar: Italo-Yugoslav Non-Aggression Pact.
		22 Apr: Austrian Chancellor visits Rome, Mussolini tells him he cannot count on Italy for armed support against Germany.
		25–28 Sep: Mussolini visits Berlin, reaffirms Axis goals.
		23 Nov: Italy, Austria, Hungary extend Pact to contest Germany in Eastern Europe.
		11 Dec: Italy withdraws from League of Nations.
		16 Dec: Italy withdraws from International Labour Organization.
1938	78	3–9 Mar: Adolf Hitler visits Rome.
		12 Mar: Deeply occupied in Ethiopia and Spain and with friendly relations with Germany, Mussolini does not react to German annexation of Austria.
		16 Apr: Anglo-Italian Pact; British recognize Italian conquest of Ethiopia, take other steps to prevent Italy from moving closer to Germany.
		3–9 May: Hitler in another state visit demonstrates friendship with Italy despite annexation of Austria.
		3 Aug: Anti-Semitic laws in Italy dismiss Jewish teachers, prohibit Jews from attending state schools, prohibit intermarriage, give Jews who had taken up residence since 1919 six months to leave country.
		29 Sep: Munich Conference; Mussolini plays key role in keeping peace.
		8 Oct: Chamber of Deputies dissolves itself, replaced by 'Chamber of Fasces and Corporations'; completion of Corporate State.
		25 Oct: Libya declared integral part of Italy.
		9 Nov: France recognizes Italian conquest of Ethiopia in attempt to woo Italy away from Germany.
		Dec: Crisis with France; Italy demands some French territory and colonies.

YEAR	HISTORY	CULTURE
1937	Japan invades China: captures Shanghai; Rape of Nanjing (250,000 Chinese killed). Irish Free State becomes Eire under Eamon de Valera's Irish Constitution. UK Royal Commission on Palestine recommends partition into British and Arab areas and Jewish state.	Jean-Paul Sartre, *Nausea*. John Steinbeck, *Of Mice and Men*. George Orwell, *The Road to Wigan Pier*.
1938	Japanese puppet government of China at Nanjing. Munich Agreement hands Sudetenland to Germany. Kristallnacht in Germany: Jewish houses, synagogues and schools burnt for whole week.	Graham Greene, *Brighton Rock*. Evelyn Waugh, *Scoop*. Films: *Pygmalion. Alexander Nevsky. The Adventures of Robin Hood*.

YEAR	AGE	THE LIFE AND THE LAND
1939	79	Jan: British Prime Minister and Foreign Minister visit Rome to move Italy away from Germany.
		26 Jan: Italian aid crucial to Spanish Nationalist capture of Barcelona; beginning of Republican collapse.
		2 Mar: Pope Pius XII elected.
		28 March: Spanish Civil War ends.
		7–12 Apr: Italy occupies Albania, incorporates it into Italy.
		20 May: Italian troop withdrawal from Spain begins.
		Aug: Italy urges negotiated settlement with Poland in secret conferences with Germany.
		3 Sep: Italy's call for Five-Power Conference to settle Polish crisis fails; Italy declares neutrality.
1940	80	10 Jun: Italy declares war on Britain and France after German blitzkrieg against France succeeds.
		24 Jun: Franco-Italian Armistice.
		6 Aug: Italians occupy British Somaliland.
		13–15 Sep: Italy invades Egypt.
		28 Oct: Mussolini invades Greece, fails.
		13 Nov: British successfully attack Italian fleet at Taranto.
1941	81	5 Jan-8 Feb: British defeat Italians in North Africa necessitating German rescue.
		Jan-Nov: British occupy Italian East Africa.
		20 Jan: German troops move into Italy to help war effort.
		22 Jun: Germany invades Russia; Italy sends troops.
		11 Dec: Italy declares war on United States.

YEAR	HISTORY	CULTURE
1939	German troops enter Prague. Germany demands Danzig and Polish Corridor: Poland refuses. Nazi-Soviet Pact agrees no fighting, partition of Poland: Japanese withdraw from Anti-Comitern Pact in protest. Second World War begins: Germany invades Poland; Britain and France declare war; Soviets invade Finland.	Béla Bartók, *String Quartet No. 6*. James Joyce, *Finnegan's Wake*. Thomas Mann, *Lotte in Weimar*. John Steinbeck, *The Grapes of Wrath*.
1940	Second World War: Winston Churchill becomes Britain's Prime Minister. Germany invades Holland, Belgium, Luxembourg. Battle of Britain. Hungary and Romania join Axis.	Graham Greene, *The Power and the Glory*. Ernest Hemingway, *For Whom the Bell Tolls*. Eugene O'Neill, *Long Day's Journey into Night*.
1941	British troops evacuate Greece; Crete falls. Japanese troops occupy Indochina. Japan attacks Pearl Harbor, invades the Philippines.	Bertold Brecht, *Mother Courage and Her Children*. Noel Coward, *Blithe Spirit*. British communist paper, *The Daily Worker*, suppressed.

YEAR	AGE	THE LIFE AND THE LAND
1943	83	19 Mar-12 May: Allies drive Axis out of North Africa.
		10 Jul-17 Aug: Allies occupy Sicily.
		25–26 Jul: Mussolini overthrown.
		28 Jul: Fascism dissolved; secret armistice negotiations with Allies.
		8 Sep: Italy surrenders to Allies.
		11 Sep: Germans occupy Italy.
		15 Sep: After being rescued by Germans, Mussolini sets up Italian Social Republic under their control in Northern Italy.
		13 Oct: Badoglio government declares war on Germany.
		10 Nov: Allies set up military occupation government in Italy.
1944	84	11 Feb: Allies restore Italian civil government in parts of Southern Italy.
		Mar: Industrial strikes in Northern Italy.
		Jun: Togliatti announces collaboration with government.
		9 Jun: Badoglio resigns, replaced by Ivanoe Bonomi.
		Jun: Rome liberated.
		9 Jun-12 Aug: Allied offensive in Southern Italy.
		23 Oct: Allies recognize Bonomi government.
		Orlando named Chamber of Deputies President.
1945	85	25 Apr: Italy liberated.
		28 Apr: Mussolini executed by partisans while trying to flee Italy.
		22 Sep: Orlando named to 'Consulta Nazionale'.
		De Gasperi government formed.

YEAR	HISTORY	CULTURE
1943	Second World War: Beleaguered Romanians and Germans surrender to Russians at Stalingrad. Allies demand unconditional surrender from Germany and Japan at Casablanca Conference. Tehran Conference: Churchill, Roosevelt and Stalin meet.	Jean-Paul Sartre, *Being and Nothingness.* Henry Moore, *Madonna and Child.* Richard Rogers and Oscar Hammerstein, *Oklahoma!*
1944	D-Day landings in France. Claus von Stauffenberg's bomb at Rastenburg fails to kill Hitler. Churchill visits Stalin in Moscow. Franklin D Roosevelt wins unprecedented fourth term as US President.	T S Eliot, *Four Quartets.* Tennessee Williams, *The Glass Menagerie.* Carl Jung, *Psychology and Religion.*
1945	Hitler commits suicide in Berlin; city surrenders to Soviets. VE Day: 8 May. US drops atomic bombs on Hiroshima and Nagasaki.	Evelyn Waugh, *Brideshead Revisited.* Richard Strauss, *Metamorphosen.* George Orwell, *Animal Farm.*

YEAR	AGE	THE LIFE AND THE LAND
1946	86	10 Feb: Treaty of Rome settles Italian Peace Terms, establishes border with Yugoslavia.
		May: Vittorio Emanuele III abdicates in favor of son.
		2 Jun: Referendum does away with Monarchy and establishes Republic.
		2 Jun: Orlando elected to Constituent Assembly; founds 'Unione Democratico Nazionale' with Francesco Saverio Nitti, Benedetto Croce, Ivanoe Bonomi.
1947	87	Jan: De Gasperi visits United States.
		Apr: Orlando's university chair restored.
		May: Communists and Socialists excluded from national government.
		Jul: Orlando speaks against ratification of Treaty of Paris ending Italy's role in Second World War.
		27 Nov: Orlando fails to form government.
1948	88	1 Jan: Italian Republican Constitution enters into force.
		18 Apr: Popular Front (Communists and Socialists) defeated by Christian Democrats in crucial first national elections of Republic.
		22 Apr: Orlando named Life Senator.
		11 May: Supported only by Left, Orlando loses first regular Presidential election of the Italian Republic to Luigi Einaudi.
1949	89	Mar: Orlando's campaign against NATO fails as Italy joins Atlantic Alliance.
1952	92	1 Dec: Orlando dies from cerebral hemorrhage.

YEAR	HISTORY	CULTURE
1946	Churchill declares Stalin has lowered 'Iron Curtain' across Europe, signalling formal start of Cold War. Nuremberg establishes guilty verdicts for war crimes. Greek Civil War begins.	Bertrand Russell, *History of Western Philosophy*. Films: *Great Expectations. It's a Wonderful Life*. Radio: Alistair Cook's *Letter from America* begins (series ends in 2004). *Woman's Hour*. *Dick Barton*.
1947	Hungary reassigned its 1938 frontiers. Moscow Conference fails over problem of Germany. Communists win Hungarian election. New Japanese constitution renounces use of war.	Edinburgh Festival is founded. Albert Camus, *The Plague*. Anne Frank, *The Diary of Anne Frank*. Tennessee Williams, *A Streetcar Named Desire*.
1948	US Congress passes Marshall Aid Act: contributes $5.3 billion to European recovery. Western Allies organise Berlin Airlift after USSR blockades Berlin. Gandhi assassinated in India: last British troops leave.	Nobel Prize in Literature: T S Eliot (Great Britain). Jackson Pollock, *Composition NO.1*. Graham Greene, *The Heart of the Matter*.
1949	North Atlantic Treaty Organisation (NATO) founded.	George Orwell, *Nineteen Eighty-Four*.
1952	Mau-Mau Rising in Kenya.	

Further Reading

Readers will discover that biographies of Vittorio Emanuele Orlando are old, brief and rare. In English they are non-existent, and the most recent accessible one in Italian is Massimo Ganci's *Vittorio Emanuele Orlando*, published in 1991. Scholarly articles devoted to Orlando in English are absent. In 2002, the 50th anniversary of Orlando's death, the Italian Senate sponsored an exhibition and a conference on him and published the papers in a short volume: *Vittorio Emanuele Orlando: lo scienziato, il politico e lo statista*. It is a shame that such an important statesman has been so little studied both in English and Italian; and it remains an extremely challenging task to find in-depth interpretations of 'Il Presidente della Vittoria' and of his multifaceted career as government minister, war leader, and diplomat. At the Paris Peace Conference, historians bring up his tendency to weep, but inform us very little about his thinking on the issues. Even ordinary details of his personal life are hard if not impossible to identify, unlike with his colleagues at the Conference. We know that Orlando was married, had four children and grandchildren, and was a good Catholic – but did he like good food and have love affairs? He travelled to the United States and Argentina during the Fascist period, but who did he meet, and did he criticize Mussolini's regime in his talks with them? Even his memoirs tell us very little about his personal life. In their two-page introduction the editors tell us that he kept his handwritten pages in folders of different colours and never completed his life story but little else. Before Orlando can come to life for readers – and he never does so completely – they must peruse rare works such as Umberto Galeota's *V.E. Orlando* (1958), not a biography at all but a brief collection by an obscure poet of some his rare letters, writings, and photographs. Otherwise, the reader must rely on official documents such as speeches to interpret the man. While this formal material is sufficient, the state of the Orlando Papers in the Archivio dello Stato in Rome harbours a bitter surprise for the researcher. The notes detailing Orlando's meetings with Wilson, listed in the finding aid, are nowhere to be found. The archivists undertook a thorough search at my behest, but had no luck.

Another detail related to Orlando that the reader will quickly discover is the bias regarding Italy's role during the First World War, and the effects this attitude had already at the Paris Peace Conference. In fact, chances are that the reader of this book has already been affected by these biases that perpetuate diplomatic and military myths, in addition to legends on all kinds of supposed moral failings. Moreover, these tendentious interpretations are unfortunately compounded by odious and superficial judgments concerning Italy's role in the First and the Second World Wars. Here is an example from a general work currently in the bookstores: 'In the two World Wars, Italy's story is the same. Neither ideals nor irresistible outside pressures compelled Italy to abandon neutrality and become a belligerent. In both cases, the Government in Rome dallied, waiting to see how the fight would go, then carried the people into war for the spoils. But the jackal-like nature of the entry was recognized as such only when Mussolini ordered it.' (S.L.A. Marshall, *World War I*, p 169) Hew Stachen's *The First World War* and Norman Stone's *World War I: A Short History* continue to spread the biases. Regrettably, the historical literature is replete with this, despite the evidence that would contradict such stances in archival documents, and by a seeming inability to place events in their historical context.

There are some notable exceptions to the prevailing myths, for example, John Keegan's treatment of the Italian war in his *The First World War*. Recently there seems to have been a move towards a more objective analysis of the Italian front, including Mark Thompson's *The White War* (2009) and, more unbiased in his treatment of both Italians and Austrians, John Schindler's *Isonzo: the Forgotten Sacrifice of the Great War* (2001). It remains to be seen if the trend will continue and whether it will penetrate more 'popular' history.

Having said this, readers will also find excellent works, if not on Orlando then on the situations of which he was an integral part. For example, Olindo Malagodi's interviews of Italian and foreign statesmen during the First World War, including the Paris Peace Conference, *Conversazioni della guerra*, 2 vols, is a treasure that any historian of Italy during the period cannot ignore. In those interviews, given in the heat of the moment, Vittorio Emanuele Orlando and other characters take on life. René Albrecht-Carrié's *Italy at the Paris Peace Conference*, originally written in 1938, is an unsurpassed diplomatic history. Physicist Mario Silvestri's writing rivets the reader with his recounting of the fighting on the Italian front; *Isonzo 1917* puts many a professional historian to shame. It is unlikely that there will be a better description of trench warfare than the memoir of soldier-turned-politician Emilio Lussu's *Un anno sull'altipiano,* which is in the same league as more famous first-hand accounts such as *Storm of Steel* and *All Quiet on the Western Front.* Lussu's book has been translated as the difficult-to-find English edition, *Sardinian Brigade,* but a search will greatly reward anyone who undertakes it.

Bibliography

Please note: this bibliography does not include articles, which the reader will find cited in the footnotes.

Agarossi, Elena, *A Nation Collapses: The Italian Surrender of September 1943* (Cambridge University Press, Cambridge: 2000).

Albertini, Luigi, *The Origins of the War of 1914,* 3 vols (Oxford University Press, London: 1952–1965).

Albrecht-Carrié, Rene, *A Diplomatic History of Europe Since the Congress of Vienna* (Harper, New York: 1958).

_____, *Italy at the Paris Peace Conference* (Archon Books, Hamden: 1966).

Alessi, Rino, *Dall'Isonzo al Piave* (Mondadori, Milan: 1966).

Alfassio Grimaldi, Ugoberto and Gherardo Bozzetti, *Bissolati* (Rizzoli, Milan: 1983).

Alloggio, Sabino, *Vittorio Emanuele Orlando* (Casa Editrice Sabina, Naples: 1928).

Baker, Ray Stannard, *Woodrow Wilson and World Settlement. Written From His Unpublished and Personal Material,* 2 vols (Peter Smith, Gloucester: 1960).

Birdsall, Paul, *Versailles Twenty Years After* (Reynal and Hitchcock, New York: 1941).

Bissolati, Leonida, *La politica estera dell'Italia dal 1897 al 1920* (Treves, Milan: 1923).

Borgese, G.A. *Goliath: The March of Fascism* (The Viking Press, New York: 1937).

Bosworth, Richard, *Italy and the Approach of the First World War* (MacMillan, London: 1983).

Burgwyn, H. James, *Italian Foreign Policy in the Interwar Period 1918–1940* (Praeger, Westport: 1997).

_____, *The Legend of the Mutilated Victory: Italy, the Great War, and the Paris Peace Conference, 1915–1919* (Greenwood Press, Westport: 1993).

Cadorna, Generale Luigi, *La guerra alla fronte italiana*, 2 vols (Treves, Milan: 1921).

Candeloro, Giorgio, *Il movimento cattolico in Italia*. (Riuniti, Rome: 1972).

_____, *Storia dell'Italia moderna*, Vols 5–8 (Feltrinelli, Milan: 1968–1978).

Caprin, Giulio, *Sistema e revisione di Versaglia nel pensiero e nell'azione di Mussolini* (Istituto per gli Studi di Politica Internazionale, Milan: 1940).

Cataluccio, Francesco, *La politica estera di E. Visconti Venosta* (Marzocco, Florence: 1940).

Cianferotti, Giulio, *Il pensiero di V.E. Orlando e la giuspubblicistica italiana fra ottocento e novecento* (A. Giuffrè, Milan: 1980).

Colapietra, Raeffale, *Leonida Bissolati* (Feltrinelli, Milan: 1958).

Clough, Shepard and Salvatore Saladino, *A History of Modern Italy: Documents, Readings & Commentary* (Columbia University Press, New York: 1968).

Coppola, Francesco, *La pace democratica* (Zanichelli, Bologna: 1921).

Croce, Benedetto, *Scritti e discorsi politici (1943–1947)* (Laterza, Bari: 1963).

_____, *Storia d'Italia dal 1871 al 1915* (Laterza, Bari: 1962).

Croce-Orlando-Sforza, *Per la pace d'Italia e d'Europa* (Il Filo di Arianna, Rome: 1946).

De Felice, Renzo, *Mussolini il rivoluzionario* (Einaudi, Turin: 1965).

De Grand, Alexander, *The Hunchback's Tailor* (Praeger, Westport: 2001).

_____, *The Italian Nationalist Association and the Rise of Fascism in Italy* (The University of Nebraska Press, Lincoln: 1978).

Di Scala, Spencer M, *Dilemmas of Italian Socialism: The Politics of Filippo Turati* (University of Massachusetts Press, Amherst: 1980).

_____, *Italy: From Revolution to Republic, 1700 to the Present*, 4th ed (Westview Press, Boulder: 2009).

_____, '"Red Week" 1914: Prelude to War and Revolution,' in Frank J. Coppa (ed), *Studies in Modern Italian History from the Risorgimento to the Republic* (Peter Lang, New York: 1986).

_____, *Renewing Italian Socialism: Nenni to Craxi* (Oxford University Press, New York: 1988).

Drake, Richard, *Byzantium for Rome: The Politics of Nostalgia in Umbertian Italy, 1878–1900* (The University of North Carolina Press, Chapel Hill: 1980).

Etna, Giacomo, *Le menzogne di Orlando* (edizioni erre, Venice-Milan: 1944).

Fragola, Ottorino, *V.E. Orlando* (Istituto Editoriale Romano, Rome: 1920).

Ganci, Massimo, *Vittorio Emanuele Orlando* (La Navicella, Rome: 1991).

Galeota, Umberto, *V.E. Orlando* (Ricciardi, Naples: 1958).

Gentile, Emilio, *La Grande Italia: The Myth of the Nation in the 20th Century* (The University of Wisconsin Press, Madison: 2009).

_____, *"La nostra sfida alle stelle": Futuristi in politica* (Laterza, Rome: 2009).

Giolitti, Giovanni, *Memorie della mia vita* (Garzanti, Milan: 1967).

Harper, John Lamberton, *America and the Reconstruction of Italy, 1945–1948* (Cambridge University Press, Cambridge: 1986).

Hoffman, Max, *The War of Lost Opportunities* (K. Paul, French, Trubner & Co Ltd, London: 1924).

Imperiali, Guglielmo, *Diario 1915–1919* (Rubbettino, Catanzaro: 2006).

Istituto Giangiacomo Feltrinelli, *Dalle carte di Giovanni Giolitti. Quarant'anni di politica italiana. III: Dai podromi della grande guerra al fascismo 1910–1928* (Feltrinelli, Milan: 1962).

Keegan, John, *The First World War* (Vintage Books, New York: 2000).

Killinger, Charles, *Gaetano Salvemini* (Praeger, Westport: 2002).

Labriola, Arturo, *Storia di dieci anni* (Il Viandante, Milan: 1910).

Link, Arthur Stanley, *The Papers of Woodrow Wilson*, 69 vols (Princeton University Press, Princeton: 1966–1994).

Lloyd George, David, *War Memoirs of David Lloyd George*, 6 vols (Little, Brown, and Company, Boston: 1934).

Lussu, Emilio, *Un anno sull'altiplano* (Einaudi, Turin: 2005).

Lotti, Luigi, *La settimana rossa* (Le Monnier, Florence: 1965).

Lyttelton, Adrian, *The Seizure of Power: Fascism in Italy 1919–1922* (Charles Scribner's Sons, New York: 1973).

Orlando, Vittorio Emanuele, *Miei rapporti con la S. Sede* (Forni, N.p: 1980).

———, *Memorie (1915–1919)* (Rizzoli, Milan: 1960).

Malagodi, Olindo, *Conversazione della guerra*, 2 vols (Ricciardi, Milan-Naples: 1960).

Marshall, S.L.A., *World War I* (Mariner, Boston-New York: 2000).

Miller, James Edward, *The United States and Italy, 1940–1950* (The University of North Carolina Press, Chapel Hill: 1986).

Morselli, Mario A., *Caporetto: Defeat or Victory?* (Cass, London: 2001).

Mosier, John, *The Myth of the Great War: A New Military History of World War I* (Perennial, New York: 2001).

Mussolini, Benito, *My Autobiography* (Hutchinson & Co., London: n.d.[originally published, 1928]).

Partito Socialista Italiano, *Resoconto stenografico del XIII congresso nazionale* (Unione Arti Grafiche, Città di Castello: 1913).

Pelloux, Luigi, *Quelques souvenirs de ma vie* (Istituto per la storia del Risorgimento italiano, Rome: 1967).

Pieri, Piero, *L'Italia nella Prima Guerra Mondiale* (Einaudi, Turin: 1965).

Nenni, Pietro, *Tempo di guerra fredda. Diari 1943–1956* (SugrarCo, Milan: 1981).

Rossini, Daniela, *Woodrow Wilson and the American Myth in Italy: Culture and War Propaganda* (Harvard University Press, Cambridge: 2008).

Salandra, Antonio, *L'Intervento [1915]. Ricordi e pensieri* (Mondadori, Milan: 1930).

_____, *La neutralità italiana [1914] ricordi e pensieri* (Mondadori, Milan: 1928).

_____, *Memorie politiche, 1916–1925* (Garzanti, Milan: 1951).

Salomone, A. William, *Italy in the Giolittian Era: Italian Democracy in the Making* (University of Pennsylvania Press, Philadelphia: 1960).

Salvemini, Gaetano, *The Origins of Fascism in Italy* (Harper and Row, New York: 1973).

Salvatore, Nick, *Eugene V. Debs: Citizen and Socialist* (University of Illinois Press, Urbana and Chicago: 1982).

Schindler, John R., *Isonzo: The Forgotten Sacrifice of the Great War* (Pager, Westport: 2001).

Scottà, Antonio, *Conferenza di pace tra ieri e domani (1919–1920)* (Rubbettino, Catanzaro: 2003).

Senato della Repubblica, *Vittorio Emanuele Orlando: Lo scienziato, il politico e lo statista* (Rubbettino, Rome: 2002).

Seton-Watson, Christopher, *Italy From Liberalism to Fascism 1870–1925* (Methuen, London: 1967).

Silvestri, Mario, *Isonzo 1917* (Einaudi, Turin: 1965).

Sonnino, Sidney, *Carteggio 1914–1916,* 2 vols (Laterza, Rome-Bari: 1975).

_____, *Diario*, 3 vols (Laterza, Rome-Bari: 1972).

Spadolini, Giovanni, *Giolitti e i cattolici (1901–1914)* (Le Monnier, Florence: 1960).

Strachen, Hew, *The First World War* (Penguin, New York: 2003).

Stone, Norman, *World War I: A Short History* (Basic Books, New York: 2009; Advanced Uncorrected Proof).

Thompson, Mark, *The White War: Life and Death on the Italian Front* (Basic Books, New York: 2009).

Tranfaglia, Nicola, *La prima guerra mondiale e il fascismo. Storia d'Italia dall'Unità alla fine della Prima Repubblica* (TEA, Milan: 1995).

Valiani, Leo, *Il partito socialista italiano nel periodo della neutralità 1914–1915* (Feltrinelli, Milan: 1963).

Wallace, Lilian Parker and William C. Askew, (eds), *Power, Public Opinion and Diplomacy* (Duke University Press, Durham: 1968).

Walworth, Arthur, *Wilson and His Peacemakers: American Diplomacy at the Paris Peace Conference* (W.W. Norton, New York: 1986).

Whittam, John, *The Politics of the Italian Army, 1861–1918* (Croom Helm, London: 1977).

Wilson, Woodrow, *A History of the American People. Vol. V. Reunion and Rationalization* (Harper Brothers, New York and London: 1902).

Archival and Parliamentary Sources
Archivio Centrale dello Stato, Rome, *Carte Orlando*
Atti Parliamentari (Camera dei Deputati)
Documenti Diplomatici Italiani

Peridodicals
Avanti!
Critica Sociale
Il Tempo
Idea Nazionale
The New York Times

Picture Sources

The author and publishers wish to express their thanks to the following sources of illustrative material and/or permission to reproduce it. They will make proper acknowledgements in future editions in the event that any omissions have occurred.

Illustrations courtesy of The Granger Collection, New York, and Topham Picturepoint.

Endpapers
The Signing of Peace in the Hall of Mirrors, Versailles, 28th June 1919 by Sir William Orpen (Imperial War Museum: Bridgeman Art Library)
Front row: Dr Johannes Bell (Germany) signing with Herr Hermann Müller leaning over him
Middle row (seated, left to right): General Tasker H Bliss, Col E M House, Mr Henry White, Mr Robert Lansing, President Woodrow Wilson (United States); M Georges Clemenceau (France); Mr David Lloyd George, Mr Andrew Bonar Law, Mr Arthur J Balfour, Viscount Milner, Mr G N Barnes (Great Britain); Prince Saionji (Japan)

Back row (left to right): M Eleftherios Venizelos (Greece);
Dr Afonso Costa (Portugal); Lord Riddell (British Press);
Sir George E Foster (Canada); M Nikola Pašić (Serbia);
M Stephen Pichon (France); Col Sir Maurice Hankey,
Mr Edwin S Montagu (Great Britain); the Maharajah of
Bikaner (India); Signor Vittorio Emanuele Orlando (Italy);
M Paul Hymans (Belgium); General Louis Botha (South
Africa); Mr W M Hughes (Australia)

Jacket images

(Front): Imperial War Museum: akg Images.
(Back): *Peace Conference at the Quai d'Orsay* by Sir William
Orpen (Imperial War Museum: akg Images).
Left to right (seated): Signor Orlando (Italy); Mr Robert
Lansing, President Woodrow Wilson (United States); M
Georges Clemenceau (France); Mr David Lloyd George, Mr
Andrew Bonar Law, Mr Arthur J Balfour (Great Britain);
Left to right (standing): M Paul Hymans (Belgium); Mr
Eleftherios Venizelos (Greece); The Emir Feisal (The
Hashemite Kingdom); Mr W F Massey (New Zealand);
General Jan Smuts (South Africa); Col E M House (United
States); General Louis Botha (South Africa); Prince Saionji
(Japan); Mr W M Hughes (Australia); Sir Robert Borden
(Canada); Mr G N Barnes (Great Britain); M Ignacy
Paderewski (Poland)

Index

Makers
of the
Modern
World

UK PUBLICATION: November 2008 to December 2010
CLASSIFICATION: Biography/History/
   International Relations
FORMAT: 198 × 128mm
EXTENT: 208pp
ILLUSTRATIONS: 6 photographs plus 4 maps
TERRITORY: world

Chronology of life in context, full index, bibliography innovative layout
with sidebars